Enhancing the Effectiveness of the EU Public Procurement Framework

Europäische Hochschulschriften Recht

European University Studies in Law

Publications Universitaires Européennes de Droit

Band/Volume 6151

Asta Gerhardt

Enhancing the Effectiveness of the EU Public Procurement Framework

Case studies of Lithuania and Germany

PETER LANG

Bibliografische Information der Deutschen Nationalbibliothek
Die Deutsche Nationalbibliothek verzeichnet diese Publikation in der Deutschen Nationalbibliografie; detaillierte bibliografische Daten sind im Internet über http://dnb.d-nb.de abrufbar.

Library of Congress Cataloging-in-Publication Data
A CIP catalog record for this book has been applied for at the Library of Congress.

ISSN 0531-7312
ISBN 978-3-631-79976-5 (Print)
E-ISBN 978-3-631-81343-0 (E-PDF)
E-ISBN 978-3-631-81344-7 (EPUB)
E-ISBN 978-3-631-81345-4 (MOBI)
DOI 10.3726/b16594

Peter Lang – Berlin · Bern · Bruxelles · New York · Oxford · Warszawa · Wien

This publication has been peer reviewed.

www.peterlang.com

I dedicate this work to my honourable parents and my husband.

Acknowledgement

The presented work was accepted as a dissertation in the summer 2017 by the Humboldt University in Berlin. The choice of topic was based on my relevant public procurement experience in the public and private sector. Recent developments in public procurement within the European Union and the member states had to be taken into account, but above all the further relevant case-law of the European Court of Justice.

First and foremost I would like to thank, my distinguished doctoral supervisor, Prof. Dr. Dr. h.c. Ulrich Battis, who supported me excellently in my work and promoted a remarkably quick and uncomplicated doctoral procedure. The members of the Jury, Prof. Dr. Dr. h.c. mult. Christian Tomuschat, Prof. Dr. Philipp Dann and my supervisor are also acknowledged. Their comments helped to improve this PhD research thesis.

My thanks goes without the affection, the work would be without the impulse, the inspiration and the patience as the support of my parents, Rita and Kazimieras my brothers and sisters in law, Kazimieras and Daiva, Vaidas and Irma and parents in law Jean Paul and Alexandra. My heartfelt biggest thanks goes to my lovely husband Cyrille who encouraged me mentally every day and provided the strength, positive energy and compassion to complete the thesis. Without his support the thesis would not have been accomplished so swiftly.

I cannot thank my friends and diligent proof-readers enough for their patience and support during such a challenging and interesting journey during my PhD thesis.

Luxembourg, November 2019

Contents

Introduction

The reform of the EU public procurement framework and recently adopted new public procurement rules in Lithuania were indisputably the most significant revisions of this regime since 2004. The aim of this thesis is to provide a critical examination of the EU Directive 2014/24/EU and its transposition into the national law systems of Lithuania and Germany. The author will discuss in more detail the transposition advantages, disadvantages of Lithuanian national law system, and provide comparison analysis with German national law system. Further analysis will be provided on peculiarities of public procurement disputes in Germany and Lithuania. Through this examination, the thesis also aims to contribute towards a sound future development of public procurement rules, both at the EU level and national law and practice.

Methodology of the thesis

The objective of the thesis is to assess the effectiveness of the transposition of the EU public procurement Directive 2014/24/EU into the Lithuanian national law system and its impact on national remedies system in comparison with the German national law system.

To achieve this goal, the following tasks had to be undertaken:

1. Disclose and analyse the concept and specificities of the EU and Lithuanian public procurement history.
2. Analyse the EU public procurement reform and its impact on the national legislation of Lithuania and Germany.
3. Analyse the effectiveness of the transposition of the EU Directive 2014/24/EU into the Lithuanian and German national law systems.
4. Identify public procurement regulatory gaps and problems in public procurement procedures.
5. Analyse peculiarities and main problems of the dispute settlement process of public procurement in Lithuania and Germany.
6. Propose solutions, alternative methods and improvement ideas in order to promote procurement effectiveness and more efficient use of the remedies system.

Research methods

Theoretical method

A variety of different categories of methods for collecting information were applied. Desk research to acquire theoretical information was used. Books, magazines, articles, previously conducted research, journals, websites, and online books as well as laws and regulation texts were used.

Empirical method

Field exploration was used for empirical research to support the findings of this thesis. Interviews were conducted and answers were obtained to questions from different procurement experts. Procurement professionals were also contacted to find fresh ideas and obtain examples on reporting procurement efficiency. The empirical research method was used for measuring procurement effectiveness.

Systemic method

The thesis covers the systematic assessment of the transposition of public procurement rules into the Lithuanian and German national law systems. The experience and issues in the application of public procurement rules of foreign countries were compared in order to come up with practical recommendations for decision making. The EU public procurement regulatory developments, challenges, and development of causation were assessed.

Statistical method

Statistical analysis, surveys and studies on public procurement were used. A series of documents such as legislation of the Member States, the EU directives and regulations, and the jurisprudence of the investigative measure were analysed.

Extrapolation method

The findings were analysed and summarised. The improvements and recommendations for the effectiveness of the EU public procurement framework were proposed.

Structure of the dissertation

The first chapter of the thesis will discuss the scope of the EU Directive 2014/24/EU and the fundamental principles including the major analysis of the case law.

Historical development of the Lithuanian public procurement will be outlined in the second chapter of the thesis. The implementation of public procurement rules in Lithuanian and German legal frameworks will be addressed in the third chapter. The author will demonstrate a detailed analysis and suggestions for improvements of the EU public procurement procedures application at the national level. The fourth chapter presents key weaknesses of the EU public procurement framework. Through system analysis and comparative methods, the author has identified flexible procedures, reduction of administrative processes, and better conditions for small and medium-sized enterprises to enter public procurement procedures. The fifth part examines the remedies system in Lithuania and its effective enforcement. The enforcement of remedies system in Germany will be discussed in the sixth chapter of the thesis. The seventh chapter will provide analysis of advantages and disadvantages of remedies systems in Lithuania and Germany. The author will summarise the findings in the final chapter of the thesis.

I Public procurement legislation in the EU

This chapter looks at how the Treaty on the Functioning of the European Union (TFEU)[1] applies to public procurement and guides through general principles of public procurement[2]. At first, the TFEU has references to public contracts and a number of generic provisions regarding free movement of goods[3], which are important to the field of public procurement. These provisions are essential for proper operation of the single market. The TFEU is a primary source for public procurement-related legislation in the European Union, as well as the basis of all secondary legislation, adopted within the power of the European Union to establish regulations relevant to the internal market.

Secondly, case law plays a major role in public procurement, namely the European Court of Justice (CJEU) has an instrumental role in interpreting and applying EU rules on the subject. Those rules are contained both in the TFEU and in various public procurement directives adopted by the EU Council. The following articles of the TFEU are particularly relevant to procurement, which will be further analysed: Article 34 TFEU on free movement of goods, Article 49 TFEU on freedom of establishment, and Article 56 TFEU on freedom to provide services. These provisions apply to public purchasing in that they prescribe what public contracting authorities cannot do when awarding public contracts, namely, discriminate against bids or bidders from other EU Member States.

The overview of relevant TFEU provisions and fundamental principles of the EU public procurement legislation are important for this thesis as it lays the foundations for a proper functioning of public procurement in the EU and its Member States.

1 Treaty provisions relevant to public procurement

The European law on public procurement relies on the following pillars: certain provisions in the TFEU, EU directives on public procurement and fundamental principles deriving from the CJEU jurisprudence. The cornerstone of the European procurement regulations lies in the provisions of the TFEU, removing

1 Consolidated version of the Treaty on the Functioning of the European Union, OJ C 326, 26 October 2012.
2 Sue Arrowsmith, EU public procurement law: An introduction, 2011, p. 52.
3 Article 26 TFEU.

obstacles for intra-Union trade, and ensuring the freedom to provide services and freedom of establishment. The CJEU has identified a number of relevant cases, which have contributed to the interpretation of the TFEU provisions and fundamental principles. In this chapter, the most relevant cases such as Dundalk, UNIX, and Vestergaard will be discussed in more detail in order to further understand the importance of Article 34 TFEU[4] on free movement of goods.

1.1 Article 34 TFEU on free movement of goods

Article 34 TFEU[5] defines the goods that can move without restrictions between Member States. This provision puts a ban on quantitative restrictions on the free import and export of goods and other measures of equivalent effect between the Member States.

Technical requirements for goods introduced by the EU and other countries in the name of public policy can create significant barriers to international trade[6]. However, certain measures will not breach Article 34 TFEU if the necessary requirements are satisfied as stated in the Dassonville case[7].

The Community has led the way of using mutual recognition to overcome such barriers. The central ruling in the achievement of free movement of goods in the Community has been the case of Cassis de Dijon[8], which relies on the principle of mutual recognition[9].

The ruling stipulates that a specific blackcurrant liqueur, a product recognised and approved in one of the EU Member States, should also be permitted to be imported and sold in any other EU Member State without the need to perform any additional testing and give approval. However, an authority may take measures to ban or limit the importation of products if they believe those products cause danger to the environment, consumer interests, or the health and life of

4 Sue Arrowsmith, The law of public and utilities procurement, para. 4.08, 2014.

5 Peter Van den Bossche, The law and policy of the World Trade Organisation, p. 581, 2005.

6 COM (2007) 36, laying down procedures relating to the application of certain national technical rules to products lawfully marketed in another Member State and repealing Decision 3052/95/EC.

7 Case 8/74, *Procureur du roi/Dassonville,* 1974, ECR 837.

8 Case 120/78, *Rewe Zentral AG v Bundesmonopolverwaltung für Branntwein*, 1979, ECR 649.

9 COM (2003) 262/02, Commission interpretative communication on facilitating the access of products to the markets of other Member States: The practical application of mutual recognition.

humans, animals, or plants, and as long as these measures correspond to the risks arising from the product and are applied in a way that is non-discriminatory. Due to the exceptions arising from the case of Cassis de Dijon, the CJEU narrowed the meaning of the mandatory requirements, because they constitute an exemption from the fundamental principle of free movement of goods. The CJEU can limit its scope by applying the principle of non-discrimination and the principle of proportionality to such restrictions. These two principles must be applied hand in hand[10].

1.2 Prohibition of measures interfering with the free market

Article 34 TFEU specifies that quantitative import restrictions and all measures of equal effect are prohibited. A "measure of equal effect" is any action by the Member States that could hamper intra-Community trade, directly, effectively or potentially[11]. Article 34 TFEU offers a number of (limited) grounds that would justify a regulation that is (in principle) banned.[12] National rules are nevertheless prohibited if they result in arbitrary discrimination or in a disguised restriction to trade between Member States.

According to Article 34 TFEU, the EU is based on a customs union and therefore it bans the following three sets of restrictions to the free movement of goods in public procurement: 1) direct discrimination[13] or quantitative restrictions on imports and exports between Member States 2) indirect discrimination[14] or measures of equivalent effect and 3) measures that may restrict trade without being directly or indirectly discriminatory[15].

These forms of restrictions will be further discussed in more detail.

---

10 Christoph Benedict, Sekundärzwecke im Vergabeverfahren, Öffentliches Auftragswesen, seine teilweise Harmonisierung im EG/EU-Binnenmarkt und die Instrumentalisierung von Vergaberecht durch vergabefremde Aspekte, p. 205, 2012.

11 Sue Arrowsmith, EU public procurement law: An introduction, 2011, p. 67.

12 Case C-324/93, *Evans Medical*, 1995, ECR I-00563, the protection of public decency, public order, public safety, public health and human life animal and plant life, the national artistic, historical and archaeological heritage and the protection of industrial and commercial property.

13 Case C-263/85, *Commission v. Italy*, 1991, ECR I-2457; Case C-21/88, *Du Pont de Nemours v. Unita Sanitaria Locale*, 1990, ECR I-00889; Case C-243/89, *Commission v. Denmark*, 1990, ECR I-03353.

14 Case C-8/74, *Procureur du Roi v. Dassonville*, 1974, ECR 837; Case C-120/78, *Rewe-Zentrale v. Bundesmonopolverwaltung für Branntwein "Cassis de Dijon"*, 1979, ECR 649; Case C-272/91, *Comission v. Italy*, 1994, ECR I-01409.

15 Cases C-267/91 and C-268/91, *Keck v. Mithouard*, 1993, ECR I-06097.

1.3 Article 34 TFEU on specification requirements and standards

In 1983, the Commission stated that national standards, compliance with which is rendered obligatory de jure or de facto by the State involvement, would be considered under Article 34 TFEU, which implies that import restrictions stated in an agreement between undertakings not to accept products based on national standards would be subject to judgement under the competition law.[16]

The application of the Treaty regime on the free movement of goods to technical standards is found in the voluntary nature of standards. The CJEU held that in case 45/87, Commission v. Ireland (Dundalk)[17] that Ireland failed to abide by its obligations under Article 34 TFEU by permitting a clause that required the asbestos cement pressure pipes in question to be certified as complying with a certain Irish standard in the contract specification. Such provision put a constraint on the supply of pipes that were necessary for the Dundalk scheme to Irish manufacturers alone and indirectly impeded the supply of equivalent pipes from countries outside Ireland. The Court ruled that Ireland should have verified compliance with the technical requirements by supplementing the reference to the Irish standard in the notice with the words 'or equivalent'. This case shows elements of indirect discrimination.

In the next case Commission v. The Netherlands[18], the Court ruled that the use of the mark of the product UNIX in the contract notice failed to comply with the principle of free movement of goods. The fact that the words 'or equivalent' were not added to the term UNIX[19] did not only breach the provisions of the Directive, but could have also discouraged other suppliers from entering the tendering procedure.

The technical specifications must be drafted in such a way that it would objectively formulate performance requirements. When providing an accurate description, public contracting authorities must take precautions not to infringe the Treaty principles. Thus, specifications must not discriminate either directly or indirectly suppliers from other Member States. Industrial objectives are therefore generally ruled out.

In order to avoid the restriction of competition, the EU has adopted a standardisation and certification policy implemented by specific directives aimed at standardising the public contracting authorities. They have to adopt standards,

---

16 Question No. 835/82, MEP R. Schwarzenberg and Commission response C-93/1, 1983.

17 Case C-45/87, *Commission v. Ireland*, 1988, ECR 4929.

18 Ibid.

19 Sue Arrowsmith, The law of public and utilities procurement, para. 4.11, 2014.

i.e. technical specifications agreed upon by a recognised standardising body, for repeated and continuous application that will ensure competition to a greater extent.

Whether national standards belong to the regime seems to depend on the particular agreements between public contracting authorities and the National Standards Bodies. In 1985, the EC developed a "new approach" to technical harmonisation and standards. This means that European Institutions decide only on the essential health and safety requirements that products need to meet. Detailed guidance on how to meet these requirements is then provided by the European standards organisations: the European Committee for Standardisation (CEN)[20], the European Committee for Electrotechnical Standardisation (CENELEC)[21] and the European Telecommunications Standards Institute (ETSI)[22]. Product manufacturers must show that their goods conform to the European law by affixing the "CE" marking to the product concerned. The "CE" marking is the passport for the free circulation of this product on the internal market.

The CJEU outlined that even non-binding measures adopted by Member States may constitute a barrier to trade in that the measures may be capable of influencing the conduct of traders and consumers in that State[23] and therefore, dismissed the argument that Article 34 TFEU applies only to binding measures.[24]

1.4 De minimis rule under Article 34 TFEU

Article 34 TFEU covers measures that may potentially hinder trade and which clearly may apply where products are excluded from the government market or any part of it. The question is whether there is a de minimis rule,[25] which excludes Article 34 TFEU where the potential effect is negligible[26]. The de minimis rule exists in relation to the Treaty's competition law provisions. This issue was raised

---

20 https://www.cen.eu/Pages/default.aspx (05.06.2017).

21 https://www.cenelec.eu/aboutcenelec/whoweare/ (05.06.2017).

22 http://www.etsi.org/ (05.06.2017).

23 Case C-249/81, *Commission v. Ireland*, 1981, ECR 4005.

24 Harm Schepel, Legal aspects of standardisation in the Member States of the EC and EFTA, p. 57, 2000.

25 MEMO/06/482, State aid: Revised *'de minimis'* Regulation – frequently asked questions, 2006.

26 Case C-195/04, *Commissio v. Finland*, 2004, ECR I-03351, also Opinion of Advocate General Sharpston, 2007.

in Dundalk case,[27] were Advocate General Darmon suggested that given the importance of contracts with public bodies for suppliers in the industry and the importance of the particular contract, the effect of the measure was sufficiently significant not be de minimis. Even if there is no de minimis rule, a limitation of the applicability to "measures" of Article 34 TFEU has to be discussed further.

In the case Commission v. France[28] concerning a complaint that the French authorities had persistently failed to approve a British company's machines without good cause, the CJEU stated that to constitute a "measure" the administrative practice must exhibit a degree of consistency and generality[29]. Furthermore, in the Dundalk[30] case Advocate General Darmon concluded that in the praxis the specifications should not be treated separately as it was referring to the Irish national standards in an Irish government contract.

With reference to the procurement cases, the Treaty also applies to the individual procurement contracts. Thus, in Re Data Processing[31], Storebaelt[32], Bent Mousten Vestergaard[33] and the UNIX[34] cases, the CJEU found violations of the Treaty arising from acts relating to individual contracts. In all the above-mentioned cases with the exception of Vestergaard, the issue was discussed in more general practice.

1.4.1 Introduction of the Dundalk case

The case of Dundalk[35] and Cassis de Dijon are the milestones that falls within the scope of the public procurement on the internal market. The key principle of mutual recognition and free movement of goods were established in the case Cassis de Dijon[36]. The Dundalk case further elaborated the key principles. Article 34 TFEU also applied to measures concerning product requirements which equally hinder the sale and production of domestic products equally. On this basis, a specification may contradict Article 34 TFEU when it excludes products

---

27 Ibid.

28 Case C-21/84, *Commission v. France*, 1985, ECR 01355.

29 Sue Arrowsmith, The law of public and utilities procurement, para. 4.6, 2014.

30 Para. 8 of the case.

31 Case C-3/88, *Commission v. Italy*, 1989, ECR 4035.

32 Case C-243/89, *Commission v. Denmark*, 1993, ECR, I-3353.

33 Case C-59/00, *Bent Mousten Vestergaard v. Spøttrup Boligselskab*, 2001, ECR I-9505.

34 Ibid.

35 Ibid.

36 Christopher Bovis, EC public procurement: Case law and regulation, para. 8.01, 2006.

meeting public contracting authority's functional requirements, even if it affects foreign and domestic products equally. This was accepted by the UNIX case.

In 1987, Ireland was summoned before the CJEU after the Commission had received complaints that it had failed to comply with Directive 71/305/EEC on public works contracts[37] with regards to the construction of a water main for transportation of drinking water.[38] The Dundalk Urban District Council was in favour of Dundalk's drinking water supply. One of the contracts in the scheme required the construction of a water pipe to transport water from a river to a treatment plant and into the then present town supply system. That contract contained specifications about the water pipes to be used and in particular provided the following: "asbestos cement pressure pipes shall be certified as complying with Irish Standard Specification 188:1975 in accordance with the Irish Standard Mark Licensing Scheme of the Institute for Industrial Research and Standards"[39]. The Commission complained, among other things, that this stipulation infringed Article 34 TFEU regarding the free movement of goods between the Member States. The CJEU pointed out that Article 34 TFEU prohibits all Member State to include such restrictions in the tender specifications. In this case, only one company had been certified by the IIRS to I.S. 118:1975 to apply the Irish Standard Mark to the pipes in question and that company was located in Ireland. Therefore, the Court held that the reference to the specification in the invitation to tender had the effect of limiting the supply of the pipes needed for the Dundalk scheme to only Irish manufacturers.[40] The Court concluded that by permitting the said requirement in the invitation to tender, Ireland had failed to fulfil its obligations under Article 34 TFEU.

1.4.2 Case discussion and commentary remarks

The possibility of intervening in a fast and effective manner to prevent arising infringements or to bring infringements to an end is one of the most useful means of ensuring that the obligations of Member States under the EU law are respected. Article 10 of the Directive for works 71/305/EEC permits the definition of technical standards but only in certain conditions. Thus, Article 10 provides for that: "unless such specifications are justified by the subject of the

37 Ibid.

38 Christopher Bovis, The EU public procurement law, 2007, p. 127.

39 par. 1.2 of the case.

40 Timothy Millet, The rule of the European Court of Justice in relation to public procurement., P.P.L.R., Nr. 1, pp. 70–79, 1992.

contract[41]". Member States shall prohibit the introduction into the contractual clauses relating to a given contract of technical specifications, which mention products of a particular make or source or of a particular process and therefore favour or eliminate certain undertakings. Above all it will be prohibited to refer to particular trademarks, patents, types etc. However, if such reference includes the words "or equivalent", it shall be allowed in cases where the public contracting authorities are unable to provide a description that would include specifications that are sufficiently precise and eligible to all parties involved.

The Irish government featured such specifications that would exclude from the tender the pipes produced in another Member States with guarantees of safety, performance and reliability equivalent to those afforded by the Tegral pipes.[42] The Irish government insisted that Article 34 TFEU did not apply since trading was not impeded, or in any event, it was not impeded as a result of a commercial specification or other measure adopted by Ireland. The legal basis for this argument was not convincing. They argued that it was very usual that materials should be required to be in compliance with a certain technical standard, even a national standard, in order to ensure they are appropriate and safe to use. It was clear that such a specification would have the effect of completely cutting off competition from those who could offer pipes manufactured by providers outside Ireland.

Indeed the provisions in Case 194/88R Commission v. Italy[43] defines that interim measures will be granted to stop contracts from being awarded in breach of Community law.[44] If Member States are allowed to get away with breaching the requirements of Community law concerning public procurement only risking a suit for damages after a final judgement of the CJEU as a sanction, the tendency to award contracts infringing Article 34 TFEU will not be diminished.

Whether the specification was impeding imports into Ireland or not, the Court noted that the clause could cause economic operators who produced or used pipes equivalent to the pipes certified to the relevant Irish standard to refrain from tendering. Furthermore, as has already been noted, only one company, namely an Irish company, was certified for the size of pipe involved.

41 Article 10, Council Directive 71/305/EEC concerning the procedures for the award of public works contracts, 1971.

42 Sue Arrowsmith, The law of public and utilities procurement, para. 17.10, 2014.

43 Case C-194/88 R, *European Communities v Italian Republic,* 1988, ECR 05647.

44 Sue Arrowsmith, The award of interim measures in procurement case: Implications of the recent order in the Wallonia buses case, P.P.L.R., Nr. 4, CS130–136, 1994.

The author concludes that products meeting standards that offer equivalent guarantees of safety and reliability must be considered on their merits and cannot be denied the chance to compete. It is advisable that Member States add "or equivalent" rather than merely going through the motions of looking at products manufactured to different standards.[45]

1.4.3 *Introduction of the UNIX case*

The Dutch public contracting authority in 1991 published a contract notice in the OJEU to purchase the supply and maintenance for the meteorological station. The Commission found that the notice failed to comply with Community law requirements for two main reasons. First, the contract notice did not specify the opening committee, as well as the time, date, and place of opening, according to Article 9(5), as amended by Article 9 of the Directive 88/295, in relation to Annex III of the supplies Directive 77/62[46]. Secondly, the general terms and conditions of the contract referred to a particular operating system, UNIX[47], which was the name of a data-processing system manufactured by Bell Laboratories of ITT without being followed by the words "or equivalent". According to the Commission, the reference to a specific item was explicitly prohibited under Article 7(6) of the Directive 77/62 (as amended by Article 8 of the Directive 88/295) unless such a specific reference was necessary for the subject of the contract.

The Commission previously used a specific "swift" procedure provided in Article 3 of the Remedies Directive 89/665[48]. This provision implies that if the Commission, prior to a contract being awarded, considers the public contracting authority to have committed a clear infringement of public procurement rules, it has the right to notify the Member States and the respective public contracting authority of its motifs to believe the infringement has occurred and request it to be corrected. Not later than 21 days after the notification, the Member State shall provide its confirmation to the Commission that the infringement has been

45 Laurence Gormley, Quantitative restrictions and measures heaving equivalent effect: Grandfather clauses in Community law, E.L. Rev. 1989, 14(3), pp. 156–162.

46 Council Directive 88/295/EEC amending Directive 77/62/EEC relating to the coordination of procedures on the award of public supply contracts and repealing certain provisions of Directive 80/767/EEC, 1988.

47 Case C-359/93, *Commission v. Netherlands* (UNIX), 1995, ECR I-00157.

48 Ibid.

removed, the reasons explaining why no correction has been made or give notice of the contract award procedure suspension.

The Commission notified the government of the Netherlands of the alleged "clear and manifest" infringements on Friday, 25 June 1992; that is, more than six months after announcing the tender in the OJEU. The relevant ministry received the notification only four days later, on Monday, 29 June 1992, on the day the contract was awarded. The Commission also communicated to the Dutch Government that it should treat the notification as a formal letter of notice. Thus, the Unix case helped to further clarify public procurement rules and application of the provisions "or equivalent" similar to the Dundalk case.

1.4.4 Case discussion and commentary remarks

If the duty of cooperation between Member States and Community institutions has been infringed, it is unlikely to expect that an award procedure, initiated a few months before, would be suspended within the time limit of one working day. The Commission itself had previously made reference to the UNIX system as the technical specification to be complied with by tenderers in a contract notice concerning the procedure to be awarded at the Community level. This was a sufficient justification for the Dutch public contracting authority to believe that the reference to UNIX complied with Community law.[49]

With respect to the second point concerning the failure of the Dutch public contracting authority to add the words "or equivalent" when requiring the UNIX system to be the operating system supplied by the successful tenderer, the Dutch government argued that UNIX was in fact a class of products, in so far as the UNIX system is normally considered as a technical specification generally recognised by traders in the relevant sector. The absence of the words "or equivalent" was, according to the defendant, purposely intended to convey to the potential tenderers that the public contracting authority meant to refer not to a particular product but to a product with well-defined technical characteristics. In fact, eventually the contract went to a supplier that used a system resembling UNIX, but not UNIX itself.

The CJEU rejected the Dutch allegations and after referring to Article 7(6) of the Directive 77/62 that prohibits references to trade-marks unless accompanied by the words "or equivalent"; it concluded that the UNIX system could not be considered a standardised system that is a technical specification approved by

49 Jose M. Fernandez Martin, Note on case C-359/93 Commission v. the Netherlands (the Unix case), P.P.L.R., Nr. 4, CS74–79, 1995.

international standard institutions. The parties came to an agreement that UNIX does in fact refer to a specific make of a product. Therefore, the absence of the words "or equivalent"[50] constituted an infringement of Article 7(6) of the aforementioned Directive.

Moreover, an exclusive reference to UNIX as the desired operating system could not only deter suppliers offering systems resembling UNIX from participating in the tendering procedure but also interfere with the imports in intra-Community trade by giving the contract to tenderers that use only the specific system, thus the public contracting authorities' conduct also infringing Article 34 TFEU.[51]

1.5 Conclusions on the main cases

The cases discussed above are of great significance for the free movement of goods in the EU. The use of specific indicators of requirements in tenders, such as trademarks, patents, specific origin or production, is forbidden by public procurement laws. A product brand may only be specified in exceptional circumstances. However, where it is otherwise impossible to describe the product in a sufficiently precise manner, it is required that said designation be accompanied by the words "or equivalent"[52]. The reason for this interdiction is that if tender documents and specifications include a reference to a specific make of a product they may prevent potential bidders from submitting a tender for works, products or services similar to the specified make. In turn, this may impede internal market trade by making the contract exclusive to suppliers that are able to offer only that particular product, which is prohibited by Article 34 TFEU.[53]

Technical specifications can be based on references to national standards transposing European standards, European technical approvals, common technical specifications, international standards, other technical reference systems established by the European standardisation bodies or national standards, only if each reference is followed by the words "or equivalent"[54]. Alternatively, technical specifications can also refer to performance or functional requirements.

---

50 McLean Sieverding, Choice in government software procurement: A winning strategy, P.P.L.R., Nr. 6, 338–351, 2006.

51 Sue Arrowsmith, The application of the EC Treaty rules to public and utilities procurement, P.P.L.R. Nr. 6, 255–280, 1995.

52 Case C-324/98, *Telaustria and Telefonadress*, 2000, ECR I-10745.

53 Sue Arrowsmith, The law of public and utilities procurement, para. 17.6, 2014.

54 Christopher Bovis, EU public procurement law, 2016, p. 164.

As discussed above, in the case of UNIX, the tender's specifications required the operating system to be UNIX. The CJEU ruled that featuring references to goods of a specific make or source or of a particular process in technical specifications deterred suppliers providing systems other than UNIX from entering the tender, which would as a result favour or eliminate certain companies or products causing an infringement of public procurement law. Despite this, the Court allowed such an indication, if accompanied by the words "or equivalent".[55]

Even if public contracting authorities award contracts outside the scope of the directives, including those below the thresholds, they must follow the fundamental principles of the Treaty.[56] However, the Court did not express a requirement for "a degree of advertising" that was implied from the Treaty principles in Telaustria[57] in respect of service concessions, and applies the same way to the contracts below the Directive's thresholds.[58]

The discussed cases identified the different forms of hindrance to the market access and therefore restricting the free movement of goods. In conclusion, references to a particular make of products should be reserved only for cases where the requirements, if expressed in any other way, shall lack precision and intelligibility to all those concerned.

1.6 Articles 49 and 56 TFEU on the right of establishment and right to provide services

Article 49 TFEU defines the right for freedom of establishment whereby all EU nationals and firms can set up firms and businesses in other Member States. This freedom of establishment includes the right to set up activities as a self-employed person and pursue undertakings on an equal basis with nationals of the host State[59].

Accordingly, non-nationals established in any Member State cannot be restricted to the public procurement contracts. Both Article 49 and Article 56

---

55 Case C-59/00, *Bent Mousten Vestergaard v. Spottrup Boligselskab*, 2001, ECR I-09505.

56 Adrian Brown, Case T-258/06: The German challenge to the commission's interpretative communication on contracts not subject to the procurement directives, P.P.L.R., Nr. 3, NA84–87, 2007.

57 Ibid.

58 Ibid.

59 Case C-221/89, *Factortame*, 1991, ECR I-157; Case C-76/81, *Fearon*, 1984, ECR 3677.

TFEU prohibit direct and indirect discrimination[60]. Article 56 TFEU aims to open up markets for persons registered in one Member State who intend to provide services in another on a temporary basis without the need to set up a permanent office[61]. A breach of Article 56 TFEU occurs if a Member State reserves the access to public contracts for domestic suppliers or applies certain quality and performance requirements to companies from other Member States that do not apply to domestic bidders in the same way.[62] The breach of Article 56 TFEU was identified in the Case-360/89, "Commission v. Italy"[63] whereby Italian law defined preferential requirements for domestic bidders through the reservation of 15 % to 30 % of public works for contractors located in the region. There is no doubt such requirements favoured local Italian companies and breached the principle of equal treatment. The case law requires eliminating any restrictions favouring domestic providers or those of other Member States alike.[64]

2 The EU public procurement Directive 2014/24/EU

The current section will provide an overview of the main EU public procurement Directive 2014/24/EU.[65] The development of secondary legislation of European public procurement started in 1970. Through the decades, a number of new directives were adopted. The latest Directive 2014/24/EU was adopted in 2014.

The Directive 2014/24/EU does not directly define the aim of public procurement, yet two key objectives may be identified. According to the provisions of Article 2 (1)(5) of the Directive, "the aim of public procurement is the rational use of funds under the procurement contract that must be of direct economic benefit to the public contracting authority in the acquisition of the necessary goods, services or works[66]".

---

60 Case C-369/89, *Commission v. Italy*, 1992, ECR I-3353; Case C-3/88, *Commission v. Italy*, 1989, ECR 4035.

61 Andrea Usai, Caught between the public procurement principles and the 'public procurement function' of Directive 2006/123/EC still a 'grey zone' in search for legal certainty, 9 EPPPL 228, 2014.

62 Ibid.

63 Case C-360/89, *Commission v. Italy*, 1992, ECR I-3401.

64 Constant De Koninck, Thierry Ronse, William Timmermans, European Public Procurement Law, The Public Sector Procurement Directive 2014/24/EU explained through 30 years of case law by the Court of Justice of the European Union, 2015, Chapter 4.

65 Ibid.

66 Article 2 (1)(5) of the Directive 2014/24/EU.

Above all, public procurement rules are defined to ensure that public funds are used efficiently. Strict regulations concerning public funds in enforcing the public procurement rules arbitrarily reduces the possibility of fraud among civil servants and helps to prevent corruption. Public contracting authorities should buy high quality, innovative, longer life-cycle goods to make public procurement a better use of common societal goals.[67] These goals can be identified as follows: protection of the environment, stimulating innovation and social inclusion, and acquiring high quality service. In order to implement these objectives, it is necessary to improve the transparency in public procurement procedures.

Simplified and successful conduct of public procurement procedures could help public contracting authorities to use the minimum time and available public funds needed to achieve the most efficient procurement outcomes. Increased-efficiency procedures for all economic operators would ensure a better access to small and medium-sized enterprises (SMEs) and promote cross-border participation in public procurement. For this aim to become reality, firstly, strong competition in the internal market for public contract awarding must be created.[68]

The second aim of public procurement has to do with ensuring fair competition. The CJEU has established the aim of Directive 2014/24/EU as being the elimination of restrictions to fair competition and providing access for bidders from different Member States to tender procedures thus ensuring the compliance with Article 49 and Article 56 TFEU on the right of establishment and right to provide services.[69]

If applied correctly, public procurement procedures ensure fair competition for all economic operators. Conditions set must allow the bidders to compete on equal terms and the said procedures must not interfere with fair competition.[70] Member States often seek to also implement secondary objectives such as the maintenance of industry and trade by encouraging the purchase of domestic production. In order to create new jobs and develop regional and local trade in a Member State, it is aimed at protecting against competition from foreign companies and therefore resulting in a discrimination against foreign suppliers.[71]

---

67 The European Commission's Green Paper on the modernisation of EU public procurement policy — towards a more efficient European Procurement Market, 2011, p. 4.

68 The European Commission's Green Paper on the modernisation of EU public procurement policy — towards a more efficient European Procurement Market, 2011, p. 5.

69 Case C-412/04, *Commission v Italy,* 2008, ECR I-00619.

70 Sue Arrowsmith, The law of public and utilities procurement, 2014, p. 26.

71 Rima Ambrazevičienė. Viešųjų pirkimų valstybinio reguliavimo politikos raida Lietuvoje, Jurisprudencija, 59 (51), p. 111, 2004.

Consequently, Article18 of the Directive defines fundamental principles of non-discrimination and equal treatment that public contracting authorities must observe when carrying out public procurement procedures[72].

Public contracting authorities must also ensure transparent use of taxpayers' money. Public procurement operations are often criticised for leaving too much room for possible corruption and therefore particular focus should be placed on the transparency of public procurement procedures. This can only be achieved, if the principles of public procurement are respected.

The principles of public procurement must be considered as the cornerstone and guidelines embodying the essence of the procurement process.[73] The principles of public procurement constitute a primary source for the rights and obligations of both public contracting authorities and suppliers in the context of public procurement.[74] It is sufficient to detect an infringement of principles of public procurement without further references to other provisions for the court to deem the activities of the public contracting authority as unlawful.[75]

Accordingly, in awarding a public contract the State, regional or local authorities, or other bodies governed by public law, shall abide by the following principles laid down in the Directive: the free movement of goods, freedom of establishment, freedom to provide services, equal treatment, non-discrimination, mutual recognition, proportionality, and transparency.[76]

It is essential that the fundamental principles of public procurement are complied with during the public procurement procedures, which includes drafting technical specifications and tender documents, selecting the procurement procedure, publishing the contract notice, nominating the successful bidder and publishing the award contract. To fully grasp the essence of these principles they must be discussed in more detail, in particular, the key principles of public procurement are equal treatment and non-discrimination.[77]

---

72 Article 18 of the Directive 2014/24/EU.

73 Jakštas V., Jovaišas K. Viešieji pirkimai. Viešųjų pirkimų įstatymo komentaras. "Verslo ir komercinė teisė", Vilnius, 2004, p. 31.

74 Judicial practice for February 2008, p. 9: https://www.lat.lt/data/public/uploads/2018/01/2009-liepa-rugpjutiss.doc (07.06.2017).

75 Lietuvos Aukščiausiojo Teismo Civilinių bylų skyriaus teisėjų kolegijos 2009 m. vasario mėn. 2 d. nutartis civilinėje byloje UAB "Kauno keliai" v. Klaipėdos miesto savivaldybė, bylos Nr. 3K-3-25/2009. https://www.lat.lt/data/public/uploads/2018/01/2009-liepa-rugpjutiss.doc (06.07.2017).

76 Recital 1 and 7 of the Directive 2014/24/EU.

77 Christopher Bovis, Public procurement in the European Union, UK, 2005, p. 73.

2.1 The principle of equal treatment

According to the Directive, the award of public contracts must duly respect the principles of the Treaties, including those of the free movement of services, freedom of establishment, and the principles derived from them, such as equal treatment, non-discrimination, mutual recognition, proportionality and transparency[78]. This implies that contracts must be awarded based on objective criteria that ensure the afore-mentioned principles are complied with. For example, to ensure that the principle of equal treatment is respected in the process of contract award,[79] public contracting authorities are required to provide the necessary transparency levels to reasonably inform tenderers of the criteria and procedures that will be followed in the contract award decision. Subsequently, the public contracting authorities have to clearly determine the contract award criteria and the weight of each criterion.

The Directive emphasises equal and non-discriminatory treatment of economic operators, in addition to the requirement for contracting entities to act in a manner that is both transparent and proportionate.[80] In addition, competition shall not be artificially narrowed if certain tenderers are favoured or disadvantaged.

The CJEU has dealt with a series of cases in which the principle of equal treatment has been an issue.[81] The principle of equal treatment requires the public contracting authority to ensure a fair playing field for all suppliers and equal opportunities to participate across the European Union countries.[82] The public contracting authority is allowed to disqualify suppliers from the public procurement procedure if they have been unlawfully involved in the preparatory work they engaged in as far as contractual matters are concerned.[83]

It should be reminded that the principle of equal treatment applies at all phases of public procurement process[84], it also means that all suppliers should

---

78 Ibid.

79 Recital 90 of the Directive 2014/24/EU.

80 Article 18 of the Directive 2014/24/EU.

81 Case C-249/89, *Trave-Schiffahrtsgesellschaft mbH & Co. KG v Finanzamt Kiel-Nord,* 1991, I-00257; Case C-3/88, *Commission v Italy,* 1989, ECR 4035.

82 Florian Neumayr, Value for money v. equal treatment: the relationship between the seemingly overriding national rationale for regulating public procurement and the fundamental E.C. principle of equal treatment, P.P.L.R. 215, 2002.

83 Case C-21/03 and C-34/03, *Fabricom SA v Belgium*, 2005, I-01559.

84 Peter Braun, A matter of principle(s) – the treatment of contracts falling outside the scope of the European public procurement directives, P.P.L.R. 2000, P. 39.

be given an equal access to procurement procedures and the right to dispute the decisions of public contracting authority thus ensuring there is effective competition between suppliers.[85] In particular, the goal of the provisions of Directive 2014/24/EU is to create the favourable conditions for competition in their areas of application.[86]

As for the technical specifications[87], public contracting authorities must always secure equal access for all economic operators to the procurement procedure and by no means have the effect of unreasonably hindering fair competition in the public procurement process.

Equality of treatment must be ensured among whole participants[88]. The information must be provided in such a way that it would not discriminate against certain suppliers as this may give other tenderers an advantage over the others during the procurement procedures[89]. An example of this could be providing some participants with more information than others.

The European procurement legislation had not regulated the question directly on the submission of additional documents during the procurement process until the new Directive was adopted. According to the CJEU, the request for clarification was regulated under the national legislation and ultimately seeking clarifications was up to the public contracting authority to decide. The only limits are the ones laid down in the above-mentioned case law. Since 2014 they are also defined in Article 56 (3) of the Directive. This provision can also be seen as an example of how European and national legislation interacts, where the Member States enjoy discretion rights as long as they comply with the set of principles and rules.[90]

---

85 Lietuvos Aukščiausiojo Teismo Civilinių bylų skyriaus teisėjų kolegijos 2009 m. vasario mėn. 2 d. nutartis civilinėje byloje UAB "Kauno keliai" v. Klaipėdos miesto savivaldybė, bylos Nr. 3K-3-25/2009. https://www.lat.lt/data/public/uploads/2018/01/2009-liepa-rugpjutiss.doc (06.07.2017).

86 Case C-21/03 and C-34/03 *Fabricom SA v Belgium*, 2005, I-01559; Case C-513/99, *Concordia Bus Finland*, 2002, I-07213.

87 Case C-432/02 *Commission v Trombin*, ECR I-9665.

88 Article 42 of the Directive 2014/24.

89 Case C-195/04, *Commission of the European Communities v Republic of Finland*, 2007, ECR I-03351, Opinion of Advocate General Sharpston, 18 January 2007.

90 Case C-599/10, *SAG ELV Slovensko a.s. and Others v Úrad pre verejné obstarávanie*, 2012, ECR I-10873.

There is some uncertainty as to what type of clarifications and amendments can be made after the deadline for submission of the offers. In the Slovensko case[91], the CJEU drew up a framework within which public contracting authorities might ask for clarifications to candidates or tenderers. While Slovensko showed that it is not precluded for a public contracting authority from exceptionally requesting clarifications of unclear aspects of a tender, the arguments in the case Manova[92] raised the issue of whether the public contracting authority can ask a candidate for the documents that were not submitted within the deadlines.[93] It seems that such a broad interpretation of equal treatment bends the principle of the discretion of public contracting authority stemming from a more flexible approach. However, as it was the case with Slovensko, in particular situations the public contracting authority may request clarifications of tenders already submitted. It cannot request any documents that would add information to the scope of the offer, and that request must not favour or discriminate the tenderer to which it is addressed.[94] Consequently, the public contracting authority can request any kind of additional information as long as it was available before the deadline and it was defined in the contract documents.[95]

It is debatable which additional documents should be allowed to be submitted by suppliers and whether the late submission should be allowed if it does not produce any significant advantage to the submitting tenderer.[96] It must be ensured that the scope of the offer would not change.

The Slovensko case enshrined both the public contracting authority's discretionary power to request clarifications and certain limits on these discretionary powers. The CJEU not only accepted discretionary powers but also laid down preventative measures to protect the equal treatment of tenders and avoid the line between discretion and arbitrariness becoming blurred. Thus, accepting and seeking certain clarifications after the deadline is not automatically forbidden. The next step can also be witnessed in the Manova case where the

---

91 Case C-336/12, *Ministeriet for Forskning, Innovation og Videregående Uddannelser v Manova A/S*, 2013, ECLI:EU:C:2013:647.

92 Ibid.

93 Albert Sanchez-Graells, Reformation or deformation of the EU public procurement rules, 2016, p. 247.

94 Ibid.

95 Ibid.

96 Ibid., p. 248.

focus falls on the principle of competition pushing aside the principle of equal treatment of tenders.

The author would like to underline that the case law had a strong influence in the reform of public procurement and, therefore, the new Directive has expressly envisaged the interpretation of arguments addressed in the Slovensko and Manova cases in Article 56 (3). The practical consequences of this provision must be examined case by case. However, the author agrees that flexibility must be achieved through reducing requirements and the need to provide certain documents, and not by bending the rules or creating exceptional situations that could be used to favour certain suppliers.

The majority of the case law considers the principles of equal treatment and non-discrimination as a cornerstone to public procurement.

2.2 The principle of non-discrimination

There has been a great focus on the non-discrimination principle in all successive versions of the directives.[97] According to the CJEU, the principle of non-discrimination should be applied in a way that tenderers are treated in the same manner unless such application is justifiable by objective reasons.[98] This general principle aims to prevent not only the obvious discrimination based on nationality, but also other forms of discrimination.[99] The main judgements "Commission v France"[100] and "Vestergaard,"[101] have placed a great emphasis on complying with the principle of non-discrimination.

Public contracting authorities and contracting process in the selection of suppliers have to avoid any action that would imply to discriminate bidders. Therefore, the CJEU has emphasised that technical specifications must consist of describing certain common features of the item to be acquired according to

---

97 Recital 9 of Directive 71/305/EEC and Recital 2 of Directive 77/62/EEC (and their subsequent revisions: see Recital 6 of Directive 88/295/EEC and Recital 14 of Directive 89/440), and Recital 20 of Directive 92/50/EEC. See also Recital 14 of Directive 93/36/EEC and Recital 10 of Directive 93/37/EEC. In the following generation of Directives, the references were much more numerous: see, especially, Recitals 2 and 46 of the Directive 2004/18/EC and Recitals 40 and 55 of Directive 2004/17/EC; Recitals 1, 37, 40, 45, 68, 90, 114 of the Directive 2014/24/EU.

98 Case C-810/79, *Peter Überschär v Bundesversicherungsanstalt für Angestellte.*

99 Ibid.

100 Case C-264/03, *Commission of the European Communities v French Republic,* 2005, ECR I-08831.

101 Ibid.

the corresponding criteria, but it is also necessary to outline the characteristics of equivalent and similar items[102]. To prevent discrimination against other candidates it is required to refrain from making any references to specific national standards and requirements in specific documents or from setting such requirements that would hinder suppliers from other Member States of the EU to enter the competition[103] that the neutrality requirements are breached.[104]

The TFEU imposes certain requirements similar to some of those of the procurement directives. It argues, firstly, that tenderers throughout the EU should know the rules of the respective procurement in advance and that an equal amount of information should be provided to them at the same time. All offers should be considered during the selection stages of the award procedure in conformity with the tender specification in order to guarantee an objective comparison between them. Non-compliant bids should be rejected and its variants should be dismissed unless it has been expressly permitted in the contract notice.[105] Member States are precluded from reserving public contracts for domestic companies and from giving preferences to bidders originating from a less developed region,[106] or preferences for domestic products.[107] Finally, the contractor should be chosen on an objective basis.

It is essential to ensure that public procurement procedures are designed so as to promote competition among bidders. This is the underlying rationale of the modern public procurement design as defined in the new Directive 2014/24/EU.[108] The doctrine of the CJEU enables public contracting authorities to correctly interpret and implement public procurement legislation, as well as confirming compliance with the relevant characteristics of the fundamental principles in practice.

To guarantee that the principles of equality and non-discrimination are followed in the contract award procedures, it is first and foremost necessary to ensure transparency. It is the responsibility of public contracting authority to

---

102 Ibid.

103 Case C-45/87, *Commission v Ireland, 1988 -04929*, 1995.

104 Barbara Buhr. Die Richtlinie 2004/18/EC und das Deutsche Vergaberecht, Beiträge zum Europäischen Wirtschaftsrecht, Band 51, Berlin, 2007, S. 54.

105 Ibid.

106 Ibid.

107 Case C-263/85, *Commission v. Italy*, 1991, ECR, I-2457.

108 Carmen Estevan de Quesada, Competition and transparency in public procurement markets, PPLR, 2014, 5, 229–244.

inform on the criteria of the procurement procedure and that the contract notice is widely published to ensure the market is open to competition[109].

2.3 The principle of transparency

The new Directive establishes that transparency is one of the principles governing public procurement.[110] Transparency is essential to maintain the integrity of the public procurement system. Transparency is not only linked to the integrity principle and the fight against corruption but, in general terms, it is also related to the maintenance and promotion of competition. The information on the availability of public contract opportunities and the existence of transparent procurement processes are essential to ensure open competition. It also ensures the accountability of public contracting authorities by providing economic operators with enough information to monitor the activities in the course of procurement procedures.

The procurement principle of transparency was also referred to expressly in the preambles of various procurement directives, indicating that this principle is also embodied in the directives rather than in the TFEU Treaty. This principle seeks first to ensure that participants know the clearly defined rules in the procurement procedures. Suppliers must therefore be informed throughout the process with precise information concerning the conduct of the entire procedure.[111] In addition, by reviewing public procurement procedures public contracting authorities maintain impartial and free from corruption.[112] The transparency principle should not be confused with the principle of non-discrimination that constitutes a fundamental principle of the Community law enforcement mechanism.

Furthermore, the principle of non-discrimination deserves a wider interpretation.[113] In the R.I.S.A.N[114] and Unitron[115] judgements, the Court did not clarify what an authority must do so that the obligation of transparency is observed, until the Telaustria case[116] was ruled out. The CJEU specified that in order to

---

109 Ibid.

110 Article 18 and Recital 1 of the Directive 2014/24/EU.

111 Case T-203/96, *Embassy Limousines & Services v European Parliament*, 1998, II-04239.

112 Case C-250/07, *European Communities v Hellenic Republic*, 2009, I-04369.

113 Ibid.

114 Case C-108/98, *RI.SAN. Srl v Comune di Ischia, Italia Lavoro SpA and Ischia Ambiente SpA.*, 1999, I-05219.

115 Case C-275/98, *Unitron Scandinavia A/S and 3-S A/S, Danske Svineproducenters Serviceselskab v Ministeriet for Fødevarer, Landbrug og Fiskeri*, 1999, I-08291.

116 Ibid.

comply with the transparency obligation, public contracting authorities must advertise public contracts in a way that they would be open to competition from potential bidders across the EU, even though outside the scope of the Directive.

The obligation of transparency also applies to the public contracting authority so that its interpretation of the award criteria would remain consistent throughout the entire procedure.[117] Thus, the aim of the mandatory public contract notice is to ensure an acceptable level of transparency. Nevertheless, it is important to note that there is a number of exceptions found within the case law[118]. Due to specific circumstances, such as very low economic benefits, it would be reasonable to argue that suppliers that may be established in another Member State would not be interested in the potential dispute.[119] Further requirements of consistent application of principles across the Member States will be discussed in the next chapter.

2.4 The principle of proportionality

The content of the proportionality principle defines the appropriate proportionality between the objectives to be achieved and the measures envisaged to achieve these objectives. The proportionality principle should be taken into consideration when public contracting authorities set minimum qualification requirements for candidates or participants. First, they may not unduly restrict competition, limit the rights of participants, regard them as inequitable, or discriminate against others. Therefore, qualification and other requirements must be clear, precise and corresponding with all aspects to the object of the purchase and conditions set.[120] Second, they may not unduly limit competition and restrict the rights of participants and discriminate against others.[121]

---

117 Case-IEHC 56, *Gaswise Limited v Dublin City Council High Court of Ireland* (Finlay Geoghegan J.), February 14, 2014; Case C-21/03, *Fabricom SA v Belgium*, 2005, ECR. I-1559.

118 Case T-258/06, *Federal Republic of Germany v European Commission*, 2010, II-02027; Case-87/94, *Commission of the European Communities v Kingdom of Belgium*, 1996, I-02043; Case C-470/99, *Universale-Bau and Others*, 2002, I-11617.

119 Case C-231/03, *Consorzio Aziende Metano (Coname) v Comune di Cingia de' Botti*, 2005, I-07287.

120 The European Commission's proposal for a Directive of the European Parliament and of the Council on public procurement, p. 6, COM (2011) 896.

121 Deividas Soloveičikas, Viešųjų pirkimų principai: jų taikymas remiantis Europos Teisingumo Teismo ir Lietuvos teismų praktika, Justitia, 2008, t. 3 (69).

In the domain of public contracts, the principle States the necessity of the definition of performance and technical specifications. Moreover, the definition must be appropriate in terms of the objective it is aimed at. It is thus not permitted for authorities to lay down excessive and disproportionate technical, professional or financial criteria when selecting candidates[122].

It is interesting to note that before the adoption of the new Directive 2014/24/EU in 2014, there was generally little concern with proportionality in the EU secondary legislation in terms of public procurement. Currently, the proportionality principle is listed not only as one of the main procurement principles, but it also imposes specific obligations to public contracting authorities outlined in the provisions of the said Directive. It requires that public contracting authorities shall treat economic operators equally, without discrimination and shall act in a transparent and proportionate manner.[123] Following a number of judgements ruled out by the CJEU, the new rules were introduced in the recent Directive 2014/24/EU. Previously, the CJEU stated in the case Presse text[124] "that modifications of a public contract during the term require a new contract to be awarded: when they are materially different in character from the original contract and, therefore, demonstrate the intention of the parties to renegotiate the essential terms of that contract"[125]. Under the case law, a general distinction has been made between modifications of public contracts that were material, and, as such, in principle, inconsistent with EU law, and modifications that were not material and, in consequence, consistent with thc EU law.[126] Consequently, the author would like to analyse whether the CJEU's interpretation of the proportionality principle is aligned with the new rules of the Directive 2014/24/EU.

Article 72 (4) of the Directive 2014/24/EU States that public contracts may be amended without initiating a new procurement procedure as long as the modifications, irrespective of their value, are not material[127]. The author believes that in some cases such modifications could be interpreted as being material. Article 72 also describes in which circumstances public contracts could be

122 Case C-213/07, *Michaniki AE v Ethniko Symvoulio Radiotileorasis and Ypourgos Epikrateias*, 2008, ECLI-731.

123 Article 18 (1), Article 36 (1), 19 (2), 47 (3), 58 (1) of the Directive 2014/24/EU.

124 Case C-454/06, *Pressetext Nachrichtenagentur GmbH v Republik Österreich (Bund), APA-OTS Originaltext-Service GmbH and APA Austria Presse Agentur registrierte Genossenschaft mit beschränkter Haftung*, 2008, ECR I-04401.

125 Ibid.

126 Sue Arrowsmith, The law of public and utilities procurement, 2014, p. 597.

127 Article 72 (4) of the Directive 2014/24/EU.

changed without publishing a contract notice. In the author's opinion, the interpretation of this provision would fall outside the scope of the Directive.

Although the modifications specified in Article 72 may be substantial, they can be carried out without a new procurement procedure so long as these conditions are met. This is contrary to the arguments defined in the case Presse text. Following the implementation of the Directive 2014/24/EU, it is necessary to clarify which modifications in the EU public procurement law are permitted to public contracts and comply with the EU law and which are not allowed and fail to comply[128].

This burden is put on public contracting authorities, which in practice decide whether to allow a modification or not. Having assessed the modification's substantiality, public contracting authorities have to consider whether or not it corresponds with the EU law and is in line with the fundamental principles. If the public contract is modified it may also violate equal treatment.[129] Based on the author's experience, if the contract is already in place, the costs of a new procurement procedure and switch of the supplier may be higher than awarding a new contract. If an incumbent supplier already exists it might happen that the costs of the process can be easily reduced, which is not necessarily possible with new procurement procedure. In practice, terminating an existing public contract and putting it out again to tender, with its original amended scope, is a costly decision in terms of, firstly, time and legal uncertainty and secondly, responsibility and liability. Consequently, public contracting authorities will typically be open to modifications of the public contract when they consider that there is likelihood of contract performance that could lead to a successful procurement process.

The final question would be what kind of decision the public contracting authority would take in case of doubts on whether or not to modify or retender the public contract. Based on the author's experience, in most cases this is case dependent. One way or another, it is very important that public contracting authorities treat modifications of public contracts with caution so that the transparency, non-discrimination and equal treatment of tenderers are ensured.

2.5 The principle of mutual recognition

The principle of mutual recognition constitutes an integral part of the set of fundamental principles and is defined in the new Directive 2014/24/EU[130]. Recital 42 of the previous Directive 2004/18 States that it is necessary to apply

128 Steen Treumer, Modernising public procurement: The new directive, 2014, p. 296.
129 Sue Arrowsmith, The law of public and utilities procurement, 2014, p. 578.
130 Ibid.

corresponding Community rules on mutual recognition of diplomas, certificates or other evidence of formal qualifications in cases where the participation in a procurement procedure or a design contest requires a particular qualification and it has to be proved[131].

Article 59 of the Directive 2014/24/EU introduces the European Single Procurement Document (ESPD), which replaces certificates issued by public contracting authorities[132]. The aim of the ESPD is to confirm that the respective economic operator meets the necessary requirements and is not excluded from tender procedures[133].

The ESPD would be applied in cross-border participation in public procurement procedures as this document will be acknowledged by all Member States. According to the principle of mutual recognition, public contracting authorities must accept products and services supplied by operators from other Member States, provided that the said products and services are able to meet the legitimate requirements set by the recipient Member State. This principle refers to the fact that technical specifications, diplomas and qualifications have to be accepted by the receiving Member State if they are acknowledged as equivalent to those required by the Member State where the service is to be provided[134]. In this case, for example, a Lithuanian contracting organisation must accept official documents of foreign tenderers and, applying the same rule, documents issued in Lithuania must be acknowledged in other Member States.[135]

To summarise, in authors view the new Directive 2014/24/EU sets a more simplified procedure in recognition of supporting documents for all Member States and ensures that a single harmonised document by ESPD would be electronically standardised and recognised in all Member States during the tender processes.

2.6 Conclusion of the fundamental principles

The authors view is that the CJEU had and continues to have a major role in the interpretation of the fundamental principles of public procurement. Whether it

131 Recital 42 of the Directive 2004/18.

132 Article 59 of Directive 2014/24/EU.

133 Rhodri Williams, The European single procurement document, PPLR, 2016, p. 2.

134 Article 3.1.4. Mutual recognition, Commission Interpretative Communication on Concessions under Community Law. 2000, p. 7.

135 Deividas Soloveičikas, Lietuvos viešųjų pirkimų sistemos tobulinimo ir plėtros strategijos studija, 2007 m. rugpjūčio mėn. 14 d. p. 163.

is through preliminary rulings ensuring the effect of the respective EU rules, or through infringement actions stating the failure of a Member State to fulfil its EU obligations or even through interim orders suspending the award of a procurement contract.

The fundamental principles first operate as an invaluable aid to interpreting the detailed rules and, in particular, in filling the gaps between the provisions of the directives. Another important purpose of the principles is that they allow for flexibility where complex and detailed rules of the directives cannot cope with the practical issues posed by a continually changing procurement environment. Accordingly, the fundamental principles will not only serve as an aid to interpretation but also as the basis for possible reforms to the European procurement regime. In order to increase legal certainty and to remove any remaining doubts as regards the question of the interpretation of principles, the author suggests that public contracting authorities should always apply fundamental principles with due diligence. The author would like to point out the occurrence of situations in which the public contracting authority at their discretion will have to make a decision regarding the extent of substantiality of contract modifications and application of fundamental principles to contracts falling outside the scope of Directive 2014/24/EU. Only substantial knowledge and solid public procurement experience can assure a proper interpretation and application of fundamental principles in the application of public procurement procedures. If all Member States together and unanimously seek the same purpose of properly using public funds, not distorting fair competition and reducing administrative burdens, then the sound application of the fundamental principles will help to achieve that vision across the EU.

3 Low-value contracts outside the scope of Directive 2014/24/EU

Low-value contracts provide significant opportunities for European businesses, in particular for SMEs[136] and start-ups. They are beneficial for public contracting authorities as they guarantee a wider range of potential suppliers and the opportunity to get better value for their money. The Directive 2014/24/EU does not govern such contracts as their value is below the EU thresholds.[137] Yet, the CJEU

136 MEMO 06/303, Frequently Asked Questions (FAQs) on interpretative communication on contract awards not or not fully subject to the public procurement Directives, 2006.

137 Article 1 of the Commission Delegated Regulation (EU) 2017/2365 amending Directive 2014/24/EU of the European Parliament and of the Council in respect of the application thresholds for the procedures for the award of contracts, 2017.

has ruled out a number of cases providing interpretation that the principles of transparency and non-discrimination applies to these contracts on the basis of the TFEU. The author will analyse these cases as to whether fundamental principles are also applicable to the low-value contracts governed by the Directive 2014/24/EU.[138] The CJEU does not provide an answer to the Commission's view nor to the contradictory opinion of General Advocate Sharpston.[139] Sharpston's opinion raises a number of key issues, which will be addressed in the next section in order to find the best answers to these issues.

3.1 The TFEU principles applicable to low-value contracts

A detailed analysis of relevant provisions of TFEU and the fundamental principles of Directive 2014/24/EU calls for a need to understand whether the fundamental principles apply outside the scope of this Directive 2014/24/EU. It is for this reason that the EU has adopted Directive 2014/24/EU, containing highly detailed procedural rules regarding procurement obligations of the Member States, outlining, *inter alia*, in what conditions and what types of procedures may be followed. For instance, various public procurement rules describe in detail under which circumstances a public contracting authority may proceed with awarding a contract without any prior call for competition whatsoever. There is no doubt that the general principle of non-discrimination on grounds of nationality, as defined in Article 18 of the TFEU, is far too general of an instrument to provide a sufficiently transparent legal basis in assessing such issues.

Thc rules and general principles[140] of the TFEU define that public contracting authorities must apply the rules regulating the free movement of goods, the right of establishment the freedom to provide services[141] and the general principles[142] of non-discrimination and equal treatment, transparency, proportionality and mutual recognition.[143] The important question, however, is the way these rules and general principles are enforced and followed outside the scope of Directive 2014/24/EU in practice. It is in this regard that the current Interpretative

138 Ibid.

139 Ibid.

140 Paul Craig Gráinne de Búrga, EU law, III edition, p. 614, 2003.

141 Ibid.

142 Florian Neumayr, Value for money v. equal treatment: The relationship between the seemingly overriding national rationale for regulating public procurement and the fundamental E.C. principle of equal treatment, PPLR 4, 215–234, 2002.

143 Peter Braun, A matter principle(s) – the treatment f contracts falling outside the scope of the European public procurement Directives, PPLR 1, 39–48, 2000.

Communication,[144] the Commission's view and especially the opinion of General Advocate Sharpston are of most interest to be further discussed.[145]

The Advocate General stated in his response that one had to examine whether it was possible that the exceptions expressly provided for in primary TFEU law or justified on grounds recognised in the case law on fundamental freedoms could be applied.

In short, the Advocate General's opinion is helpful in acknowledging the existence of some flexibility when applying the requirement for advertisement under the TFEU: the degree of advertising may vary according to the circumstances and may be dispensed with altogether in some situations. However, it is regrettable that neither the judgement nor the opinion give any clear guidance on what the TFEU requirements actually entail in particular circumstances.

Furthermore, it is well established that Directive 2014/24/EU, as a secondary law, cannot override the requirements of the TFEU, as a primary law, where the secondary legislation regulates the issue in question exhaustively. The Directive 2014/24/EU fails to comprehensively regulate those contracts that fall entirely or partially outside the scope of the Directive.

The key issue is not whether the principles of the TFEU[146] continue to apply to contracts outside the scope of the Directive 2014/24/EU, but rather whether these principles justify the introduction of a positive obligation of advertising, rather than a mere "negative" prohibition on taking measures that may discriminate against suppliers from other Member States. The best practise is that public contracting authorities continue awarding these contracts directly to local providers without any competition.

3.2 The counter arguments of General Advocate Sharpston

Advocate General Sharpston made a statement in the case Commission v. Republic of Finland[147] arguing that it should be national law, rather than the

144 Commission interpretative communication on the Community law applicable to contracts awards not or not fully subject to the provisions of the public procurement Directives, 2006/C 179/02.

145 Case T-258/06, *Federal Republic of Germany v European Commission*, 2010, ECR II-02027; Adrian Brown, Case T-258/06: The German challenge to the Commissions interpretative communication on contracts not subject to the procurement Directives, PPLR 3, NA84–87, 2007.

146 Green Paper on public-private partnerships and community law on public contracts and concessions, COM (2004) 327.

147 Ibid.

EU law that decides on the transparency degree in the award of contracts bellow the EU thresholds. If her opinion is taken into account by the CJEU, it would establish that national rules apply for low value contracts and constitute a meaningful development of the CJEU's case law.[148]

The Commission did not share the view of the General Advocate Sharpston. The Commission found that the public contracting authority had not secured a sufficient degree of advertising and as a consequence Finland breached its obligations under Article 34 TFEU. The key concern in this case was the degree of contract advertising and award transparency, regardless of the fact that the value of the contract was below the respective threshold established by the public procurement regulations. The Commission considers that the low value contracts require a certain level of advertisement to ensure the transparency obligations under Article 34 TFEU.

3.3 Transparency obligation

Articles 49 and 56 of the TFEU[149] lay down the principle of an obligation of transparency as previously discussed. The main concern is whether the obligation for transparency outside[150] the scope of Directive 2014/24/EU still applies during the public procurement procedures.

In order to respect the rules and principles of the TFEU and Directive 2014/24/EU the award process has to be in line with principles of non-discrimination, equal access, reasonable time limits for application of procedures, etc.[151]

However, these provisions of the TFEU do not in all cases preclude a direct contract award, i.e. without publication of a contract notice or call for competition available beforehand. In order to assess whether such a direct award is permissible, it is considered, in the framework of a market analysis, which economic operators would be interested in the proposed contract, taking into account potential competition. The value and object of the contract play a decisive role in this regard.

148 Totis Kotsonis, The extent of the transparency obligation imposed on a public contracting authority awarding a contract whose value falls below the relevant value threshold: Case C-195/04, Commission v Finland, opinion of Advocate General Sharpston, PPLR 3, NA71–83, 2007.

149 Peter Trepte, Public procurement in the EU, para. 1.22, 2007.

150 Ibid.

151 Matthias Krugner, The principles of equal treatment and transparency and the Commission interpretative communication on concessions, PPLR 5, 181–207, 2003.

In the "Commission v. Republic of Finland" case, Finland tried to prove the following two aspects. First, it stated that the entire process had to be assessed as a whole. The second argument was that it being a low value contract the obligation of transparency did not require a specific form of publication; also that the application of the transparency obligations is circumstantial and mostly governed by national law[152].

Advocate General Sharpston argued that the position of the Commission was inadmissible and had failed to prove the breach of the transparency obligations under Article 34 FEU.[153] Advocate General Sharpston held that the requirements for advertising are governed by States. First, she argued that the award of contracts below the established threshold was a matter of national law regardless of the amount of the advertising invested. Following the principles of subsidiary, the European Commission should rather focus on starting infringement proceedings against Member States that failed to secure sufficient transparency through national legislation, rather than on dealing with individual contract cases of low value contracts. Second, she explained that imposing a requirement of publicity without having the details would lead to a substantial legal confusion in any legislative texts[154].

Advocate General Sharpston brought to attention the fact that the Commission was only vaguely able to suggest what forms of publicity would have been sufficient to fulfil the transparency obligation in this case.[155] Further analysis of the CJEU will show that the fundamental principles have to be applied for below-value contracts by States regardless of the Advocate General Sharpston opinion.

3.4 Interpretation of the further case law

In the cases[156] on contracts below the EU thresholds, the CJEU was of the opinion that does not necessarily absolve the Member State from application of

---

152 Dawn Hendry, Transparency obligations in public procurement – Two cheers for Advocate General Sharpston, 2007. http://www.worldservicesgroup.com/publications.asp?action=article&artid=1892 (21.05.2018).

153 Sue Arrowsmith, The law of public and utilities procurement, para. p. 239, 2014.

154 Ibid.

155 Totis Kotsonis, The extent of the transparency obligation imposed on a public contracting authority awarding a contract whose value falls below the relevant value threshold: Case C-195/04, Commission v Finland, opinion of Advocate General Sharpston, PPLR 3, NA71–83, 2007.

156 Martin Dischendorfer, "Service concessions under the EC procurement Directives: A Note on the Telaustria Case", PPLR 10, NA57, 2001.

fundamental principles. As the CJEU concluded in the case Unitron Scandinavia[157], non-discrimination principle means, above all, an obligation of transparency.[158]

On 14 September 2006, Advocate General Stix-Hackl expressed his opinion regarding two contracts that were not published above the thresholds Ireland had failed to fulfil its obligations under the TFEU[159].

The first case[160] was regarding the award of a contract that would allow people to collect their welfare benefit payments from post offices. The contract was the so-called Part B service contract, and the public contracting authority was not obligated under the old Services Directive 92/50/EEC[161] to announce the contract in the OJEU.

The second case[162] concerned the ambulance services contract, which was awarded verbally. As there was no written contract, it was considered outside the scope of the Services Directive 92/50/EEC, and, therefore, there was no obligation for advertisement. However, according to the fundamental EU principle of transparency the contracts have to be pre-advertised to ensure effective competition across all Member States. The opinion of Advocate General Stix-Hackl was in line with the CJEU's decision of Telaustria. In that case it was concluded that low value contracts must respect the general principle of transparency. The Commission's Interpretative Communication further endorsed this conclusion[163].

In the case Telaustria, the CJEU stressed out that the principle of transparency had to have a degree of advertising sufficient to enable the services market to be opened up to competition.[164] Advocate General Fennelly stated that, in determining the degree of advertising required, the first relevant question is whether

---

157 Ibid.

158 Erik Pijnacker Hordijk, A bridge too far: Why the European Commission's attempts to construct an obligation to tender outside the scope of the public procurement Directives should be dismissed, PPLR 3, 123–130, 2005.

159 ICLG, Public Procurement 2018. https://iclg.com/practice-areas/public-procurement-laws-and-regulations/eu-public-procurement-rules (21.05.2018).

160 Case C-507/03, *Commission of the European Communities v Ireland*, 2007, ECR I-09777.

161 Ibid.

162 Case C-532/03, *Commission of the European Communities v Ireland,* 2007, ECR I-11353.

163 Ibid.

164 Adrian Brown, Transparency obligations under the EC Treaty in relation to public contracts that fall outside the procurement directives: A note on C-231/03, Consorzio aziende metano (Coname) v. Comune di Cingia de'Botti, PPLR 6, NA153–159, 2005.

a publication is necessary at all. In her view, derogations permitted by the rules should also be allowed under the primary law. It would be ineffective only to allow the direct award contracts without publication in those circumstances which are laid down in the procurement directives.

One year after its ruling in Telaustria, the Court in Vestergarard[165] confirmed that TFEU principles also apply to low value contracts. Even if the transparency requirements specified in Telaustria were very vague, the issue was not repeatedly reviewed until the case Coname[166] over four years later. In the Coname case, Advocate General Christine Stix-Hackl examined the transparency issues at much greater length than the Court itself. She first discussed in general terms whether the Treaty's free movement principles could impose positive obligations on Member States. She deduced from the Court's jurisprudence on mutual recognition that the fundamental freedoms do impose certain positive procedural obligations on Member States. Consequently, the Advocate General recognised that these may be misapplied on certain grounds, for example when justified by public security or public policy under the Treaty or by "general interests" in the context of the Cassis de Dijon law case[167]. The case law significantly contributed to the application of the TFEU provisions in the public procurement procedures.

3.5 Conclusions

Having analysed the case praxis, the author believes that the transparency obligation under the EU law should not impose such a requirement for contracts whose value is lower than the threshold. Public contracting authorities would be obligated, for each contract below the threshold that might be "potentially" significant, to assess the interest in the market in an unspecified number of Member States with their failure to do so correctly putting them at the risk of

165 Case C-59/00, *Bent Mousten Vestergaard v. Spøttrup Boligselskab*, 2001, ECR I-9505 and Case C-264/03, *Commission of the European Communities v French Republic,* 2005, ECR I-08831. In those cases the Court stated that authorities awarding contracts outside the scope of the Directives, including those below the thresholds, are "nevertheless bound to comply with the fundamental rules of the Treaty". However, the Court did not expressly stipulate that the positive requirement for "a degree of advertising", which was implied from the Treaty principles a year earlier in Telaustria in respect of service concessions, applies equally to contracts below the directives thresholds.

166 Case C-231/03, *Consorzio Aziende Metano (Coname) v Comune di Cingia de' Botti,* 2005, ECR I-07287 also see opinion of Advocate General Stix-Hackl.

167 Ibid.

a penalisation. Such a situation is the opposite of legal certainty. In the author's opinion, such a requirement would likely affect small public contracting authorities (such as local authorities), which often have lower value contracts to announce than bigger public contracting authorities. It is likely to impose on them an unnecessary and disproportionate administrative burden.

Another reason to criticise the Commission's point of view is that the cost of advertising must be in proportion to the value of the contract. Obviously, the publication of the contract notices give opportunities to suppliers to compete.[168] The cost of the publication itself, as well as the cost implied by the necessity to examine numerous applications or tenders, should normally not exceed the gains that may be expected from competition. However, this cost should not be blown out of proportion as the contracts above the EU thresholds, which need to be advertised in the OJEU or in its national counterparts, may be published in a wide variety of journals or other information media.

In many cases it will be unclear, however, whether one or more of the above situations are covered by a particular contract. For example, how low should the contract value be that suppliers from abroad would be considered to have no interest in it[169]?

The conclusion can be drawn from these somewhat indeterminate approaches is that if a notice before the award of a contract has not been published it will almost always require a special justification of the reasons behind it. On the other hand, if the case is appropriately justified, a contract may lawfully be awarded by direct negotiation without advertising. Therefore, it depends on the CJEU how it will rule in ambiguous cases and how the circumstances of non-publication will be interpreted.[170]

---

168 Case C-496/99 *Commission of the European Communities v CAS Succhi di Frutta SpA.* 2004, ERC I-03801.

169 Adrian Brown, Seeing through transparency: The requirement to advertise public contracts and concessions under the EC Treaty, PPLR 1, 1–21, 2007.

170 Rhodri Williams, Contracts awarded outside the scope of the public procurement directives, PPLR 1, NA1–10, 2007.

II The development of public procurement law in Lithuania

The objective of this section is to analyse the history and evolution of the Lithuanian public procurement law in the global and European context. The global and European procurement practices had a major impact on the development of the Lithuanian public procurement framework.

Public procurement history in Lithuania is young in comparison with Germany or Austria[171]. Until 1991, the public procurement law had hardly any latitude under the Soviet Union's authoritarian regime in Lithuania. The public procurement directives of the European Union have significantly influenced the Lithuanian public procurement legislation. The development of Lithuanian public procurement law within the EU began through the tendering of the international public procurement procedures, organised by the World Bank, European Bank of Reconstruction and Development, and European Investment Bank. Lithuania had to adapt the rules of these international organisations and to accomplish the projects without any influence of the Lithuanian authorities. The first steps in the practical procurement law approach began with the EU procedure for external assistance.

The infrastructure and cohesion programmes such as PHARE[172], ISPA[173], and SAPARD[174] made an important contribution in supporting Lithuania's integration into the European Union. The projects under these programmes were financed by the European Commission. External aid programmes are accomplished together by the national authorities and the European Commission. It is important to note that after Lithuania had joined the EU, structural and the coherence funds were harmonised including the Lithuanian national public procurement rules.

---

171 Michael Holoubek/Claudia Fucks/Kerstin Holzinger, Vergaberecht, 2014, S. 22.

172 PHARE means Poland and Hungary Assistance for the Restructuring of the Economy.

173 ISPA means Structural Pre-Accession Instrument supports the candidate countries to prepare accession to the European Union in the field of environment and transport.

174 SAPARD means the Special Accession Programme for Agricultural and Rural Development was a key financial instrument to support the beneficiary countries of Central and Eastern Europe in dealing with the structural adjustment in their agricultural sectors and rural areas.

1 The development of public procurement worldwide

Efficient public procurement and the rational use of funds from the state budget remains one of the most challenging and pressing issues for all countries. In one way or another, all countries in the world use public procurement as a means for economic growth and establish the rules for its execution, which is then controlled by the relevant legislation.

There are three public procurement regimes in the world today: The United Nations UNCITRAL[175] Law Model[176]; the Government Procurement Agreement (GPA)[177] of the World Trade Organisation (WTO) and the EU directives[178]. All the EU Member States seeking to open up their markets to international or European trade are obliged to follow procurement regulations and to introduce the provisions into their national legislation.

Thus, all the above-mentioned international agreements deal with the international market. The agreements define international procurement thresholds contained within the detailed procurement rules. International Treaties also give a certain degree of discretion to set their own rules.

2 GPA

The procurement relationships of the EU and its Member States with its major trading partners are mostly addressed by the GPA[179]. The GPA was negotiated during the Tokyo Round and adopted in 1996 with its main purpose to open up the international market and make government procurement more transparent. The main objective of this Agreement is to liberalise procurement internationally.

---

175 Sue Arrowsmith, EU public procurement law: An introduction, 2014, p. 27. https://www.nottingham.ac.uk/pprg/documentsarchive/asialinkmaterials/publicprocurementregulationintroduction.pdf (12.05.2018).

176 United Nations Commission on International Trade Law: UNCITRAL Model Law on Procurement of Goods, Construction and Services, adopted in 1994. http://www.uncitral.org/pdf/english/texts/procurem/ml-procurement/ml-procure.pdf (07.07.2017).

177 The EU is a member of the GPA agreement including Lithuania since 1st of May 2004. https://www.wto.org/english/tratop_e/gproc_e/memobs_e.htm (07.07.2017).

178 The EU Directive 2014/24/EU of the European Parliament and of the Council of 26 February 2014 on public procurement and repealing Directive 2004/18/EC.

179 Consequences of Brexit in the area of public procurement, Study for the IMCO Committee, 2017, p. 27. http://www.europarl.europa.eu/RegData/etudes/STUD/2017/602028/IPOL_STU(2017)602028_EN.pdf (12.05.2018).

The GPA's ratification was necessary, involving the exercise of competence of both the European Commission and Member States.[180]

The GPA establishes the requirements for government procurement. The Agreement is based on a number of general principles such as transparency and non-discrimination.[181] According to this Agreement, parties have to treat the products, services and suppliers of any other party to the Agreement "no less favourable" than that they would treat their domestic products, services and suppliers and respect fundamental principles.[182] To ensure that stakeholders apply the basic principle of non-discrimination and that foreign products, services and suppliers have access to the market. The Agreement places a heavy focus on procedures for providing transparency of laws, regulations and practices regarding government procurement.[183]

The entities covered and the type of procurement and monetary thresholds are set out mainly in Appendix I to the Agreement. Under the EU procurement regime, the EU directives provide general definitions for the entities, contracts covered and thresholds coverage, which are the same for Member States. Under the GPA uniform rules on coverage for parties do not exist and they can vary by the State. The type of the negotiations undertaken between the parties can explain these differences: these negotiations will differ for each Member State and extent of procurement that each Member State is willing to open up to competition.[184]

The Agreement is applicable only to specific parties:[185] central government entities, sub-central government entities and other entities such as utilities for the provision of goods services and construction services[186]. Similar European regime aspects will be discussed further in details.

---

180 Sue Arrowsmith, The law of public and utilities procurement, par. 20.11, 2014.

181 Peter Van den Bossche, The law and policy of the World Trade Organisation, p. 479, 2005.

182 Christopher Bovis, EU public procurement law, P. 47, 2016.

183 Agreement on Government Procurement, Article III, 1994.

184 Sue Arrowsmith, The law of public and utilities procurement, par. 20.12, 2014.

185 Vinod Rege, Transparency in government procurement, Journal of World Trade, 35 (4), p. 492, 2001.

186 Agreement on Government Procurement, Appendix I, 1994.

3 The development of public procurement in Europe

From a historical perspective, it is important to highlight that the single market was established by signing the Treaty of Paris, which established the European Coal and Steel Community[187] in 1951 between six Member States: France, the Federal Republic of Germany, Italy, Belgium, the Netherlands and Luxembourg. Today, after more than 68 years, there are 28 members merging into a single entity, the European Union, establishing general economic policy in the single market. For this mechanism to operate smoothly it was necessary to create a more level playing field that would eliminate any trade barriers. Therefore, the EU directives on public procurement were established to ensure equal access and treatment to all parties in competition for public contracts in any country within the EU.

Under the Treaty of Rome, which established the European Community in 1957[188], it was already possible to detect the origins of international public procurement rules. However, the application of these rules has proven to be difficult as their provisions were of a more political nature. In 1971, the first European Union Directive was adopted covering contracts for public works.[189] This Directive defined key procurement principles, which had to apply to all public procurement regardless of their value. This Directive however did not achieve the desired results because not all Member States properly applied the rules. Therefore, the European Commission decided to establish a more effective EU public procurement regime. In 1985, the White Paper[190] was published to rejuvenate the whole European single market policy[191] and underlined key public procurement areas for action and prompted major legislative initiatives.

Directive 89/440/EEC[192] was developed and entirely replaced the previous Directive.[193] Six years later a similar Directive 77/62/EEC[194] was adopted for supply contracts. Due to the difficulties encountered when implementing these

---

187 Treaty establishing the European Coal and Steel Community (ECSC), 1951.

188 Treaty establishing the European Economic Community (TEEC), 1957.

189 Council Directive 71/305/EEC concerning the procedures for the award of public works contracts, 1971.

190 White Paper from the Commission of the European Communities, COM (85) 310 final, 1985.

191 Sue Arrowsmith, Regulating public procurement, national and international perspectives, 2000, p. 220.

192 Amending Directive 71/305/EEC concerning coordination of procedures for the award of public works contracts.

193 Folsom Ralph, European Union law after Maastricht: Practical guide for lawyers outside the common market, 1993, p. 97.

194 Council Directive 77/62/EEC of 21 coordinating procedures for the award of public supply contracts, 1976.

directives, many Member States disregarded their application. Further changes were introduced through two new directives 89/440/EEC[195] on public works and 88/295/EEC[196] on public supplies. The new provisions included a new negotiated procedure that allowed for negotiations during the procurement process. New time limits were also introduced to extend the procurement process. These directives amended the original Directive. Thus in 1993, new directives were adopted to consolidate the existing text into the following: Directive 93/36/EEC[197] on public supply contracts, Directive 93/37/EEC[198] on public works and Directive 93/38/EEC[199] on water, energy, transport and telecommunication contracts. Due to the lack of regulation in the non-construction services area in the EU, a new Directive 92/50/EEC[200] was adopted to regulate these services in 1992. This Directive took on a similar approach as the previous ones, the main difference being that not all of the services were fully regulated.

In 1985, the White Paper on completing the internal market[201] also adopted legislative initiatives for improving an enforcement of public procurement mechanism and completing the internal market. Initially the Commission had the power to enforce the EU law. However, in accordance with the White Paper recommendations, the new Directive 89/665/EEC[202] was adopted to cover the enforcement rules in the public sector and the Directive

---

195 Council Directive 89/440/EEC amending Directive 71/305/EEC concerning coordination of procedures for the award of public works contracts, 1989.

196 Council Directive 88/295/EEC amending Directive 77/62/EEC relating to the coordination of procedures on the award of public supply contracts and repealing certain provisions of Directive 80/767/EEC, 1988.

197 Council Directive 93/36/EEC concerning the coordination of procedures for the award of public supply contracts, 1993.

198 Council Directive 93/37/EEC concerning the coordination of procedures for the award of public works contracts, 1993.

199 Council Directive 93/38/EEC coordinating the procurement procedures of entities operating in the water, energy, transport and telecommunications sectors, 1993.

200 Council Directive 92/50/EEC concerning the coordination of procedures for the award of public service contracts, 1992.

201 Commission of the European Communities, Completing the internal market, White Paper from the Commission to the European Council, COM (85) 310 final, 14 June 1985.

202 Council Directive 89/665/EEC on the coordination of the laws, regulations and administrative provisions relating to the application of review procedures to the award of public supply and public works contracts, 1989.

92/13/EEC[203] to deal with the remedies in the utilities sector. Both these directives remain in place today with the purpose of ensuring an effective remedies system. In 2007 new amendments to these directives were proposed.

According to the Green Paper recommendations[204] made in 2004, the previous Directive 93/38/EEC was replaced by Directive 2004/17/EC[205] for the utilities sector and Directives 93/36/EEC; 93/37/EEC and 92/50/EEC were replaced by a single consolidated Directive 2004/18/EC[206] on works, supplies and services contract in the public sector. These directives were in force for ten years. The aforementioned Green Paper identified the major points concerning the simplification and clarification of the rules for entities, which should apply the existing rules in praxis and in particular, facilitating the development of electronic procurement.

Meanwhile at the global level, technology developed swiftly through the growth of electronic services and the need for electronic public procurement, leading to the adoption of the new Public Procurement Directives 2004/18/EC and 2004/17/EC, and the necessity to introduce new reforms[207].

Wider review was introduced in 2010 following the report of Mario Monti on a new strategy for the single market[208], which pointed out the need to simplify public procurement rules, promote innovation and enable better access to procurement for small and medium-sized enterprises (SMEs). The key objective was to establish a single market and a sustainable economic and monetary union. The implementation of public procurement rules remained an essential point to

203 Council Directive 92/13/EEC coordinating the laws, regulations and administrative provisions relating to the application of Community rules on the procurement procedures of entities operating in the water, energy, transport and telecommunications sectors, 1992.

204 Resolution on the Commission Green Paper on public procurement in the European Union: Exploring the way forward (COM(96)0583 C4-0009/97), 1996.

205 Directive 2004/17/EC of the European Parliament and of the Council coordinating the procurement procedures of entities operating in the water, energy, transport and postal services sectors, 2004.

206 Directive 2004/18/EC of the European Parliament and of the Council on the award of public works contracts, public supply contracts and public service contracts, 2004.

207 Public Procurement 2018, https://iclg.com/practice-areas/public-procurement-laws-and-regulations/eu-public-procurement-rules (12.05.2018).

208 Report from Mario Monti to the President of the European Commission, A new strategy for the Single Market at the service of Europe's economy and society, 2010. https://www.google.de/url?sa=t&rct=j&q=&esrc=s&source=web&cd=2&ved=2ahUKEwiQofGWxPvlAhXIalAKHQGFARUQFjABegQIAhAC&url=https%3A%2F%2Fec.europa.eu%2Focsroom%2Fdocuments%2F15501%2Fattachments%2F1%2Ftranslations%2Fen%2Frenditions%2Fpdf&usg=AOvVaw3enoPvnaG2ZtXPk5aYnqKI (16.07.2017).

prevent barriers to the free movement of goods and services and the freedom of establishment.[209]

After extensive consultations introduced by the European Commission in 2011, new directives were adopted in 2014, namely, the Directive 2014/24/EU[210], which replaced Directive 2004/18/EC regulating the award of contracts for supplies and services, and the Directive 2014/25/EU[211] replaced Directive 2004/17/EC to regulate the award of contracts in the utilities sector. A new Directive 2014/23/EU[212] was adopted for the sector of concessions. Forty-eight years have passed since the adoption of the first Directive in 1971. Certainly, it is difficult to evaluate the extent to which the current directives affect the internal market's supply and demand. Throughout this period, these directives aimed to establish a competitive market and to promote economic efficiency in the public sector of the Member States.[213] Despite the major developments that took place throughout the last forty-eight years, the fundamental principles in public procurement have remained unchanged.[214]

Currently, it is expected that Member States have already implemented the new directives ensuring transparent application of public procurement procedures that do not discriminate against foreign suppliers and ensure free and competitive opportunities for all suppliers in any country.

4 The development of public procurement in Lithuania

If compared to the public procurement system in Germany, the Lithuanian public procurement system with its 28 years of history is relatively young. From 1991 to 1997, the public procurement procedures were governed by government resolutions[215]. Prior to 1991, the public procurement in Lithuania was

---

209 The European Commission's Green Paper on the modernisation of EU public procurement policy: Towards a more efficient European procurement market, 27 January 2011.

210 Ibid.

211 Directive 2014/25/EU of the European Parliament and of the Council on procurement by entities operating in the water, energy, transport and postal services sectors and repealing Directive 2004/17/EC, 2014.

212 Directive 2014/23/EU of the European Parliament and of the Council on the award of concession contracts, 2014.

213 Sue Arrowsmith, The law of public and utilities procurement, 2014, p. 28.

214 Directive 2014/24/EU of the European Parliament and of the Council on public procurement and repealing Directive 2004/18/EC, 2014.

215 Lietuvos Respublikos Vyriausybės 1991 m. lapkričio 26 d. nutarimą Nr. 489 „Dėl Lietuvos Respublikos valstybinio užsakymo nuostatų.

not regulated. The model of public procurement did not exist in the socialist economy. The term "government contract," is therefore often associated with the mechanism of the State orders and the State purchases. The public sector had to familiarise itself with completely new rules for putting contracts out for competition and the private sector had to be made aware of the new opportunities for winning contracts.

The first legal act introduced by the Government of the Lithuanian Republic on public procurement was Resolution No 335 of 15 May 1992 on the procedure of acquisition of goods (services) by budgetary institutions.[216] The provisions laid down in the resolution are mainly applicable to the institutions and organisations financed from the national budget which consists of the State budget, municipal budgets and the State social insurance fund[217]. The public procurement law was drafted by the Ministry of Economics, which together with other ministries concerned presented the drafts for discussion in the Cabinet meeting.

During the first year in 1992, institutions and organisations financed by the national budget were authorised to purchase goods and services at the lowest market prices as those could not be subject to price regulation by the State. Contracts where the values were above 1,000 Rubbles had to be awarded by means of an invitation to tender. If the total value of goods or services exceeded 100,000 Rubbles, the procurement was organised by means of tender, which had to be announced a week before in the national press.[218] A number of at least three bidders was deemed to be sufficient. If these rules were not followed, financial penalties would apply. These fines were required to be paid by the party who breached the rules.

The second Lithuanian Government Resolution, No 444 of 9 June 1992 on the provisions relating to the invitation to tender, established the requirements for tender and contract evaluation methodology as well as losses in the event of non-compliance with contractual obligations.[219] In 1993, the procurement procedures were simplified so that the list of institutions was more precise and included the organisations and enterprises that increased their productive capacity from

---

216 Lietuvos Respublikos Vyriausybės 1992 m. gegužės 15 d. nutarimą Nr. 355 "Dėl Lietuvos Respublikos valstybinio užsakymo nuostatų".

217 Ibid.

218 Ibid.

219 Lietuvos Respublikos Vyriausybės nutarimas Nr. 444 "Dėl valstybinio užsakymo konkurso nuostatų, valstybinio užsakymo sutarties nuostatų, valstybinio užsakymo įsipareigojimų nevykdymonuostolių įvertinimo metodikos patvirtinimo", Valstybės žinios, Nr. 24–716, 1992.

the State allocations. The threshold to apply the public procurement rules was increased from 10,000 Rubbles to 15,000 Litas[220] and the penalty system was revised. Exemptions were introduced for particular cases where the provisions of the Resolution could not be applied, especially concerning the law on people with disabilities. Both domestic and foreign suppliers were able to participate in public procurement procedures on equal terms.

In 1995, the Government of the Republic of Lithuania adopted the new Resolution on the Provisional Government Procurement Rules[221] regulating public procurement procedures that defined the rules for the acquisition of national goods and services. Article 2.2 of the Resolution defined that the priority for purchases of goods and services should be given to companies registered in the Republic of Lithuania. Foreign goods or services were allowed to be purchased only if the officially registered Lithuanian companies were unable to produce the required products or the companies did not produce enough quantities of the products. In addition, foreign products and services were accepted if technical characteristics of national goods or services were much worse than those of their foreign equivalents and/or if local goods and services were priced higher than their foreign counterparts.

In addition, the Parliament, the President and the Government of the Republic of Lithuania were granted exclusive rights to be exempted from public procurement rules adopted by this Resolution in certain cases.[222] Until 1999 the public contracting authorities had the discretionary power to decide whether foreign suppliers would have an interest in bidding and, if not, to invite only Lithuanian suppliers to attend the process.

The legislation provided for the possibility of applying preferential adjustments to the assessment of offers for local suppliers. Neither of these legal acts established principles for non-discrimination and equal treatment necessary to ensure efficient application of public procurement procedures. The only attempt was that the officials in public procurement had to sign a Declaration of Impartiality that had no connection with the suppliers involved in the procurement.

The latest Resolution on the Provisional Government Procurement Rules established a direct discrimination between local and external suppliers and

---

220 Litas currency was introduced after the Lithuanians independency in 1993.

221 Ibid.

222 Lietuvos Respublikos Vyriausybės nutarimas Nr. 510 "Dėl valstybinio pirkimo laikinųjų taisyklių patvirtinimo", Valstybės žinios, Nr. 33–778, 1995.

priority was given to companies registered in Lithuania, which produced goods or services.

The EU and international rules for public procurement define different provisions, which also had to be aligned with the Lithuanian public procurement law system. To foster the Lithuanian integration, the EU adopted the Resolution[223] on the conclusion of a Europe Agreement between the European Communities and their Member States in order to facilitate the eventual integration of Lithuania into the European Union.

4.1 First Lithuanian public procurement law

Lithuania was under pressure deriving from various international bodies to establish its own public procurement law system. These legal instruments included: the GPA,[224] EU directives, the UNCITRAL Model Law,[225] the regulations of lending institutions (the World Bank, European Bank of Reconstruction and Development, and European Investment Bank.) and the procurement rules of the EU funding mechanisms (mainly PHARE and the ISPA).

All these instruments to a certain extent influenced the drafting of national regulation on the subject. That reality had its side effects, mainly that the first public procurement law was established based on the UNCITRAL Model Law and this law is considerably different from the EU directives, further providing for possibilities that are not compatible with the directives.

The first law on public procurement was adopted in 1996[226], which completed the period of government resolutions and laid down the fundamental principles for the modern procurement system. UNCITRAL, established in 1966 is the United Nations General Assembly's International Trade Law Commission, which issues conventions, laws and other legal instruments aimed at developing,

---

223 Legislative resolution on the proposal for a Council and Commission Decision on the conclusion of a Europe Agreement between the European Communities and their Member States, of the one part, and the Republic of Lithuania, of the other part (COM(95)0207 - C4-0326/95 - 95/0128(AVC)) (Assent procedure), Official Journal C 323, 04/12/1995.

224 The EU is a member of the GPA agreement including the Lithuania since 1 May 2004, https://www.wto.org/english/tratop_e/gproc_e/memobs_e.htm (17.06.2017).

225 United Nations Commission on International Trade Law: UNCITRAL Model Law on Procurement of Goods, Construction and Services, adopted in 1994. http://www.uncitral.org/pdf/english/texts/procurem/ml-procurement/ml-procure.pdf (17.06.2017).

226 Lietuvos Respublikos Viešojo pirkimo įstatymas, Nr. I-1491, 1996 m. rugpjūčio 13 d.

liberalising, harmonising and uniting world trade. Lithuania became a member of UNCITRAL in 1995.

UNCITRAL-based law served a useful purpose in transforming Lithuanian procurement practices from the limited ad hoc supervision of the early post-Soviet years to a comprehensive and recognisable system of regulated government purchasing. For the first time, government agencies were required to follow uniform rules whenever they spent money on public contracts. Gradually, however, the ease with which the public procurement authorities were circumventing the purpose behind the rules indicated major shortcomings in the statutory mechanism. Thus, by the end of the nineties a general consensus was formed that new and improved regulatory tools were necessary to meet the goal of transparent and effective Lithuanian government procurement.

For the first time in the history of Lithuania, the modern public procurement law allowed for the legalisation of the concept of public procurement. The provisions of this law were applied to purchases, which had a value greater than 25,000 Litas, and therefore this Law was not applicable for the purchases which had a value lower than 25,000 Litas and such purchases were acquired from the supplier who had offered goods or services at the lowest price[227].

The Law defined the following procurement procedures: open tender, closed tender, survey, two-stage tender, competitive negotiations and purchase from a single source. The procedure of a closed tender or purchasing from a single source was allowed only with the permission of the Government. The deadline to submit applications for tenders was at least 30 days, and inquiries by suppliers had to be sent not later than 15 days before the deadline for the submission of applications.

The Law, however, laid down a provision allowing purchases to be made only from suppliers registered in Lithuania. Such purchases could only be carried out if the value of goods and services did not exceed 100,000 Litas, and 500,000 Litas for works. An irrevocable decision to restrict or allow foreign suppliers to participate in the purchase had to be included in the procurement documents.

This Law also outlined the provisions to set up a new institution: Public Procurement Office. This Office was established by the Government of the Republic of Lithuania in 1996[228] and its purpose was to analyse complaints regarding the infringement of public procurement rules. Upon receipt of a

227 Ibid.

228 Lietuvos Respublikos Vyriausybės 1996 m. gruodžio 19 d. nutarimas Nr. 1473 "Dėl Viešojo pirkimo tarnybos prie Lietuvos Respublikos Vyriausybės įsteigimo".

supplier's complaint, the Public Procurement Office would forward it to the responsible public contracting authority and suspend the procurement procedure only if the complaint was justified or if the suspension of the procedure would not result in any damages to the supplier or the public contracting authority.

After the freedom was restored, Lithuania finally established the first procurement law, which envisaged the main procurement procedures and thresholds to be applied. The instrumental first steps towards the accession to the European Union were already embedded.

4.2 PHARE assistance programme

Lithuania was significantly supported by a number of the EU assistance programmes for the EU accession. One of them was PHARE. The main objective of the PHARE[229] programme was to assist Central and Eastern European countries in their preparation of accession through Partnership and National Programme for the adoption of Acquis.[230] In preparation for accession to the European Union, Lithuanian extensively applied the PHARE project financed by the European Union. The PHARE programme of the European Community was established in 1989 in order to support the process of economic and social reform in Central and Eastern Europe. Originally, the PHARE programme applied to Poland and Hungary only. Gradually more countries were included under the programme so that it provided assistance to 12 Central and Eastern European countries,[231] including Lithuania.

The PHARE programme was one of the three EU financial instruments supporting the preparation of the candidate countries including Lithuania for the EU accession. The other two programmes were: the instrument for structural Policies for Pre-Accession (ISPA)[232] and the Special Action for Pre-Accession for Agriculture and Rural Development (SAPARD)[233].

---

229 Ibid.

230 Lithuania country study guide, Volume 1, Strategic information and development, 2015, p. 131.

231 Council Regulation (EEC) No. 3906/89 of 18.12.1989, [1989] O.J. L375/11, last amended by Council Regulation (EEC) No. 1366/95, June 12, 1995.

232 The Instrument for Structural Policies for Pre-Accession (ISPA) was designed to address environmental and transport infrastructure priorities identified in the Accession Partnerships with the 10 applicant countries of Central and Eastern Europe. Its aim was to enhance economic and social cohesion in the applicant countries. https://ec.europa.eu/neighbourhood-enlargement/policy/glossary/terms/ispa_en (17.07.2017).

233 The Special Accession Programme for Agricultural and Rural Development (SAPARD) was a key financial instrument to support the beneficiary countries of Central and

The EU decided to implement comprehensive administrative reform programmes so that all new EU members, including Lithuania would have effective civil services and monitoring instruments. Lithuania received additional support in 1998 to accelerate its preparations for the membership. The programme helped Lithuania to complete the process of economic and social reforms, to attract investment and to fight corruption.

Under the PHARE programme, assistance was given by means of non-refundable grants financing both technical assistance and investments. These grants were particularly spent on projects in the areas of agriculture, industry, investment, energy, training, environmental protection, trade and services. What exactly the grants were spent on within these areas depended to a large extent on the recipient's country.

In line with the new PHARE orientations, the PHARE programme for Lithuania focused on sectors highly relevant to the country's accession to the European Union. PHARE support to Lithuania in 1998 was based on the short-term priorities of the Accession Partnership. In addition to the two main components of the programme: institution building and investment support, for the first time in 1988 the PHARE also contributed to Lithuania's participation in the EU programmes. PHARE support for Lithuania's accession preparations was channelled through four main programmes; in addition to the National PHARE Programme (with a budget of EUR 32 million), Lithuania received support under the Cross-Border Cooperation Programme, the Large-Scale Infrastructure Facility and the Catch-Up Facility, which together added another 12 million euros, bringing total support to EUR 44 million euros in 1998. The creation of the National Fund and the beginning of the decentralised and deconcentrated system in Lithuania brought about major changes to programme implementation.[234]

Lithuania also implemented the major PHARE twinning project strengthening the public procurement policy.[235] The EU funded programme played a significant role in the development of the national public procurement system, which as a result had to harmonise its legislative framework with the EU Public Procurement

---

Eastern Europe in dealing with the structural adjustment in their agricultural sectors and rural areas. https://ec.europa.eu/neighbourhood-enlargement/policy/glossary/terms/sapard_en (17.07.2017).

234 PHARE programme, Annual report 1998, COM (2000) 183 final, 2000, p. 51.

235 PHARE programos Dvynių projektas "Viešųjų pirkimų politikos stiprinimas" Nr. LI99/IB-FI-03, galutinė ataskaita, Rugsėjo 10 d. 2002 m.

directives, relevant EU requirements and facilitate the integration of candidate countries into the European Union's internal market.

The PHARE programme for Lithuania was significant in terms of policy learning; it strengthened the Lithuanian internal reforms considerably and thus advanced the emergence of adequate governmental capabilities to manage EU matters and increased the ability to meet the obligations for the EU membership.

In preparation for the EU accession in 2001, Lithuania became a member of the WTO.[236] The WTO is one of the most influential international organisations with the objective of developing common rules to govern international trade and the harmonisation and liberalisation of trade policies to remove international trade barriers. Beyond this preliminary step, between 2000 and 2002 Lithuania has implemented several PHARE programmes.

Paramount technical assistance gave Lithuania an opportunity to implement a proper public procurement system after its independence and, in a more general sense, to have access to the internal market.

4.3 Pre-accession of Lithuania to the European Union

The relations with the European Union were strengthened in 1998. Lithuania entered the Europe Agreement, launched the accession process in March, signed the Accession Partnership and published first regular report[237]. The regular report underlined that Lithuania had made considerable progress, although it was noted that additional measures were needed before it could be considered to meet the Copenhagen economic criteria[238]. Lithuania demonstrated not only the country's limited capacity to fulfil the obligations of the EU membership, but also a limited capacity to negotiate favourable terms of accession to the EU.[239]

At the end of 1999, the EU formally invited Lithuania to commence the negotiations for joining the EU. At this time, Lithuania started the national procurement law harmonisation with public procurement legislation of the EU.

---

236 World Tarde Organisation (WTO). https://www.wto.org/english/thewto_e/countries_e/lithuania_e.htm (12.05.2018).

237 Regular report from the Commission on Lithuania's progress towards accession, 1998. http://aei.pitt.edu/44570/1/lithuania_1998.pdf (12.05.2018).

238 The Copenhagen economic criteria apply for those countries who want to join the EU. https://ec.europa.eu/info/business-economy-euro/economic-and-fiscal-policy-coordination/international-economic-relations/enlargement-and-neighbouring-countries/enlargement/economic-accession-criteria_en (12.05.2018).

239 Jacques Rupnik, Vello Pettai, Jan Zielonka, the Road to the European Union, Volume 2, Estonia, Latvia, Lithuania, 2003, p. 133t.

Formal negotiations were launched in 2000 for accession to the European Union. In the process of the negotiations, Lithuania as a candidate country was obliged to change the legal regulation of public procurement in a way that would open up the market to competition. Lithuania was further required to achieve the free movement of goods, persons, and capital within the EU.

The integration process required Lithuania to modify its public procurement rules to harmonise them with the EU directives[240] and create a public procurement system that would be based on fundamental principles of equal treatment and non-discrimination, applicable to all suppliers and that would eliminate inconsistencies of the rules in the nation law. The public contracting authorities would be required to no longer restrict the participation of foreign suppliers in public procurement procedures.

The Lithuanian public procurement legislation had to be harmonised with the EU directives. In 1999 Swedish experts carried out an analysis of the Lithuanian Law on Public Procurement that identified a number of articles failing to comply with the Directive and therefore it was decided to adopt a new law rather than amend the existing one.[241]

To this end, in 1999 the new Public Procurement Law was introduced.[242] This law reflected the practices of the old European Union Member States and the main concepts of the European Union directives on public procurement. The law applied to those contracts with a total value of minimum 75,000 Litas when purchasing the goods or services and minimum 300,000 Litas when purchasing works. Lower values for procurement were governed by a special procedure approved by the Government.[243]

240 The Lithuania had to adopt the following directives Council Directive 92/13/EEC coordinating the laws, regulations and administrative provisions relating to the application of Community rules on the procurement procedures of entities operating in the water, energy, transport and telecommunications sectors, 1992.

Council Directive 93/36/EEC concerning the coordination of procedures for the award of public supply contracts, 1993; Council Directive 93/37/EEC concerning the coordination of procedures for the award of public works contracts, 1993; Council Directive 93/38/EEC coordinating the procurement procedures of entities operating in the water, energy, transport and telecommunications sectors, 1993.

241 Rima Ambrazevičienė, Viešųjų pirkimų valstybinio reguliavimo politikos raida Lietuvoje, Jurisprudencija, 59(51); 105–113, 2004.

242 Lietuvos Respublikos Viešojo pirkimo įstatymas Nr. I-1491, 1999 m. birželio 3 d.

243 Lietuvos Respublikos Vyriausybės 1999 m. rugsėjo 29 d. nutarimo Nr. 1079 "Dėl prekių, paslaugų ar darbų, kurių vertė yra mažesnė už nurodytą Lietuvos Respublikos viešųjų pirkimų įstatymo 1 straipsnio 1 dalyje, tvarkos patvirtinimo" pakeitimo.

With the adoption of a new version of the Law on Public Procurement[244] in December 2002, all obstacles preventing the completion of the single market in the EU were removed. This legal act not only completely eliminated all forms of discrimination against foreign suppliers, but also established a number of safeguard measures for foreign suppliers against indirect discrimination: publication of tender documents in the EU, established rules for qualification requirements and the preparation of technical specifications. It was prohibited to create indirect obstacles for foreign suppliers and others. This new law was a first step towards Lithuanians preparation for the EU accession.

4.4 Lithuanian accession to the EU

Bearing in mind the above-mentioned development of the law on public procurement one can conclude that by 2003 Lithuania had not yet implemented two EU directives 98/4/EC[245] and 97/52/EEC[246]. The coordination of these directives was carried out in 2003.

The enlargement and harmonisation of the national law with the EU public procurement directives remained highly complex. This is evidenced by taking into account that although the EU public procurement directives had been in force since the early 1970s, various obstacles were constantly encountered regarding their application, forcing the professionals to deal with this sector to continually search for ways to ameliorate the regulatory framework and make it more efficient. It is obvious that eastern European countries including Lithuania faced problems in fully incorporating the EU public procurement rules since concepts like public procurement, competition, the free market, extraterritorial freedom to provide services were simply non-existent.

The Public Procurement Office played an active role in Lithuania's integration into the EU, and made a substantial contribution to the progress of the EU integration and in the implementation of the EU programme and the Acquis

---

244 Lietuvos Respublikos viešųjų pirkimų įstatymo pakeitimo įstatymas, Valstybės žinios, Nr. 118-5296, 2002.

245 Directive 98/4/EC of the European Parliament and of the Council amending Directive 93/38/EEC coordinating the procurement procedures of entities operating in the water, energy, transport and telecommunications sectors, 16 February 1998.

246 European Parliament and Council Directive 97/52/EC amending Directives 92/50/EEC, 93/36/EEC and 93/37/EEC concerning the coordination of procedures for the award of public service contracts, public supply contracts and public works contracts respectively, 13 October 1997.

Communautaire[247] (implementation of the EU legislation) measures on public procurement. The contribution of Public Procurement Office was highly appreciated by the European Commission. The progress made by the country in the area of public procurement was significant.

The author believes successful procurement processes do not depend on the formal and detailed requirements for the procedures provided for by the law yet rather, as demonstrated by the experience of the EU countries, on the qualifications and competences of the staff involved in the procurement processes.

Upon Lithuania´s accession to the EU, intensive cooperation and consultation with the European Union's member States was underway. In 2004 and 2005, in collaboration with the Finnish Institute of Public Administration, the PHARE Twinning project preparation for public procurement was successfully completed.

All these developments resulted in full harmonisation of the Lithuanian public procurement law with the EU directives by 2004, following the adoption of a new public procurement law[248].This law was fully aligned with the new EU public procurement directives and its provisions were fully transposed into national law. Although the national law on public procurement was improved and amended at least once a year, it remained unchanged for a decade.

On 1 May 2004 Lithuania successfully joined the European Union and GPA. These treaties[249] allowed Lithuania not only to open its market and invite foreign suppliers seeking to participate in the national public procurement procedures, but also to equally participate in the tender processes organised by foreign countries.

5 Conclusion

In conclusion the author is of the view that one of the key issues of economic policies is the rational use of budget funds in public procurement, whereas an effective public procurement system is one of the ways to achieve economic growth. When seen from the historical perspective, the public procurement experience

247 The acquis therefore comprises the objectives of the European Union, its policies and the rules governing these policies; Under the PHARE programme a twinning project 'Preparation for the implementation of the acquis on public procurement. https://ec.europa.eu/agriculture/glossary/acquis-communautaire_en_en (12.05.2018).

248 Lietuvos Respublikos 2004 m. birželio 1 d. Viešųjų pirkimų įstatymas Nr. I-1491.

249 https://www.fdfa.be/sites/default/files/atoms/files/564_Final%20act%20in%20English.pdf (02.05.2018).

in Lithuania is only 28 years old and since 1996 the procurement law has been amended almost annually[250]. In Europe the first public procurement rules can be found in the Treaty of Rome of 1957. However, in Lithuania, the first attempts to establish a public procurement system were made only after the Lithuanian independence in 1991.

The analysis of the historical development of public procurement in Lithuania since its independence until its accession to the European Union allows the author to conclude that the fundamental stage of modernisation in the national public procurement system began with Lithuania's preparation to join the European Union. This historical moment led to an updated procurement law in 2004 that no longer contained any discriminatory provisions permitting the purchase of goods, services or works from only Lithuanian suppliers. Such change not only resulted in the growth of competition and the opening up of the market to foreign suppliers, but also enabled the suppliers of this country to compete in single European market with equal rights alongside other European suppliers.

---

250 http://vpt.lrv.lt/lt/teisine-informacija/viesieji-pirkimai-2/lietuvos-respublikos-istatymai-1/viesuju-pirkimu-istatymas (08.07.2017).

III Implementation of the EU public procurement rules in Lithuanian and German national law systems

1 Introduction

This chapter aims to clarify if, and to what extent, the new Directive 2014/24/EU has been transposed into the Lithuanian and German national law systems and explains the problems encountered in the process thereof. To this end the chapter will provide an overview of the implementation of the EU public procurement rules in Lithuanian and German national law systems. Having analysed the successful transposition, the chapter will move on to discuss the main opportunities and challenges for the application of the new public procurement rules. One of the main topics that will be discussed is the simplification and transparent application of public procurement procedures. Both countries are very different, first of all in terms of historical development of public procurement, since Lithuanian public procurement system is very young, only 28 years old compared to Germany, which is more than 98 years old. Secondly, at the same time both countries are similar because both systems developed detailed national procurement rules ensuring coherent application of the TFEU and the Directive 2014/24/EU.

2 The EU Public Procurement Reform

The overview of the main aspects of the public procurement reform calls for a repeated emphasis that the EU was founded to identify, protect and maintain the single market of Member States, which today consists of 28 different legal frameworks and national legal traditions.

The cornerstone of Europe's integration and sustainable growth, the single market, is far from being fully implemented in many areas and due to certain missing links cannot act as a powerful tool for development and delivery of full benefits to its consumers.[251] Founded in 1992, the single market offered new opportunities for Member States but even to this day has not been fully

251 Mario Monti's Report to the President of the European Commission José Manuel Barroso of 9 May 2010. "A New Strategy for the Single Market at the Service of Europe's Economy and Society". https://www.kfw.de/migration/Weiterleitung-zur-Startseite/Homepage/KfW-Group/Research/PDF-Files/Monti_Report.pdf (21.11.2019).

integrated as such; the movement of goods, services, capital and people still faces new challenges and obstacles.

The strategic objective of the single market requires the inclusion of a wide range of policy areas, which are a key factor in developing a stronger single market. One of the pillars of the single market is European public procurement.

Welcoming foreign suppliers to the national public procurement market is beneficial at both European and global levels. In order for this to happen and in spirit of mutual benefit, it is necessary to ensure equal conditions and fair competition for European and foreign companies alike.[252]

Across Europe effective spending is essential and, for this reason, hundreds of billions of euros are spent annually on public procurement. Back in 1994, the public procurement expenses of the EU-15 amounted only to 11.5 % of GDP.[253] It is obvious that today's spending on public procurement has grown and should be even more transparent.

Despite progress being made in the area of public procurement since the establishment of the single market in 1992, some of its objectives have failed to be fully implemented. Namely, the implementation of more eco-friendly, sustainable, environmentally sound, socially responsible and innovative public procurement[254]. Therefore, the effects of the public procurement reform are greatly significant, as they will help to fully implement the objectives of public procurement and provide SMEs with an easier access through simpler and more flexible procedures.[255]

3 Transposition of the Directive 2014/24/EU into national systems

The public procurement institute is a subject of law, which is regulated by EU directives and national law.[256] The Lithuanian Supreme Court has noted that the

---

252 Communication from the Commission to the European Parliament, the Council, the European Economic and Social Committee and the Committee of the Regions, Making Public Procurement work in and for Europe, 2017.

253 Commission Staff Working Paper, Evaluation Report, Impact and Effectiveness of EU Public Procurement Legislation, Part 1, p. i, 27 January 2011.

254 Green Public Procurement, 2018. http://ec.europa.eu/environment/gpp/index_en.htm (21.05.2018).

255 Twelve projects for the 2012 Single Market: together for new growth,13 April 2011.

256 Lietuvos Aukščiausiojo Teismo Civilinių bylų skyriaus teisėjų kolegijos 2009 m. lapkričio mėn. 17 d. nutartis,priimta civilinėje byloje Nr. 3K-3-508/2009.

Lithuanian law on public procurement aims to ensure the rational use of budget funds as well as ascertaining the good quality of goods and services necessary to ensure the effective functioning of the State and municipalities, and in turn the promotion of competition and market development[257].

The TFEU primary provisions have direct effects, which are binding and enforceable without the need to be put in place by States. However, Member States must transpose the directives in their national law reserving the right to decide on the way in which to implement them.[258] Such measures are set out in Article 288 TFEU.

In its annual reports, the Commission presents proposals for more effective implementation of directives by the Member States and for the improvement of the procurement policy itself. The Commission, in its annual report for 2016, stated that it had opened infringement procedures against most Member States including Lithuania for not transposing the Directive 2014/24/EU into the national law on time. Due to this, the Commission may propose financial penalties, even when it is the first referral to the Court of Justice under Article 258 TFEU for failure to fully transpose a Directive. Article 258 TFEU introduced in the Treaty of Lisbon aims to give Member States a greater incentive to transpose directives on time. The Commission decides on the level of financial penalties to propose in line with the policy laid down in its Communication on the implementation of Article 260(3) TFEU. In its Communication on enforcement policy, the Commission announced that for infringement cases launched after its publication, it would systematically ask the Court to impose a lump sum as well as a periodic penalty payment.[259] Today Lithuanian successfully transposed the Directive 2014/24/EU in to the nation law.

Directive 2014/24/EU has a long history. In 2012, the Commission introduced a reform programme with the aim to simplify and modernise the EU public procurement framework. Two years later, in October 2014, the EU Council adopted the following new public procurement directives: Directive 2014/23/EU on the award of concession contracts;[260] Directive 2014/24/EU on public procurement[261]; and Directive 2014/25/EU on procurement by entities operating in

---

257 Viešųjų pirkimų reglamentavimas ir teismų praktikos apžvalga, AC-38-1, 2016.

258 Sue Arrowsmith, The law of public and utilities procurement, p. 213, 2014.

259 Report from the Commission, Monitoring the application of European Union law 2016 Annual Report, COM (2017) 370.

260 To date (11 November 2019) all Member States have implemented the Directive (Luxembourg was the last country which implemented the Directive in July 2018).

261 To date (11 November 2019) all Member States have implemented the Directive (Luxembourg was the last country which implemented the Directive in April 2018).

the water, energy, transport and postal services sectors[262]. The Member States were required to transpose the directives into their national framework by 18 April 2016.

Yet, only seven Member States had implemented all the directives on time[263]. In May and December 2016, the Commission sent letters of notice for failure to implement all or some of the directives to 21 Member States and in December to 15 Member States.[264] Member States faced difficulties in transposing directives into their national legislation mainly because of the national political situations (such as Spain and Greece etc.). Member States were faced with new challenges and obligations under the new directives. It shows that the reform was too early for the Member States to properly transpose all Directives on time.

The approach of those Member States who have already implemented the directives has been very different across the EU. Therefore, experienced Member States, such as the UK were able to transpose the directives rapidly without any major departure from the Directive.[265] Some Member States took advantage of the entire implementation period and have sometimes introduced stricter provisions than those in the directives themselves.[266] An implementation of the Directive 2014/24/EU was delayed in Lithuania because of the internal reforms to public procurement with a view to addressing long and outstanding problems within the public procurement system and especially to enhance clarity and certainty in the area of the in-house related contracts. Consequently, Lithuania transposed the Directive 2014/24/EU into the national law only on 6 June 2017 after the deadline, which is in force as of 1 of July 2017.

Germany was able to successfully transpose Directive 2014/24/EU into national law on 17 February 2017 on time with the deadlines provided, and

---

262 Ibid.

263 The following Member States have implemented all three Directives: Denmark, Germany, France, Italy, Hungary, Slovakia and United Kingdom.

264 http://ec.europa.eu/growth/tools-databases/newsroom/cf/itemdetail.cfm?item_id=9057 (06.06.2017).

265 HM Government, Transposition Guidance: How to implement European Directives effectively, 2013. http://ec.europa.eu/growth/tools-databases/newsroom/cf/itemdetail.cfm?item_id=9057 (06.06.2017).

266 An example is the introduction of stricter rules for subcontracting (essentially restricting its use by stating in Article 105(1) of the new Italian Code that the value of the subcontract cannot exceed the 30 % of the overall amount of the contract).

which is in force as of 14 of April 2017. The implementation aspects of both countries will be further assessed in the new chapter.

4 New legal framework of public procurement in Lithuania

There is no doubt the jurisdiction of the CJEU plays a major role in the enforcement of law process. To overcome legal challenges in the area of public procurement, it is necessary to invoke both national and European regulations, including an examination of the legal objectives. Similarly, the CJEU has had a great impact on the development of public procurement system not only in Europe but also in Lithuania. In the next sections, the author will discuss the enormous impact of the CJEU jurisprudence on national law and the underpinned interpretation of the national courts based on the CJEU judgements[267].

The incorporation of the provisions of Directive 2014/24/EU into the Lithuanian public procurement law was different from the rapid and smooth implementation of these provisions in public procurement practice. According to the European Parliament, the monitoring of the application of the EU law consists not only of the assessment of the percentage of the transposition achieved but also the quality of the transposition and the practice of applying the EU law[268]. This means that the rapid implementation of the EU law is only an integral part of the law, because, according to the European Parliament, clear and well-described laws are a prerequisite for the good application of the EU law across the EU[269].

In Lithuania, the transposition of Directive 2014/24/EU into national law was successful, however, some problematic old in-house provisions remained. In April 2017, the president of Lithuania Dalia Grybauskaitė, voted against the amendments on the in-house provisions to be included in the new national law on public procurement. According to the president, it is necessary to unite forces for the destruction of corruption, and not to make concessions, exceptions or privileges. Therefore, the Seimas (parliament), having included the exceptional provisions for in-house provisions, created a space for corruption, lack of clarity about the use of the State funds and the unpopularity of self-government to thrive[270].

---

267 European Commission, Public Procurement Guidance for practitioners, 2018.

268 European Parliament resolution of 6 October 2016 on monitoring the application of Union law: 2014 Annual Report (2015/2326 (INI).

269 Ibid.

270 Vidaus sandoriams – prezidentes veto. (In-house provisions –president veto). http://alkas.lt/2017/04/18/vidaus-sandoriams-prezidentes-veto/ (01.06.2017).

It leads to the statement that there is a lack of capacity to apply and properly interpret EU provisions at the national level to ensure the level of compliance necessary. In changing the conditions of economic and social growth, both in Lithuania and throughout the EU, it is also necessary that legal rules be in line with the economic growth and changes of the society's development.

The need of a proper regulation of public procurement was acknowledged by the adoption of the new Law on Public Procurement, which became effective on 01 of July 2017.[271] The established procurement procedures that fell below the thresholds did not change to a large extent, whereas the procurement procedures above the thresholds are the ones that have been aligned with the new provisions of the Directive 2014/24/EU and will in turn have an enormous impact on the procurement enforcement in Lithuania.

This section will analyse the implementation of new provisions defined by the Directive 2014/24/EU in the Lithuanian national law. It is important to not only harmonise the law of Lithuania with the EU legal framework for public procurement, but also to continue effectively implementing the harmonised law. In order to implement new procurement provisions and correctly apply in-house rules it will not be enough for contracting organisations and suppliers to make efforts to improve their qualifications and attend trainings on public procurement. If inadequately transposed, these innovations could aggravate the implementation of public procurement principles (equality, non-discrimination, transparency, mutual recognition and proportionality).

4.1 Primary legislation of public procurement

Public procurement rules at the Lithuanian national level are regulated by primary and secondary legislation. The primary legislation includes the Civil Code and the Code of Civil Procedure, which define the requirements for the completion of the contracts and are generally applicable when dealing with public procurement disputes in court. However, Article 6.305 (3) of the Lithuanian Civil Code[272] allows for specific peculiarities of the purchase and sale of certain goods to be regulated by certain corresponding laws. Specific legislation includes the Law on Public Procurement and other public procurement regulatory legal acts, some of which are mandatory (Decisions of the Government of the Republic of

---

271 Lietuvos Respublikos, Viešųjų pirkimų įstatymo Nr. I-1491 pakeitimo įstatymas, 2 May, 2017. (Repulic of Lithuania, Law on Public Procurement, No I-1491, (last amended on 2 of May, 2017).

272 Civil Code of the Republic of Lithuania, 18 July 2000, No VIII-1864.

Lithuania etc.), while others are merely advisory (e.g. decrees of the director of Public Procurement Office etc.[273]) and may apply to procurement procedures.

Article 6.382 of the Civil Code applies to public procurement contracts to the extent that they are not otherwise regulated by other laws. The provisions of the Civil Code play an important role not only in the performance of a public procurement contract, but also in defining the subject-matter of a public procurement contract. In one of the cases the dispute arose concerning the definition of the product in public procurement and whether a product could be considered if it has not yet been manufactured. The Public Procurement Law does not determine whether a product as a purchase object could be a future item. Therefore, in resolving the dispute, the panel of judges relied on Article 6.305, Article 6.477, Article 6.306 and Article 6.567, of the Civil Code and Article 2 (33) of the Law on public procurement, and ruled that there were no compelling arguments to justify the prohibition of the public contracting authority to purchase a product that is yet to be created.[274]

Lithuanian courts must settle disputes between economic entities and public contracting authorities according to the regulations of the Civil Code and the Public Procurement Law, to the extent that such a process is not defined by Public Procurement Law. For example, the duration of the claim process is regulated by the Public Procurement Law and the Civil Code regulates the fees owed to the court.

Considering that the Public Procurement Law regulates the legal relations in public procurement, the provisions of the Civil Code, the Code of Civil Procedure and other legal acts must be applied in a subsidiary manner, with respect to the rules of Public Procurement Law. Thus, the Civil Code, the Code of Civil Procedure and other legal acts shall regulate public procurement relations only in the cases that the Public Procurement Law does not address.

4.2 Secondary legislation of public procurement

This chapter discusses the main source of the public procurement system in Lithuania, namely the Public Procurement Law. The law came into force very recently, on 1 July 2017. At this stage there is little literature or commentary about the new law and the impact on the enforcement of rules. In light of the

273 http://vpt.lrv.lt/lt/teisine-informacija/teises-aktu-archyvas/viesuju-pirkimu-tarnybos-direktoriaus-isakymai-3 (21.05.2018).

274 Lietuvos apeliacinio teismo Civilinių bylų skyriaus teisėjų kolegijos 2010 m. rugpjūčio 31 d. nutartis, priimta civilinėje byloje Nr. 2A-713/2010.

authors experience as a procurement expert, this paper will present the author's view on the enforcement of the new rules.

The Public Procurement Law seeks to harmonise the rules with the requirements outlined in the EU law. These rules on public procurement are simplified with the aim to ensure a higher flexibility in procurement procedures, providing public contracting authorities with a bigger role and thus relieving the administrative burden on suppliers. This will improve the efficiency of public spending money and guarantee the best results for purchases with respect to price and quality ratio. Due to simplified and more efficient procurement procedures, all economic operators, small and medium-sized businesses and foreign suppliers will have a better access to the Lithuanian procurement market.

For businesses to propose innovations in the new public procurement framework, conditions for that must be improved by aligning them more closely with the political, social and economic objectives established in the European strategy for smart, sustainable and inclusive growth by 2020[275]. The benefits of the new public procurement framework include among others the improved business environment and conditions for business innovation, job creation, social inclusion, and green procurement. Subsequently, the objectives of public procurement will be improved in a way that they will stimulate a competitive, innovation-driven economy as well as its growth.

The Public Procurement Law regulates management and implementation procedures including execution of public contracts and dispute settlement procedures and defines the rights, obligations, and responsibilities of public procurement entities.[276] In order to achieve the main goal of procurement, which is to acquire supplies, services or works necessary for the public contracting authorities, they must follow the fundament procurement principles[277].

Article 17(1) of the Public Procurement Law stipulates that the public contracting authority must ensure that in the course of procurement procedures and contract awarding stage all the following principles are observed: the principle of equal treatment, non-discrimination, mutual recognition, proportionality and transparency.

Furthermore, Article 17(2) defines the goal of procurement to be the award of public contracts in line with the requirements outlined in the Public Procurement

275 Communication from the Commission, Europe 2020, A strategy for smart, sustainable and inclusive growth, COM(2010) 2020.

276 Article 1 of the Public procurement law.

277 Article 17 of the Public procurement law.

Law, for the public contracting authority or third persons to acquire necessary supplies, services or works at the same time using the resources allocated for this purpose rationally. Planning and preparation for procurement should only be possible while observing the procedures established by this law and preventing any artificial reduction of competition. It is considered that competition is artificially reduced when the purchase unduly favours or disadvantages certain suppliers.

Thus, there are two main goals of public procurement. The first is to enable the public contracting authority to acquire goods, services and works which are needed for its proper functioning. Note that this goal is not mentioned very often when dealing with public procurement matters or settling these kind of disputes in Lithuanian courts. The other objective of the Public Procurement Law is to ensure that the public contracting authority's financial resources are used properly and efficiently. Usually Lithuanian courts[278] read the lines of Article 17 of the Public Procurement Law as meaning that most procurement procedures have to be applied in such a way that would allow the public contracting authority to save as much funds as possible and, therefore, most of the contracts are awarded using lower price criteria only.

Such a line of reasoning is short-sighted because it creates many practical problems[279]. The new Directive 2014/24/EU encourages Member States to apply the most economically advantageous criteria for their procurement procedures. Further guidance on the implementation of Public Procurement Law rules are explained in the decrees or orders issued by the Ministers[280].

The secondary Lithuanian legislation on public procurement includes the Law on Public Procurement Government Resolution, the Decree of the Minister of the Economy, Decrees of the Minister of Environment, and Decrees of the director of the Public Procurement Office.[281]

---

278 Supreme Court of Lithuania of 23rd December, 2008, *UAB "ERP" v Valstybinė mokesčių inspekcija prie Lietuvos Respublikos finansų ministerijos,* case, No. 3K-3-538/2008.

279 Deividas Soloveičikas, Public Procurement in Lithuania: The ongoing development, E.P.P.P.L., vol. 2, 2009, p. 110; Deividas Soloveičikas, Viešųjų pirkimų teisės tikslai ir jų įgyvendinimas, Teisė, 2014, p. 42.

280 http://vpt.lrv.lt/lt/teisine-informacija/teises-aktu-archyvas/ministru-isakymai-3 (21.05.2018).

281 Public Procurement Office, http://vpt.lrv.lt/lt/teisine-informacija/viesieji-pirkimai-2 (03.06.2017).

4.3 Public Procurement Office

The role of the Public Procurement Office in interpreting public procurement rules is very important. The Public Procurement Office is responsible for observing the public procurement system and monitoring its compliance with the Public Procurement Law. Other functions include drafting legal acts regulating procurement, assessing and recommending improvements to the procurement system, providing methodological assistance to public contracting authorities and monitoring their compliance with the law and its implementing legislation.[282] Within its competence, it carries out investigations, provides methodological assistance, collects, compiles and analyses information about planned and executed purchases.

Most recently several articles have been published in the media that the Public Procurement Office has provided misleading recommendations for purchasing the official police cars for the State[283]. The Public Procurement Office recommended buying one type of car for rural areas and another type for the city. Officials called this instruction null and void. The Police Department stated that the public contracting authority itself sets specifications and requirements and, therefore, will maintain its own conditions.

This implies another recent case wherein the Public Procurement Office recommendations were misleading and provided an inconsistent methodology for the interpretation of public procurement rules. New Public Procurement Office recommendations came into force in 2017 regarding travel organisation services. Institutions were required to combine all travel organisation services of the annual purchase value and publish one tender. In such a tender, there were no opportunities to compete for airline companies, which would order accommodations. Thus, the company that was awarded the contract was a travel intermediary agency, an agency that offered zero charges for their services[284]. Considering this fact, one of the tenderers lodged a claim to the court to suspend

---

282 Peggy Ford-Fyffe King, OECD Review of the corporate governance of States-owned enterprises, Lithuania, 2015, p. 39.

283 Liuzija Zubrute, VPT del policijos automobilių pirkimo pasikonsulatvo su gamintojais, 2017, https://www.vz.lt/transportas-logistika/2017/05/22/vpt-del-policijos-automobiliu-pirkimo-pasikonsultavo-su-gamintojais (21.05.2018).

284 Vakaris Deksnys, Pirkimų preivaizdai spjiovė į reikalavimus, dėl kurių skalpuoja kitus, 2017, https://verslas.lrytas.lt/rinkos-pulsas/2017/05/30/news/pirkimu-prievaizdai-spjove-i-reikalavimus-del-kuriu-skalpuoja-kitus-1477510/ (21.05.2018).

the tender procedure. As a result, the tender procedure was cancelled based on the decision of the Supreme Court of Lithuania.[285]

As a consequence, public contracting authorities, including organisations (Parliament, universities etc.) that followed these recommendations of the Public Procurement Office are currently dealing with the court and are forced to pay litigation costs.[286]

The reason for the contradictory recommendations issued by the Public Procurement Office is that the specialists who prepared the recommendations did not take into account all the possible scenarios for conducting public procurement of travel services. It is inevitable that some of the recommendations are also prepared in such a way that the lowest price criteria overrule the most advantageous criteria[287]. Thus, such cases suggest that when making future recommendations, policy makers will need to determine all the possible requirements and award criteria for establishing fare and competitive procurement procedures for travel services across the country. As a consequence the Public Procurement Office has to follow best practises and align it with their adopted methodologies.

4.4 Definitions of public procurement

The public sector uses various forms of purchasing activity, and it is important to define the definition of public procurement as accurately as possible. The Public Procurement Law enhanced the definitions of public procurement based on the recent CJEU case law. Public procurement rules do not regulate all types of contracts. They are applicable only to public contracts for the purchase of goods, services or works.

A further definition of the scope of public procurement taking into consideration the practice of the CJEU, includes other key definitions regarding the public contracting authority, public purchase contract, public works contract and centralised procurement activities. In addition, new definitions are

285 Supreme Court of Lithuania of 23rd December, 2008, *UAB* "ZIP Travel" *v* Lietuvos Respublikos valstybės kontrolės, case, No. e3K-3-1-969/2017.

286 Jolanta Lapeniene, Neišvengiamos viešųjų pirkimų rekomendacijos įklampino į teismus, Delfi, 28 May 2017, https://www.delfi.lt/news/daily/lithuania/neisvengiamos-viesuju-pirkimu-rekomendacijos-iklampino-i-teismus.d?id=74770212 (04.06.2017).

287 The order of the chairman of PPO of 26 February 2003 regarding the adoption of the methodology of the evaluation of the procurement value of goods and services, Official Gazzette, 28 February 2003, No. 22–949.

introduced such as sub-central contracting organisation, life cycle costs, unacceptable bid, inappropriate application, inappropriate bid, auxiliary procurement, subcontracting contracts[288].

The CJEU has elaborated further on the definition of public contracting authority in several cases and this has also been reflected in the Public Procurement Law. It may occur that the public contracting authority, while acting in the name of general interest, is guided by other than economic motives.[289] The presence of competition has a role to play when the need in the general interest is other than industrial or commercial. Subsequently, the CJEU determined that while assessing the nature of performed tasks, the goals set by the entity could not be achieved by an exchange of goods and services on the free market. The CJEU in the SIEPSA case[290] has pointed out that needs with no industrial or commercial nature are generally needs that the market is not able to satisfy.[291]

Firstly, Article 2 (25) of the Public Procurement Law further clarifies the definition of a public contracting authority according to the CJEU case law[292]. The definition of a public contracting authority has been changed in cases where the entity's activities are considered to be unrelated to public interest, which namely are the following: 1) the entity operates in normal market conditions; 2) seeks profit; and 3) itself suffers losses related to its activities.

In order to establish whether an entity can be treated as a public contracting authority, all legal and factual circumstances of its activities (e.g. what conditions were present at the time the entity was established and under what conditions it operates) should be established.[293] It is also important to note that entities that carry out even a small part of their activities related to the public interest,

288 Article 2 of the Public procurement law.

289 Case C-360/96, *Gemeente Arnhem and Gemeente Rheden v BFI Holding BV*, 1998, ECR I-0682.

290 Case C-283/00, *Commission of the European Communities v Kingdom of Spain*, 2003, ECR I-11697.

291 Andrzej Panasiuk The court of justice of the European union and its influence on European and national public procurement regulations: the case of Poland, E.P.P.P.L., 2017, p. 194.

292 Case C-18/01, *Arkkitehtuuritoimisto Riitta Korhonen Oy, Arkkitehtitoimisto Pentti Toivanen Oy and Rakennuttajatoimisto Vilho Tervomaa v Varkauden Taitotalo Oy*, 2003, ECR I-05321.

293 Case C-373/00 *Adolf Truley GmbH v Bestattung Wien GmbH*, 2003 ECR I-0193. Case C-18/01 *Arkkitehtuuritoimisto Riitta Korhonen Oy, Arkkitehtitoimisto Pentti Toivanen Oy and Rakennuttajatoimisto Vilho Tervomaa v Varkauden Taitotalo Oy*, 2003, ECR I-05321.

and perform non-industrial and non-commercial activities (e.g. the majority of their activities are, respectively, purely commercial), are recognised as public contracting authorities[294], provided that they meet other criteria of the public contracting authority.

Secondly, under Article 2 (24), (26) of the Public Procurement Law, the definition of a public contract has also been modified corresponding to the CJEU case law[295]. The same has been further updated to include the concept of "economic benefits". Hence, the CJEU case law[296] refers to the public procurement contracts as the ones that are completed for the pecuniary interest, and they are subject to the EU Directive 2014/24/EU, irrespectively of the form of remuneration to be paid. The pecuniary interest in a contract refers to the consideration paid to the contractor on account of the execution of works intended for the public contracting authority.[297] Such remuneration may be cash payment or for example, the right not to pay taxes or to use materials obtained during the demolition work. The remuneration for a public contract may also depend on the supplier's ability to receive funds from third parties.

Thirdly, in understanding the definition of a public works contract as provided in Article 2 (7) of the Public Procurement Law, it should be pointed out that the subject of such a contract might be of a very diverse nature. It may include works that create a new building (e.g. school, bridge, and stadium) or works that result in the refurbishing of the same building (e.g. demolition, repair, roof repair). Hence, by this definition for public works they will be purchased if the public contracting authority purchases construction works on the land it owns or if such construction works are requested by an economic operator on the land owned by the public contracting authority, which it will later take over.[298] Therefore, public contracting authorities are required to follow the procedures laid down in the Public Procurement Law whenever they decide to award a public works contract of that type.[299]

---

294 Case C-44/96, *Mannesmann Anlagenbau Austria AG and Others v Strohal Rotationsdruck GesmbH*, 1998, ECR I-00073, paras. 25, 26, 31.

295 Case C-399/98, *Ordine degli Architetti delle province di Milano e Lodi, Piero De Amicis, Consiglio Nazionale degli Architetti and Leopoldo Freyrie v Comune di Milano, and Pirelli SpA, Milano Centrale Servizi SpA and Fondazione Teatro alla Scala*, 2001, ECR I-05409, paras. 76 to 8; 84 to 86.

296 Case C-220/05, *Jean Auroux and Others v Commune de Roanne*, 2007, ECR I-00385.

297 Ibid.

298 Csase C-451/08, *Helmut Müller GmbH v Bundesanstalt für Immobilienaufgaben*, 2010, ECR I-02673.

299 Ibid.

On the grounds of what has been explained above, the aim of this chapter was to provide further explanation on the necessary updates introduced to more elaborated procurement definitions in the newly revised Public Procurement Law, which are mainly based on the outcomes of the CJEU case law. The new definitions clarify the precise definition of the public contracting authority, emphasising which activities are not considered to be related to the public interest. Furthermore, the definition of a public contract is complemented with a further explanation of economic benefits and finally the definition of a public work contract has been modified in such a way that it would ensure the compliance of public contracting authorities with the procedures set by the Public Procurement Law.

4.5 Thresholds

In 2015, the estimated total in general government expenditures on works, goods, and services represented 13.1 % of the EU GDP, which is the highest value for the last 4 years. Presently, more than 80 % of all expenditure on public procurement in the EU is regulated below the EU thresholds.[300]

The regulation of public procurement within the EU is of a dualistic nature: contracts are subject to the full EU regulation only above particular financial thresholds, if their value is lower –they fall under the scope of national rules. Between 2004 and today, the thresholds have been updated every two years as requested by the GPA agreement. Threshold levels will finally be reviewed in the near future, firstly because Article 12(7) of the revised GPA so determines and secondly, because Article 92 of Directive 2014/24/EU also demands this.[301]

However, there are different types of thresholds and determining which particular one applies depends on three factors: the sector (classic[302], utilities[303], or defence[304]), the contract nature (works, goods, or services), and the public contracting authority (central government or others).[305] The author will focus

300 Public Procurement Indicators 2015, DG Grow G4 – Innovative and e-procurement, 19 December, 2016, p. 1.

301 Pedro Telles, Public procurement financial thresholds in the EU and their relationship with the GPA, E.P.P.P.L., 2016, p. 206.

302 Ibid.

303 Ibid.

304 Directive 2009/81/EC.

305 Ibid.

mainly on thresholds established in the classical Directive 2014/24/EU. Different EU public procurement thresholds are introduced every two years by the European Commission via Regulations[306]. The proposed directives will establish thresholds going forward. Other than adding a new threshold for social care services at €750,000, the overall values remain unaltered.

A works contract has to be defined as an anti-avoidance measure that stems from the fact that the threshold above which works contracts are subject to an announcement in the OJEU is much higher than that for service contracts. The threshold of the OJEU works contracts is currently €5,548,000. The thresholds for service contracts are currently, depending (with some exceptions) on whether or not the awarding body is a central government entity, either €221,000 or €144,000.

The Public Procurement Law has transposed the EU thresholds and defined thresholds below the EU thresholds. Article 4 of the Public Procurement Law establishes the EU, simplified and small-value purchases. The law itself does not determine the major limits of the EU purchasing value; they are established by the Directive 2014/24/EU. It is thus intended to avoid amendments to be introduced in the newly adopted the Public Procurement Law.

In principle, the estimated purchase value calculation procedure has not changed. The main update is the authorisation for the public contracting authority's own departments to arrive at the estimated value of the purchase by themselves. Such a unit may not have separate legal personnel, but must independently make and perform purchasing decisions as well as have a separate budget for purchases. Where the departments fail to meet the criteria as described above, the public contracting authority must estimate the approximate value of the purchase for all departments combined.[307]

The following table provides a detailed overview of the public procurement values for the EU and national purchases in accordance with the provisions of the Public Procurement Law and the Directive 2014/24/EU.

---

306 Ibid.

307 Article 5 (2) of the Public Procurement Law.

Purchase	Purchase value
The EU threshold values Public contracts equal to or above the EU thresholds are subject to the established values in Article 4(1) and (2) of the Public Procurement Law and in Article 4 of the Directive 2014/24/EU.	1. €5,548,000 – for public works contracts[308]; 2. €144,000 – for public supply and service contracts awarded by central government authorities and design contests organised by such authorities[309]; 3. €221,000 – for public supply and service contracts awarded by sub-central public contracting authorities and design contests organised by such authorities[310]; 4. €750,000 for public service contracts for social and other specific services listed in Annex XIV[311].
Simplified procurement values Public contracts equal to or below the EU threshold are subject to Article 4(2) and (3) of the Public Procurement Law.	1. A simplified procurement is considered to be a purchase, of which the estimated value is less than the respective EU threshold. 2. Notwithstanding the public contracts value, which is equal to or higher than the EU thresholds, the public contracting authority may apply the simplified procurement procedure. Thus, the value of any of the lots, net of VAT, should be less than €80,000 for services or supplies, or €100,000 for works, provided that the aggregate value of those lots does not exceed 20 % of the aggregate value of the lots as a whole. (Article 5 (8) of the Public Procurement Law)[312].

308 Ibid.

309 Ibid.

310 Ibid.

311 Ibid

312 Article 4 (2) and (3) of the Public Procurement Law. Republic of Lithuania, Law on public procurement (official translation in English online of old version of Public Procurement Law, 1997.). http://www.who.int/medical_devices/survey_resources/medical_device_technical_specifications_lithuania.pdf (21.05.2018).

Purchase	Purchase value
Small procurement values Small public procurement values are subject to Article 4 (3) of the Public Procurement Law.	1. Small public procurement values shall mean a simplified procurement procedure where the contract value net of VAT is less than €58,000 for supplies or services, or less than €145,000 for works[313].
	2. Notwithstanding the small public contracts value, which is equal to or above the small value thresholds, the public contracting authority may apply small value public procurement procedure. Thus, the value of any of the lots, net of VAT, should be less than
	3. €58,000 for services or supplies, or €145,000 for works, provided that the aggregate value of those lots does not exceed 20 % of the aggregate value of the lots as a whole. (Article 5 (9) of the Public Procurement Law).[314]

4.6 Simplified procurement procedures

In this section, the author will briefly discuss the rules of procedure for simplified and small value public procurement regarding the purchase of goods, services or works whose value is below the EU threshold. The new Public Procurement Law introduces significant modifications regarding the application of rules for simplified and small value procurement procedures. Simplified procedures constitute a major part of the total procurements in Lithuania. Therefore, it is important that these procedures are fast and less bureaucratic. The old Public Procurement Law required that public contracting authorities draft their own rules. A simplified and small value procurement procedure had to be launched complying with the rules approved, which had to be published in the Central Portal of Public Procurement and on its website maximum three working days after the approval

313 Article 4 (3) of the Public Procurement Law.
314 Article 5 (9) of the Public Procurement Law.

respecting the procedures established in the previous Lithuanian law on public procurement.[315]

Presently, these requirements have been updated for simplified procurement procedures aswell, which must be carried out in accordance with the new Public Procurement Law.[316] In addition, the purchase of services, supplies and works of small value is regulated by the specific rules of low value procurement set out by the PPO[317], rather than the requirements laid down by the public contracting authorities themselves, as it used to be under the previous Public Procurement Law.

Importantly, the new law does not distinguish between public procurement procedures below the EU thresholds and above. Simplified procurement procedures have shorter time limits; however, the process of the procedures remains the same. In the author's opinion, the same procedures established below the EU thresholds might be deemed complicated and disproportionate to the value of the purchase. In the Vestergaard case the CJEU determined that the procedures established in the EU Directive 2014/24/EU are not suitable for public contracts of low value. The CJEU has stated that public procurement procedures apply only to contracts whose value exceeds a threshold laid down expressly in each directive. However, the mere fact that the EU legislature considered that the strict special procedures laid down in this Directive 2014/24/EU is not appropriate in the case of public contracts of small value does not mean that those contracts are excluded from the scope of the EU law.[318] Thus, the question is if such complex procedures below the EU thresholds are appropriate in terms of effort and money. In the author's view, such procedures do not justify the cost involved. This is shown in further detail in the table below wherein the simplified procurement value corresponds to 28 % of total procurement value in 2016[319].

---

315 Lietuvos Respublikos, Viešųjų pirkimų įstatymo Nr. I-1491 pakeitimo įstatymas, 85 str. 2006 m. sausio 31d. https://www.e-tar.lt/portal/lt/legalAct/TAR.C54AFFAA7622/mljgfOSVqW (03.06.2017).

316 Article 5 (8) (9) of the new Public Procurement Law.

317 Dėl mažos vertės pirkimų tvarkos aprašo patvirtinimo, 2017. https://www.ltkt.lt/admin/ckeditor/fileman/Uploads/Dokumentai%20parsisiuntimui/Mazos-vertes-pirkimu-tvarkos-aprasas_galioja-nuo-2017-07-01.pdf (21.11.2019).

318 Case C-59/00, *Bent Mousten Vestergaard v. Spøttrup Boligselskab*, 2001, ECR I-9505, para. 19.

319 Yearly statistic and analyses of public procurement in Lithuania, Public Procurement Office. http://vpt.lrv.lt/lt/statistika-ir-analize/ketvirtines-ir-metines-ataskaitos-1 (04.06.2017).

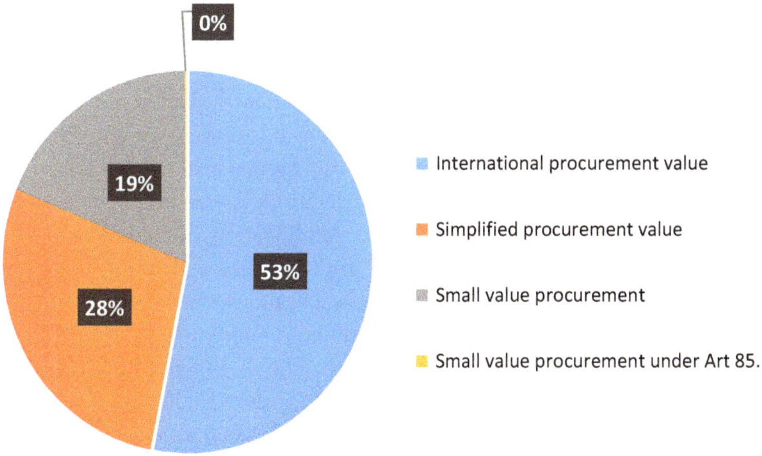

Chart 1: Percentage of the purchase value in Lithuanian in 2016.

Unlike the simplified procedures, there are only two types of low value procurement procedures: a survey conducted with the bidders orally and in writing. Despite accounting for one third of all purchases in Lithuania, the simplified procurement procedures have not been updated or improved since 2005. Consequently, it is inevitable that as of 2017 the public contracting authorities will have to follow new Public Procurement Law rules and procedures in applying the simplified procurement procedures and will no longer have flexibility in defining its own rules. Despite the new public procurement reform in Lithuania, which has the objective of introducing more simplification and flexibility in the application of rules, the simplified public procurement process has been even more rigorously regulated in the new Public Procurement Law.

To summarise, the simplified procurement procedures constitute almost 30 % of all procurement purchases in Lithuania and play an important role in purchasing services, supplies and works. Despite of the new Public Procurement Law rules, the author believes that the simplified procurement procedures are in need of updating in light of a new more flexible approach and dismissing the practice of applying the same public procurement procedures for the purchases below the EU thresholds. Thus, the simplified procurement procedures could be adjusted with the procedures which are currently applied for the small value procurement purchases.

4.7 Conclusions

Lithuania has implemented all provisions provided by the Directive; therefore the author did not discuss the new rules introduced by the Directive, which were discussed earlier in Chapter II such as the access to the SMEs, simplification and modernisation of procurement, best value for money criteria, introduction of European Single Procurement Document, electronic means etc.

This section has mainly addressed the modifications introduced in public procurement procedures in addition to the transposed requirements of the Directive. Currently, the Public Procurement Law focuses on the maximum level of transparency, resulting in even the simplified procurement procedures being aligned with the procedures above the EU thresholds and published where the contract value before VAT is within the range of under €58,000 and €221,000 for supplies or services, or between €145,000 and €5,548,000 for works. The author considers such procurement procedures to be too complex and rigid, and therefore out of proportion to the value of the procurement. Such findings are also confirmed by the CJEU and most of the survey participants[320]. The aim is that the implementation of the newly transposed rules will be effective. Therefore, the Lithuanian PPO will have to ensure methodological assistance for proper and effective implementation of these rules.

5 New legal framework of public procurement in Germany

On 18 April 2016, Germany introduced so far the biggest reform in procurement law. Germany had also a big challenge to implement new public procurement directives[321]. Therefore, at the same time the reform aimed to simplify the procurement system and to improve the user-friendliness of the rules to suppliers. One part of the reform was a full digitisation of the procurement procedures. The reform led to redesigning and abolishing the unnecessarily complex governance structures. For the first time, there will also be a valid statistical basis for public procurement in Germany.

320 Viktorija Bobrova, Magistro baigiamasis darbas, Supparastintų viešųjų pirkimų vykdymo problemos ir jų sprendimo būdai, 2009, p. 22. In this thesis the author discussed the survey results, which were made between the bidders and public authorities regarding the application of the simplified procurement procedures and the survey showed that the simplified procedures are too complex.

321 Ibid.

The implementation of the respective EU directives on national level took place according to the so-called cascade principle.[322] This meant that the German legislator was against the creation of a homogeneous set of rules[323] and rather implemented the EU directives into existing rules of different legal systems.[324]

The German law is subject to four different legal acts. Public procurement provisions are regulated by the most important law on competition, the Act against the restrains on competition (GWB)[325]. There are subsidiary norms that supplement the procurement provisions: the Ordinance of the Award of Public Contracts (VgV)[326] that is referred to in the Regulation of the Awards of Works (VOB/A).[327] As such, the VOB/A also complements the GWB. The fourth act is newly established Law for public procurement below the thresholds (UVgO).

The complex governance of procurement legal structures was advocated on German constitutionality and efficiency, however the procurement legal structure remained unchanged[328]. The Koblenz Administrative Court[329] and Administrative Court of Appeal[330] issued opinions on the cascade of the German legal system and held the view that there should be a two-step approach of the legal system. The German Federal Constitutional Court took the final decision wherein the cascade law systems does not infringe the constitution.[331]

The new structure of the German procurement legislation is illustrated in the table below.

---

322 Klaus Dieter Kapellmann, Burkhard Messerschmidt, VOB, Teile A und B: Vergabe- und Vertragsordnung für Bauleistungen mit Vergabeverordnung Rn. 10. 2015.

323 Matthias Knauff, das Kaskadensystem in Vergaberecht, ein Regelungsmodell mit Zukunft?, NZBau, 657–659, 2010.

324 Dacian Dragos, Roberto Caranta, Outside the EU procurement Directives-Insite the Treaty? 2015, p. 121.

325 Act against restraints of competition (GWB), 2016.

326 Verordnung über die Vergabe öffentlicher Aufträge (Vergabeverordnung – VgV), 2016.

327 Vergabe- und Vertragsordnung für Bauleistungen Teil A, Allgemeine Bestimmungen für die Vergabe von Bauleistungen, 2016 (VOB/A).

328 Hanna Schebesta, Towards an EU Law of Damages, p. 122, 2013.

329 Judgement of Administrative Court of Appeals Koblenz, No 6L 2617/04, 31 January 2005.

330 Judgement of Administrative Court of Koblenz, No 7B 10356/05, 25 May 2005.

331 Judgement of German Federal Constitutional Court, No 1 BvR 1160/03, 13 June 2006.

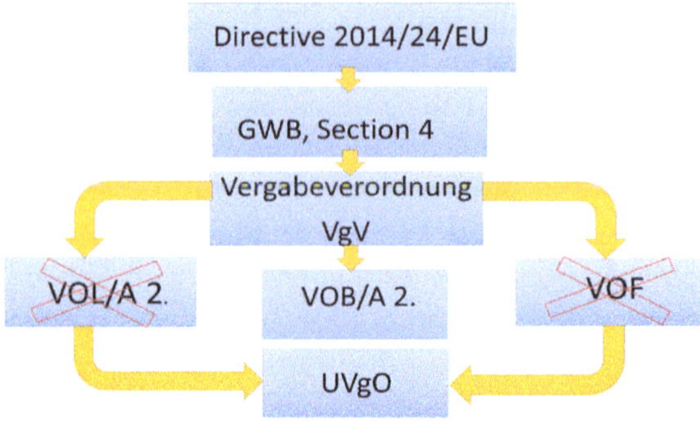

Chart 2: Overview of the German public procurement law system.

Both the GWB[332] and the VgV[333] apply the EU procedures for services and supplies, which replaced the previous VOL/A[334] and the VOF.[335] Two sections of the VgV also apply to construction works. For the building sector there is a new version of the VOB/A adapted, which is applied for below and above the thresholds. Social, ecological and economic criteria are increasingly being introduced into the law of justice.[336] A further major change is that mandatory exclusion grounds are introduced. A new rule sees taxes and duties as a compulsory reason for exclusion or even for termination of the contract. Another new feature is that, for example, a substantially bad performance is an optional exclusion reason. In practice, the proportionality will play a big role in such cases. A corresponding interpretation will ultimately be the task of the public contracting authority. The further sections will provide more details on the different public procurement rules in Germany.

5.1 Act against restraints on competition (GWB)

The GWB transposes the essential provisions of the new Directive 2014/24/EU into the national law of Germany. The fourth part of the GWB has been comprehensively reviewed and restructured.

---

332 Gesetz gegen Wettbewerbsbeschränkungen (GWB), 2018.

333 Verordnung über die Vergabe öffentlicher Aufträge (Vergabeverordnung – VgV), 2016.

334 Vergabe- und Vertragsordnung für Leistungen, 2009 (VOL); Hans-Peter Kulartz, Norvert Portz, VOL und VOF, p. 13, 2016.

335 Verdingundordnung für freiberufliche leistungen (VOF).

336 Martin Trybus, Roberto Caranta, The law of green and social procurement in Europe, p. 105, 2010.

In the field above the EU thresholds the structure of the German public procurement law is simpler and more user-friendly. In addition, the extended possibilities were introduced for better participation of SMEs in procurement procedures. The procurement procedures in the future will be electronic.

In the first stage of the procurement framework whether any public contract is restricted to a specific procurement procedure that is underway needs to be determined. § 97 GWB introduces the principles applied and similar provisions including the definition of a public contracting authority, public order and exemptions.[337]

The new Part 4 of the GWB deals with the substantive provisions on the award of public contracts in particular:

- the general principles of procurement law;
- the scope, types;
- the basic requirements for eligibility and award of the contract;[338]
- conditions of implementation, reasons for exclusion from public procurement procedures,
- the "self-cleaning" requirements of suppliers.

In order to ensure the law is properly enforced and to facilitate the procedures related to the grounds for exclusion, the screening of suppliers with respect to the performance of the contract has been introduced in the GBW for the first time. Electronic communications will be carried out following the EU Directive 2014/24/EU.

5.2 Regulation on the award of public contracts (VgV)

The VgV was adopted together with the GWB in 2016. At the second phase of the procurement framework the VgV establishes further implementation rules, e.g. preparation of procurement procedures, transparency requirements and requirements on the award of public contracts. The reform of the procurement framework in Germany resulted in including procedural rules in the VgV that had so far been separately governed by the VOL/A, section 2 and VOF, both of which have been therefore repealed. The VgV contains traditional procurement procedures, which are established in the Directive 2014/24/EU. Regarding the award of architectural and engineering services the new regulation defines

337 Alfred Katz, Kommunale Wirtschaft, 2017, Rn 77.

338 Mario Comba and Steen Treumer, Award of contracts in EU procurement, 2013, p. 95.

requirements in two independent sections. The provisions of the VgV will apply to the procedures above the EU thresholds.

5.3 Regulation on the award of works contracts (VOB/A)

The procedure for the award of public works contracts is laid down in the VOB/A of the procurement regulation. The standard paragraphs are to be applied to national awards of contracts by public contracting entities bound by budgetary law[339]. Sections 2 to 4 apply to the contracts above the EU thresholds by public contracting authorities within the meaning of § 98 of the GWB. Threshold amounts have been adjusted to comply with the EU requirements. Despite the elimination of the VOL/A and VOF rules and their consequent integration into the VgV, the VOB/A remains valid at the third stage of the procurement system for awarding works contracts above and below the EU thresholds[340]. Thus, the reform of the German procurement framework has only succeeded fragmentally[341] since the VOB/A has not been incorporated into the VgV. Thus, it could have led to the two-stage approach of the procurement framework. The author Knauff speaks of an "artificial ruin" with regard to the new structure of the law. It also carries a risk of divergent rules and represents a barrier in itself.

In addition, the VOB/A regulates the simplified regime for the award of social and other special services (§ 130 GWB), for which a higher threshold of €750,000 exists. The rules of VOB/A are complex[342] and hopefully there will be new vision on how to take the German procurement system to the next stage.[343]

Although 90 %[344] of all contract awards are now carried out at the national level, the EU is dominating in the decisions on questions for remedies. The

339 Ulrich Battis, Öffentliches Baurecht und Raumordnungsrecht, 7 Auflage, 2017, Rn 9.

340 Ralf Leinemann, Die Vergabe öffentlicher Aufträge, 2016, p. 357.

341 Matthias Knauff, Strukturfragen des neuen Vergaberechts Aufsatz, NZBau 2016, p. 195.

342 Ulrich Battis, Michael Krautzberger und Rolf-Peter, Kommentar zum BauGB, 13 Auflage, 2016.

343 Norbert Portz, Deutscher Städte- und Gemeindebund, The new rules on public procurement in 2016. https://www.dstgb.de/dstgb/Homepage/Schwerpunkte/Vergaberecht/Aktuelles/Entwurf%20%E2%80%9EGesetz%20zur%20Modernisierung%20des%20Vergaberechts%E2%80%9C%20vorgelegt/Positionspapier_%20Die%20Umsetzung%20der%20neuen%20EU%20Vergaberichtlinien.pdf (05.07.2017).

344 Die Bundesregierung, Monitoring – Bericht der Bundesregierung zur Anwendung des Vergaberechts 2017, p. 14. https://www.bmwi.de/Redaktion/DE/Artikel/Wirtschaft/reform-der-eu-weiten-vergaben.html (08.08.2017).

reason for this is the absence of legal standards at the national level. Therefore, the provisions of sections 1 of the VOB/A are neither influenced by the requirements of Directive 2014/24/EU nor by the provisions of the GWB and Public Procurement Regulations (VgV). Rather, they pursue an economical allocation of public contracts following the budgetary principles established by the Federal Budget Regulation and various Land Budget Codes.

5.4 Regulation on the award of contracts below the EU thresholds (UVgO)

Following the modernisation of the law applicable above the EU thresholds, the legal framework for contracts below the EU thresholds has also been improved. Through these changes the Federal Government considers that the new legal framework is also applied by the confederations, federal States and municipalities below the EU thresholds.

The UVgO is effective as of 2 September 2017 and federal public procurement authorities are required to apply the Regulation for the award of contracts for supplies and services below the EU thresholds (UVgO). The new UVgO is therefore applicable to all procurement procedures of supply and service contracts below the EU thresholds. Thus, section one of the VOL/A is no longer valid and the further rules of § 55 BHO[345], aswell as the general administrative provisions to the federal budget regulation (VV-BHO), have been amended accordingly.

The new UVgO has to be implemented in the federal States. When the UVgO is implemented in the federal States it does not mean that the rules will be regulated uniformly.

There is an additional hurdle in some federal States; it consists of not only the land budget regulation, but also an amendment of the respective procurement act of the land. For example, the existing regulations of the federal States of Mecklenburg-Vorpommern, Niedersachsen, Nordrhein-Westfalen, Sachsen, Sachsen-Anhalt, Schleswig-Holstein, and Thüringen apply the first section of the VOL/A rules. Meanwhile, Hamburg has amended its procurement act respectively on 9 June 2017. In contrary, the State of Hessen will omit the introduction of the UVgO and continue applying the VOL/A rules. The UVgO regulation is still not transposed[346] into the law by the States of Berlin, Mecklenburg-Vorpommern,

345 Bundeshaushaltsordnung, 2017.
346 https://www.forum-verlag.com/themenwelten/kommunales/unterschwellen vergabeordnung-uvgo-zeitplan-fuer-die-einfuehrung-in-den-bundeslaendern (22.05.2018).

and Thüringen etc.[347]. It is for the local authorities to implement and enforce through separate regulation of the competent authority necessary rules.

5.4.1 Scope of UVgO

The UVgO is addressed only to "contracting entities" and not to "public contracting authority". Therefore, the municipalities in their area have the right to decide to what extent they want to apply specific UVgO rules. The UVgO covers all awards of public supply and service contracts and framework agreements below the EU thresholds according to § 106 GWB and § 1(1) UVgO.

§ 2 (1) UVgO is innovative in setting out the principles of profitability, proportionality and equal treatment. Public contracts are awarded on the basis of competitive and transparent procedures. The principles of profitability and proportionality are respected. It suggests these principles are applied not at a specific stage of the procurement process but rather in the course of the entire procurement process and requires them to be fully respected[348].

Certain rules contained in the VgV (§ 5 to 8) were transposed in UVgO, in particular "confidentiality rules" (§ 3 UVgO), "avoiding conflict of interests" (§ 4 UVgO), and "participation in the preparation of the procurement procedure" (§ 4 UVgO).

The UVgO sets out the main requirements that are applicable below the thresholds; thus, Germany imposed the consistency of the procurement rules above. The new UVgO constitutes meaningful reform steps and facilitations. However, the UVgO is in its entirety still too cluttered for the user. In particular, the procurement laws of States are currently preventing a desirable progress for further standardisation and simplification.

5.4.2 Procedures below the thresholds

The UVgO intends to clarify that it covers competitive and transparent procurement procedures. The public contracting entity is allowed to freely choose between the open and restricted procedure in accordance with § 8 (2) UVgO. The same can be said of the rules defined in § 14 (2) of the VgV. In contrary, a new procedure, namely the restricted procedure without publication could be conducted by

347 UVgO: Umsetzung in Bund und Ländern, Vergabeblog, 2017. https://www.vergabeblog.de/2017-08-16/uvgo-umsetzung-in-bund-und-laendern/ (08.08.2017).

348 Norbert Portz, Deutscher Städte- und Gemeindebund, UVgO Unterschwellenvergabeordnung, 2016, https://www.akh.de/fileadmin/download/Vergabe_und_Wettbewerbe/Vergabetag/Vergabetag_2017/01_Portz.pdf (08.08.2017).

two conditions set out in § 8 (3) UVgO. The first condition is that an open tender would not bring economic results and second, an open tender or restricted tender with competition for the contracting entity or the candidates or tenderers would be disproportionate to the advantage gained or the value of the service.

Such a restricted invitation to tender without a contract notice has no parallel provisions in the VgV. The corresponding restricted tender procedure without publication in accordance with § 16 of the VgV must always be advertised.

For the first time the negotiated procedure ("Verhandlungsverfahren") is spelled out in § 8 (4) UVgO and has the same definition for above and below the EU thresholds. Pursuant to § 3 (5) of the VOL/A such procedure was defined as "Freihändige Vergabe.[349]" Such a definition of the procedure was introduced only to make a distinction between various negotiated procurement procedures above the thresholds. Hence, the UVgO contained the same definition of the negotiated procedure below the EU threshold; this is to be aligned with the definition above the EU threshold. Similarly, to the restricted procedure, the negotiated procedure is also subject to certain conditions. The public contracting authority may opt for the negotiated procedure with or without publication following § 8 (4) (1–14) UVgO. The negotiated procedure could also be applied in the case of one bidder according to the requirements specified in § 8 (4) (9–14) UVgO. The public contracting authorities have to apply one of the conditions specified in the § 8 (4) UVgO. The in order to apply the negotiated procedure. The application terms of the negotiated procedure are specified in Article 26 (4) and 32 of the Directive 2014/24/EU.

Each federal State has defined its threshold limits below which procurement procedures may be conducted without disclosing the reasons behind the choice of the negotiated procedure. In Bavaria the limit is usually €25,000 for authorities at the State level or €30,000 for local authorities (VAT excluded)[350].

5.5 Thresholds

The national legal framework in Germany depends on whether the value of the tendered service exceeds the relevant thresholds which are specified in § 106 GWB. Below the EU thresholds of the contract value differ considerably depending on the procurement rules of each federal State.

---

349 Kulartz, H. P., Röwekamp, H., Portz, N., Prieß, H.J., Kommentar zur UVgO, p. 112, 2018.

350 ABZ, Leaflet, Public procurement in Germany, 2013, p. 5. https://www.handelskammer-bremen.de/blob/hbihk24/gruendung_foerderung/downloads/1301404/6cf334c8b75cd488115c323207c2f5a2/Public_Contracts_in_Germany-data.pdf (06.07.2017).

Purchase	Purchase value
The EU threshold values Public contracts equal to or above the EU thresholds are subject to the established values in § 106 GWB and in Article 4 of the Directive 2014/24/EU.	1. €5,548,000 – for public works contracts[351]; 2. €144,000 – for public supply and service contracts awarded by central government authorities and design contests organised by such authorities[352]; 3. €221,000 – for public supply and service contracts awarded by sub-central public contracting authorities and design contests organised by such authorities[353]; 4. €750,000 for public service contracts for social and other specific services listed in Annex XIV[354].
Procurement values below the EU thresholds (National private tender procedure)[355] Public contracts equal to or below the EU thresholds are subject to the established procurement rules by the separate federal States[356]	1. Restricted invitation to tender concerning construction works is acceptable with thresholds not higher than €100,000,000 2. Invitation to negotiate offers concerning construction works is acceptable with thresholds not higher than €75,000. 3. Restricted invitation to tender concerning services and supplies is acceptable with thresholds not higher than €100,000. 4. Invitation to negotiate offers concerning services and supplies is acceptable with thresholds not higher than €50,000.

351 Ibid.

352 Ibid.

353 Ibid.

354 Ibid.

355 The table provides overview of procurement values below and above the EU thresholds. https://www.nbank.de/medien/nb-media/Downloads/Rechtliche-Grundlagen/Vergaberecht/%C3%9Cbersicht-Wertgrenzen-und-EG-Schwellenwerte.pdf (05.07.2017).

356 The table provides overview of the different thresholds established in the federal States. http://www.abst-brandenburg.de/wp-content/uploads/2019/08/Wertgrenzen_Bund_-Bundesl%C3%A4nder_2019.-07.08.19.pdf (05.07.2017).

5.6 E-procurement

The Directive 2014/24/EU defines the approach of the e-procurement to replace traditional hard-copy forms of procurement with e-procurement matters. The provisions in the Recital 52 of the Directive 2014/24/EU define the change in this approach: "electronic means of information and communication can greatly simplify the publication of contracts and increase the efficiency and transparency of procurement processes.[357]" Therefore, they should be used as the standard means of communication and information exchange in procurement procedures. The recital then sets out the mandatory backdrop to the new rules and States that the: "transmission of notices in electronic form, electronic availability of the procurement documents and after a transition period of thirty months fully electronic communication should be made mandatory[358]".

Therefore, Germany took a very serious approach regarding e-procurement. With the reform of public procurement, Germany committed to strengthening the e-government, because the digital public procurement services are still below the EU average. Unfortunately, Germany is lacking the interoperable electronic systems that are efficient. The Federal Government is committed to setting up a central portal for citizens which will also provide the public services and will in turn contribute to the entire country. The aim of e-procurement would be to increase the publication of the contract notices at the OJEU. Hence, currently only 1.2 % of Germany's GDP has recorded the lowest values for contracts published in the OJEU. Whereas, the average of the EU is 4.3 % of the GDP[359]. The reform of digitalisation of the services is critical at the governmental level, which should lead to simplification, effectiveness and a reduction of the burden, especially for the SMEs.[360]

The Directive 2014/24/EU sets out mandatory electronic requirements as of 18 October 2018 and for the central purchasing bodies these requirements were set on 18 April 2017[361]. Germany successfully transposed all mandatory

---

357 Recital 52 of the Directive 2014/24/EU.

358 Ibid.

359 Commission staff working document, Country report Germany 2017, Including an in-depth review on the prevention and correction of macroeconomic, SWD (2017) 71.

360 European Commission, 2016 SBA Fact Sheet, Germany, p. 10. http://ec.europa.eu/growth/smes/business-friendly-environment/performance-review-2016_en (07.08.2017).

361 Ibid.

electronic requirements into the national law. Thus, a proper implementation of all electronic means will require a great effort and political will.

Statistics below in the table show the results of a survey concerning the usage of electronic tendering by industrial companies in Germany in 2015. During the survey period, it was found that roughly 8.3 % of responding companies had been using e-procurement for coordinating suppliers and customers for three to five years prior to the survey[362].

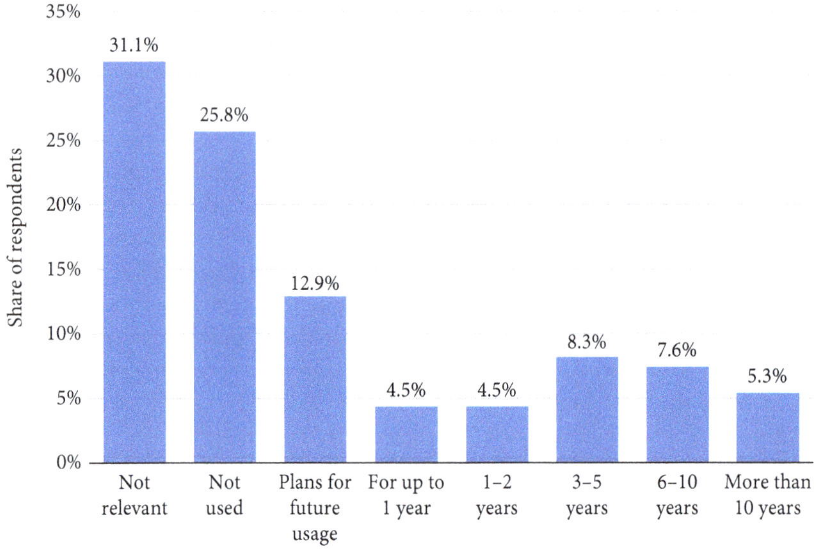

Chart 3: Electronic tendering by industrial companies in Germany in 2015.

5.7 Conclusions

The current German system of public procurement has to be viewed as the result of a long and controversial legislative process that was followed by several reforms and amendments over the decades. Hence, this is the consequence of the complex procurement structure, which is developed today in Germany. The German system of awarding procurement contracts is complex as it is modelled on the basis of the cascade of four different legal acts: 1) GWB, 2) VgV, 3) VOB/A

362 Statista, https://de.statista.com/statistik/daten/studie/214139/umfrage/nutzung-von-ausschreibungen-durch-industrieunternehmen-im-b2b/ (07.08.2017).

and 4) UVgO. Hence, this comprehensive legal structure relies on the application of the rules above the EU thresholds (GBW and VgV, partially VOB/A) and below the EU thresholds (UVgO and partially VOB/A). Directive 2004/18/EC mainly aimed at the consolidation of the rules for the award of supplies, services and works contracts and the same purpose was maintained by Directive 2014/24/EU.[363] Contrary, Germany amended the existing legal structure and did not incorporate the second or third legal acts into one legal act. Although these developments ensured conformity with the EU law for the most of the part, the German approach is still criticised as being too complex and not sufficiently friendly[364]. The latest revision of the procurement system saw the introduction of the new UVgO regulation to replace the VOL/A and VOF regulations in the domain of the award of procurement contracts for supplies and services below the EU thresholds. The UVgO determines very intricate procurement procedures similar to the ones set out for procurement above the EU thresholds. In addition, competitive dialogue and innovative partnership procedures are excluded from the application below the EU thresholds. The UVgO regulation should also be adopted at the States of Germany, which also enforce their own rules, and the above-mentioned rules are not necessarily harmonised amongst all federal States. Alternatively, Lithuanian procurement law aligns procurement procedures below the EU thresholds with those above.

The SIGMA review paper on the regulation of contracts below the EU thresholds in the Members States,[365] defines that a number of different procurement methods can be found below the EU thresholds.

In Denmark any procurement procedure below the EU thresholds may be used but central government authorities are required to announce invitations for tenders and to publish a notice for contracts. In Estonia, all procedures can be applied freely with prior publication. The Hungarian system allows for negotiating the offers during the open and restricted procedure if it has been established within the procurement documents. In Spain, it is the national threshold that determines whether a negotiated procedure can be applied, whereas in the Netherlands the regulations have a voluntary nature[366].

---

363 Ibid.

364 Steen Treumer, Enforcement of the EU public procurement rules; Marin Burgi, A report about the German Remedies System, 2011, p. 107.

365 SIGMA paper No 45, Public Procurement in the EU Member States – the Regulation of contract below the EU thresholds and in areas not covered by the detailed rules of the Directive, p. 29–45. 2010.

366 Ibid.

Taking into consideration best practices in the EU member States, the author would suggest redefining the German procurement procedures established below the EU thresholds, which would also be applied to all States of Germany. It is the author's view that Germany could apply all procedures freely without any specific requirements for choosing a negotiated procedure. Spain and Estonia already apply such an approach, which is in conformity with the Directive 2014/25/EU. The author would also recommend an equal application of all procedures (open, restricted, negotiated procedure with publication) without introducing any specific provisions. If all procurement procedures would be applied freely, the difference between these two procedures would not be marginal and only the requirement that allows negotiations during the procurement procedure would make a distinction. Therefore, if it were accepted for the tender documents to define the procurement procedure with negotiations or without them, setting up independent restricted procedures would not be required and would spare the excessive bureaucracy and complexity of the application of procurement procedures. Similar rules are established in Hungary's procurement framework as well. Such a structure would allow Germany to overcome the inefficiencies that result from the separation of the legal systems, in particular between the federal governance and federal States. Such a layout of the legal systems and in addition complex procurement procedures creates substantial costs for public contracting authorities and also for economic operators. Lack of harmonisation creates substantial difficulties and barriers to getting better access to procurement information and also to an application of the correct rules. It is the author's view that the major reform helped only to transpose new requirements of the Directive 2014/24/EU into the national legislation mainly above the EU thresholds. However, the main reform has to be adopted concerning the award of contracts below the EU thresholds as presently 90 % of the total purchases in Germany fall below the EU thresholds[367].

6 Public procurement procedures in Lithuanian and German legal frameworks

This section will review the main challenges and opportunities of the public procurement procedures above the EU thresholds transposed to the national laws of Lithuania and Germany in line with Directive 2014/24/EU. The author will offer

367 Beatrix Körner, Entscheidung über die Verfahrensart, https://www.vergabe24.de/blog/entscheidung-ueber-die-verfahrensart/ (27.05.2018).

further insights into the new aspects of public procurement procedures and their practical application.

Every reform of the EU public procurement would lead to the introduction of a new public procurement procedure. In 2004 a new competitive dialogue was established and ten years later in 2014 a new innovation partnership procedure was also introduced. The author will address the aim of the Directive 2014/24/EU, which is the simplification and flexibility to be achieved when conducting procurement procedures. The author will, in particular, analyse the process similarities of negotiated and competitive dialogue procedures and propose solutions for their better application in practice.

6.1 Open procedure

This section discusses the main steps of the open procedure following the provisions laid down in the Directive 2014/24/EU. Public contracting authorities must award contracts within the scope of the Directive 2014/24/EU. The CJEU[368] has allowed Member States to adopt contract award procedures other than the ones provided for in the Directive 2014/24/EU, on the condition that they exhibit equivalent characteristics to those of the Directive.

Open procedure consists of one single stage. According to Directive 2014/24/EU, a tender can be submitted by any interested economic operator[369]. The procedure begins with an announcement in the form of a contract notice describing the requirements of the contract published in the OJEU. This notice details the procedure, organisation of the procedure, methods of assessing offers (exclusion, selection and award criteria), the way to receive tender documents, deadline for submitting offers and date of public opening. It may also give information about the minimum economic, financial, technical and professional capacity required by the selection criteria as well as the admissibility of variant solutions[370].

It is a very binary procedure under which the technical specifications, contract terms and proposals are essentially set in stone and no changes or negotiations are permitted except for clarifications in writing. An open procedure may be suitable for specific type of contracts such as e.g. supplies where requirements

368 Case C-299/08, *European Commission v French Republic*, 2009, ECR I-11587.

369 Article 27 of the Directive 2014/24/EU.

370 Hans-Joachim Priess, Award Procedures for the EU Institutions, Chapter 16, in Gunilla Edelstam, Martin Trybus, Roberto Caranta, EU Public Contract Law, Public Procurement and Beyond, 1 Edition, 2013, p. 417.

are clearly defined, not subject to change and the standard contract terms and conditions apply.

Full information about the subject of the procurement, conditions and procedure is given in the tender documents that can be made available via the internet or in hard copy on request. Any inconsistency in procedure documents should be avoided. In particular, inconsistencies between the contract notice and the tender documents can call for suspension of the procedure. Any natural or legal person may respond to the contract notice and tender documentation and submit a bid offers electronically and opened by the opening committee. The evaluation committee assesses all offers, applying the exclusion, selection and award criteria separately. It prepares the evaluation report, including its recommendations. On this basis, the authorising officer takes the award decision and the public contracting authority sends notification to all the tenderers.

Upon informing the successful candidate of the contract award the public contracting authority asks the winning tenderer for proof that they comply with the exclusion criteria. Following verification of that evidence and after waiting for possible complaints, a minimum of 10 days after dispatch of the notification of the decision, the public contracting authority signs the contract with the winning tenderer. Following the award decision the award notice is published at the OJEU.[371]

6.1.1 New provisions

The new Directive 2014/24/EU introduces shorter time limits for open procedures. The minimum time limit to receive offers has been reduced from 52 days to 35.[372] If the prior information notice has been published and if the case is extremely urgent, time limits can be cut down to 15 days. Reductions in deadlines are reasonable and comply with the EU strategy 2020 measures[373].

One more requirement is added on the cap of turnover, which is set at the amount twice the value of the contract[374]. Such a new requirement should also help SMEs to have a better access to the market and to be able to submit the bids. This is because their turnover is much smaller than that of larger companies. Such requirements are also in line with the EU strategy 2020, which envisages

371 Article 50 of the Directive 2014/24/EU.

372 Glenn Fletcher, Minimum time limits under the new Public Procurement Directive, P.P.L.R, 2014, (3), p. 95.

373 Ibid.

374 Article 58 (3) of the Directive 2014/24/EU.

better access to procurement for SMEs. While public contracting authorities could always increase the turnover requirement, it is still required that the turnover method chosen be justified by the contacting authority.[375]

Moreover, Directive 2014/24/EU has introduced the European Single Procurement Document ("ESPD") as a new requirement.[376] The purpose of this document is to replace the single certificates issued by public contracting authorities or third parties confirming the submission of relevant documents assuring the following: 1) the supplier is not in one of the situations indicated in Article 57 of Directive 2014/24/EU, 2) it meets the criteria laid down in Article 58 and 3) complies with the objective rules and criteria laid down in Article 65.[377]

The ESPD[378] will allow all businesses to electronically self-declare that they meet the necessary regulatory criteria or commercial capability requirements, and thereafter only the awarded supplier will need to submit all necessary documentation proving that it qualifies for the contract. In this case, only the original documents based on the ESPD document would need to be submitted to the public contracting authority. Therefore, the ESPD document would only have to be filled out by the suppliers at the submission stage whereas the original documents would only have to be submitted by the awarded tenderer at the end of the procurement stage.

To make the ESPD more user-friendly, the Commission has set up a free, web-based system for Member States and businesses.[379] As Member States are officially allowed to postpone the use of electronic means until 18 October 2018, according to Articles 22, 59, 61 and 90(2)–(5) of Directive 2014/24/EU, the ESPD may be printed, filled in manually, scanned and submitted in an electronic form until that date.

To reduce the administrative workload for public contracting authorities and entities and to avoid any possible contradictions in different documents, the information that must be provided in the ESPD by the supplier is to be clearly stated prior to the call for competition[380]. All this information must be analysed

375 Ibid.

376 Articles 59 and 61 of the Directive 2014/24/EU.

377 https://ec.europa.eu/regional_policy/sources/docgener/guides/public_procurement/2018/guidance_public_procurement_2018_en.pdf (27.05.2018).

378 Andreas Neun, Olaf Otting, Die Entwicklung des europäischen Vergaberechts in den Jahren 2015/2016, EuZW 2016, 486.

379 http://ec.europa.eu/social/main.jsp?catId=1135&langId=en (04.06.2017).

380 Recital 3 of the Commission Implementing Regulation (EU) 2016/7 of 5 January 2016 establishing the standard form for the European Single Procurement Document.

in detail by the supplier in view of their possible participation and submission of tenders.

The ESPD should help to further simplify the process for public contracting authorities and suppliers by replacing numerous and diverging self-declarations with a single format document recognised at the European level. This, will also help to reduce the number of issues arising from the precise wording of formal statements and declarations of consent as well as language issues because the standard form will be available in all official EU languages[381]. The ESPD, being used in all public procurement procedures, should thereby lead to an improved cross-border competition in public procurement.[382]

6.1.2 Provisions in German law

Provisions established in the Directive 2014/24/EU for the open procedure have been fully transposed in the VoV[383] and GWB[384] legal frameworks of Germany. The open procedure is defined in § 119 (3) of the GWB as a procedure in which a public contracting authority invites an unlimited number of suppliers to submit tenders.[385]

This type of procedure together with the restricted procedure are standard procedures. The contract notice should be issued pursuant to § 39 (2) of the VgV. The notice shall include a large quantity of information on the award procedure applied, the type, scope and place of the service, the period of availability and the documents to be submitted with the tender.

According to § 41 (1) VgV, the public contracting authority must provide in the contract notice or call for confirmation of interest an electronic address where the bidding supplier can request tender documents to be sent free of charge and without restriction. There may be cases as stipulated in § 41 (2) VgV in which the public contracting authority may deliver tender documents in other ways, for example, by post etc. The tender documents contain the actual invitation to submit an offer and the so-called tender documents (description of services, general terms and conditions, as well as further details).[386]

381 Ibid.
382 Rhodri Williams, The European single procurement document, § 101 GWB, n. 4, 2011.
383 Ibid.
384 Ibid.
385 Klaus Willenbruch/Kristina Wieddekind, Kompaktkommentar Vergaberecht, 2017.
386 Jan Byok/Wolfgang Jaeger, Kommentar zum Vergaberecht, § 101 GWB, n. 602, 2011.

All relevant criteria (such as eligibility, selection and award criteria) should be set out in the tender documents as well as other information necessary to assess the bid such as price, quality and required environmental characteristics, including their weighting in accordance with § 52 (2) VgV. A minimum of 35 days will then be provided for the bidders to submit their offers pursuant to § 15 (2) VgV. If the offers are submitted electronically, the public contracting authority may shorten the time limit by five days as stipulated in § 15 (4) VgV. After receiving all the offers they are reviewed and assessed by the public contracting authority. This examination must be carried out according to a strictly formalised procedure in order to ensure a fair and non-discriminatory award.[387]

The examination and evaluation of the offers are carried out in the steps described in § 56 (2) VgV. If the offer contains formal errors, it can be automatically excluded from the further process. Formal erroneous offers are, for example, those which are received late, are not signed or for which the bidder has made changes to the tender documents. However, it is the public contracting authority that makes the final decision regarding whether an offer is eligible, non-compliant or erroneous on the basis of self-declarations, statements, certificates or other documents, which are to be provided by the bidder.

Further, pursuant to § 122 GWB, the public contracting authority verifies whether the suppliers have the qualification and permission and by extension, whether they comply with economic, financial, technical and professional standing. The suitability of a bidding company is either accepted or excluded from the further process.

In the next stage a price will be verified. Offers with an unreasonably low price may be excluded from the process pursuant to § 60 VgV. For this purpose, however, the reasons must be verified. The public contracting authority is only obliged to exclude the low value offer that meets the provisions specified in § 128 (1) GWB. Regulations serve primarily the protection of the public contracting authority before the occurrence of an economic risk. In this case, the public contracting authority would be running a risk of experiencing economic difficulties in completing services, supplies or goods.

Finally, the public contracting authority decides using one of the award criteria, the most economically advantageous criteria, from the remaining offers in the evaluation stage following § 127 GWB and § 58 (1) VgV. The public contracting authority might decide to take into account environmental or social

387 Martin Burgi, Vergaberecht, 2018, p. 154.

criteria as stated in § 58 (2) VgV. These particularly refer to quality, technical requirements, experience and accessibility of performance etc.

Pursuant to § 134 (1) GWB, once the public contracting authority has taken the award decision it must inform all successful and non-successful bidders of the reasons for not taking or taking their bid. The contract may be awarded 15 days (if notified by fax) or 10 calendar days (if notified electronically) after the date of the dispatch of the decision notification. If the contract is awarded before the stand still period, it shall be considered void following § 135 (1) GWB.

If the public contracting authority has failed to meet one of the provisions established in § 135 GWB, the contract is not valid. The award must also be announced in the OJEU 30 days at the latest after the award of the contract in accordance with § 39 (1) VgV.

Unlike other types of procedures, the open procedure allows all interested suppliers to participate and submit an offer. This means that a pre-selection of the bidders in a participating competition does not take place. The open procedure thus ensures the greatest possible competition.

6.1.3 Provisions in Lithuanian law

Lithuania also transposed all required provisions for the open procedure. Pursuant to Article 59 of the PPL, an open procedure can be selected by the public contracting authority for all cases. An open procedure means that a tender may be submitted by any interested supplier, which makes the number of tenderers in this type of competition unlimited. Open procedure consists of the following stages[388]:

1) publishing of a contract notice, calling for suppliers to submit tenders in accordance with the rules set out in Articles 31 and 34 of the PPL[389];
2) verifying whether there are any reasons for exclusion of tenderers in the procurement documents, assessing if the tenderers comply with the required qualification requirements and, if applicable, the corresponding standards to ensure the quality and/or the environmental management system;
3) analysing, evaluating and comparing the offers submitted by the tenderers against the terms laid down in the procurement documents.

---

388 Professional Association of Lawyers Soloveičikas, Markauskas, Aviža, Bagdanskis. The Study of Improvement and Development Strategy for Lithuanian Public Procurement System, 14 August 2007, p. 349.

389 Ibid.

The public contracting authority must make sure that the evaluation is conducted in an impartial and transparent manner and that the contract or framework contract is awarded to a properly qualified supplier. In this case negotiations between the public contracting authority and suppliers are not allowed[390].

After assessing the supplier qualifications and their commercial offers the public contracting authority must produce a preliminary ranking of supplier tenders[391]. Upon completing the preliminary ranking of tenderers, the public contracting authority must inform the suppliers whose offer did not make it to the ranking, communicating the reasons behind such decision[392].

Pursuant to Article 60 of the Public Procurement Law the minimum number of days to submit an offer for tender with an open procedure is 35 days, which should enable tenderers to prepare appropriate proposals or applications. In very urgent cases the deadline could be reduced to 15 days.

The public contracting authority may sign the contract at a minimum 10 days after the notification has been sent to tenderers in order to give suppliers time to apply effective remedies.[393] The need for this provision has emerged particularly after the CJEU's interpretation in the Alcatel case.[394] The dispute was caused by the public contracting authority publishing the contract award and signing the contract with the winner on the same day. Advocate General Mischo[395] stated in his opinion that the EU law cannot allow a situation where the award notice is published and the contract is signed on the same day. The Advocate General Mischo rightly pointed out that tenderers must be granted full legal protection to defend their own interests. The CJEU stated that the EU law defending supplier's rights should be applied in such a way that suppliers would be able to dispute any decisions of public contracting authorities and/or actions which breach the rights of suppliers. The Court also found the supervisory system, which does not

---

390 Lithuanian Law on Public procurement, online English version from 1997, http://www.who.int/medical_devices/survey_resources/medical_device_technical_specifications_lithuania.pdf (27.05.2018).

391 Vaidotas Jakštas, Karolis Jovaišas, Viešieji pirkimai, komentaras, 2005, p. 127.

392 Ibid.

393 Case C-31/87, *Gebroeders Beentjes BV and State of the Netherlands*, 1988, ECR I-04635.

394 Case C-81/98, *Alcatel Austria AG and Others, Siemens AG Österreich and Sag-Schrack Anlagentechnik AG v Bundesministerium für Wissenschaft und Verkehr*, 1999, ECR I-07671.

395 Opinion of Advokate General Mischo, Case C-81/98, *Alcatel Austria AG and Others, Siemens AG Österreich and Sag-Schrack Anlagentechnik AG v Bundesministerium für Wissenschaft und Verkehr*, 1999, ECR I-07671.

require the contract award notice and does not establish remedies other than compensation, fails to comply with the requirements of the directives.

7 Restricted procedure

A restricted procedure is a procurement method by which all interested suppliers are allowed to submit applications to take part in the tender but the public contracting authority only invites a restricted number of tenderers to submit their offers.[396] The restricted procedure consists of two stages. The first stage is the publication of a contract notice and the qualification-based selection of candidates who will be invited to submit their offers. The second stage is for analysing, evaluating and comparing proposals made by the invited tenderers[397]. The public contracting authority has the right to restrict participation of tenders during the second stage of the procedure. At least five candidates must be invited to the second stage.[398]

Both restricted and open procedures do not allow negotiations. In a restricted procedure the technical specifications can only be clarified but not negotiated.

The assessment of a potentially high number of tenders may cause additional workload for the public contracting authority during the evaluation stage. The public contracting authority itself selects the criteria against which the economically most advantageous tenders will be assessed such as: quality, price, technical merit[399], aesthetic and functional characteristics, environmental characteristics, running costs, technical assistance, delivery time and other criteria[400]. The conclusion might be drawn that for such procedure the economically most advantageous criteria might be the most appropriate method.

The two-stage approach was discussed by the CJEU in the Nord-Pas-de-Calais case[401]. At the first stage, the candidates should meet the minimum qualification requirements. Candidates not fulfilling the minimum criteria of qualification comparison will not be evaluated and shall not be invited to the next stage. At the second stage, an assessment and comparison of the qualifications of candidates is carried out.

---

396 Article 28 of the Directive 2014/24/EU.

397 Ibid.

398 Article 65 (2) of the Directive 2014/24/EU.

399 Christopher Bovis, EU public procurement law, 2016, p. 149.

400 Article 53 of the Directive 2004/18/EC.

401 Case C-225/98, *Commission of the European Communities v French Republic,* 2000, ECR I-07445.

The first stage requires the establishment of criteria according to which the candidates would be invited to submit proposals in the second stages of the process[402]. These criteria may include the following: operational capacity (number of years in business, license requirements, experience etc.), economic and financial capacity, integrity etc. (no conflicts of interest, declaration of non-collusion). These are obviously pass/fail requirements, so that it could be easily established or confirmed whether suppliers fulfil these requirements[403]. The technical capability can also be assessed during the first stage, when it is clearly established in the procurement documents as "minimum requirements". When the minimum requirements are clearly referred to in the procurement documents, candidates can be inquired during the pre-qualification stage to confirm whether they satisfy the minimum requirements.[404] Apart from a general question on conformity with the procurement documents, questions about specific requirements referred to in the procurement documents can also be asked, so candidates can confirm whether they have them or not and be given a pass or fail mark accordingly. It must be ensured that there is a clear distinction between the first stage and second stage of the process. Thus, technical capacity that is assessed at the first stage should not be duplicated and assessed again as an award criteria during the second stage.

Restricted procedures allow the public contracting authority to select from the submitted applications the candidates that they will invite to the next stage. The selection is carried out based on the provided information in the tender applications and formalities required to assess the minimum economic and technical requirements to be fulfilled[405]. In addition, the public contracting authorities must disclose any methodology developed when choosing suppliers to tender; also, whether the rules and criteria are beyond the specific requirements of the Directive 2014/24/EU must be disclosed to all candidates, too. Candidates meeting minimum criteria are invited to the second stage.[406]

Particularly in the UK, a common best practise approach is that on a variety of criteria all economic operators designated as qualified and those who receive a set of minimum score for each criteria are invited to tender. In some cases

---

402 Walter Frenz, Vergaberecht, EU und National, p. 496, 2018.

403 Philipp Kiiver, Jakub Kodym, The practice of public procurement, 2014, p. 112.

404 Ibid.

405 Ibid.

406 Case C470/99, *Universale-Bau AG, Bietergemeinschaft: 1) Hinteregger & Söhne Bauges.m.b.H. Salzburg, 2) ÖSTÜ-STETTIN Hoch- und Tiefbau GmbH v Entsorgungsbetriebe Simmering GmbH*, 2002, ECR I-11617.

a method is applied to pre-select the suppliers with the highest turnover and the most experience in that line of work provided other minimum criteria have also been satisfied, especially if there is no other way to choose between the candidates on the basis of the limited criteria.[407]

The deadline to submit an application to participate shall be minimum 30 days after the date of the contract notice publication in the OJEU. The deadline for submission of proposals should be at least 30 days after the invitation was sent[408].

In the light of the above considerations and referring to the case law, a conclusion should be made that the setup of procurement procedures should not allow public contracting authorities to artificially restrict competition and establish higher requirements than objectively necessary. In determining the minimum qualification requirements, the public contracting authority should always follow key principles of proportionality, non-discrimination and transparency.

In the author's view, the open and restricted procedures have the same structure and meaning of the evaluation of proposals and there is only a minimum difference between these two procedures, namely the time for submissions and the established two-stage approach in the restricted procedure. In the first stage of the restricted procedure, the minimum requirements have to be assessed in order to invite the prequalified candidates to the second stage. Whereas in the open procedure – one stage approach – the proposals won't even be evaluated if the minimum requirements are not met. Thus, the open procedure has also kind of first stage approach where the proposals won't even be evaluated if the minimum requirements are not met. The question is what was the purpose of the legislature to establish two almost identical procedures: restricted procedure with two stage approach and open procedure with one stage approach? Negotiations cannot be also pursued in both procedures and the assessment of the minimum requirements of candidates has the same procedure. In conclusion, the restricted procedure is more cumbersome and requires more time to conduct than the open procedure.

To sum up, it might be said that the public contracting authority must carefully assess the time period necessary to carry out procurement procedures, as well as the availability of human resources and their readiness to successfully conduct the procedures.

407 https://www.gov.uk/guidance/public-sector-procurement-policy (27.05.2018).
408 Article 28 (2) of the Directive 2014/24/EU.

7.1 Provisions in Germany

As far as the situation in Germany is concerned, similarly to Lithuania, the choice of an open procedure over a restricted procedure is significant. According to the statistics of 2017, Germany applied only 2 % of the restricted procedure out of total available procurement procedures.[409] It is very common that at the State and commune level, open procedures are more frequently used than restricted procedures. The reasons could be different however the main one is that the process of open procedure is much shorter. The restricted procedure is similar to the open procedure and is available for all public contracting authorities at its choice[410].

The definition of restricted procedure is defined in § 119 (4) GWB: the restricted procedure is a procedure in which a public contracting authority, following previous public invitation to submit applications to participate, selects a limited number of suppliers based on objective, transparent and non-discriminatory criteria (competitive tender) and invites them to submit a proposal. A further detailed description of the process of the restricted procedure is provided in the VgV.

According to § 16 VgV, the deadline for submissions of applications is 30 days after the publication of the notice and the deadline for submissions of proposals is also 30 days. There is a new requirement deferring from the Directive 2014/24/EU pursuant to § 16 (7) "with the exception of the supreme federal authorities, the public contracting authority may set a different time limit to receive tenders following a mutual agreement with the candidates invited to tender, provided that all the candidates are given the same time for submitting the tenders." If the deadline to receive tenders cannot be determined by mutual agreement, the minimum amount of time shall be 10 days from the day when the invitation to tender was issued. The author believes that such a provision is not justified because a 10 day limit is a very short time in which to prepare the offers. It is stated that it should be a mutual agreement between all tenderers, however in the author's view, it should be the public procurement authority's responsibility and burden to take a decision on how long the preparation of offers may take, in particular taking into consideration the complexity of the specific requirements. In particular, if the timeline were not mutually agreed among the tenders, the timeline of 10 days would still apply. In addition, it is also necessary to verify if this provision is correctly reflected in the national law, especially taking into consideration that

409 https://opentender.eu/lt/dashboards/market-analysis (05.07.2018).

410 Article 14 (3) VgV.

the non-supreme federal authorities have little time for the offer preparation. Following such provisions, it should be further investigated whether there is any discrimination between the different types of public procurement authorities, which should have equal rights to apply the same provisions defined in the VgV and GWB.

In addition, another new provision introduced in § 38 (4) VgV is more reasonable than the one discussed above. The VgV also provides a new requirement for German procurement authorities with an exception for supreme federal authorities. According to § 38 (4) VgV, the omission of the publication of a contract notice is allowed in restricted or negotiated procedures if a prior information notice has contained certain required information. Such requirements are absent in Directive 2014/24/EU, as it only foresees the possibility to reduce the time limit from 30 to 10 days under the condition that a prior information notice has been published.[411]

7.2 Provisions in Lithuania

In Lithuania, like in Germany, a restricted procedure in comparison with an open procedure is rarely used. According to the statistics of 2017, Lithuania only conducted two restricted procedures during the entire year.[412] It is difficult to assess what the main reasons for not using such a procedure are, however in the author's view, one of the reasons is that the successful outcome of such a procedure is mainly based on the application of most advantageous criteria and not only cost criteria.[413] Accordingly, a common practice in Lithuania is to apply the lowest price criterion when conducting procurement procedures and consequently opt for the open procedure as the most suitable procedure for using the lowest price criterion as the decisive one.

Lithuania has successfully transposed the provisions of Directive 2014/24/EU concerning the restricted procedure. Pursuant to Article 61 of the Public Procurement Law, the restricted procedure shall be conducted in two stages. The public contracting authority shall establish time limits to submit applications and later on tenders in line with the provisions of Article 39 of the PPL. The deadline for the submission of applications shall be minimum 30 days after the day of a respective announcement made by the PPO and 10 days after the day on which

---

411 Article 28 (2) (3) of the Directive 2014/24/EU.

412 Public Procurement Office, yearly analysis of the purchasing in Lithuania, http://vpt.lrv.lt/lt/statistika-ir-analize/ketvirtines-ir-metines-ataskaitos-1 (07.08.2017).

413 Article 67 of the Directive 2014/24/EU.

such a notice was published in the Central Public Procurement Information System or in the case of simplified procurement procedure, the day on which the invitation to confirm their interest was communicated to suppliers[414]. Publication of a contract notice where the public contracting authority allows the proposals to be sent electronically can reduce the time limit for the submission of tenders by 5 days. The deadline for the submission of tenders shall be minimum 30 days after the dispatch of invitations to tender to suppliers.[415]

The accelerated procedure is also allowed in the urgent cases. However, the use of the accelerate procedure requires the public contracting authority to indicate the reasons for using this particular type of procedure, because the deadline for submissions would be shortened to 15 days.

The Directive 2014/24/EU has also introduced the possibility to request additional information during all procedures.[416] It must be noted, however, that such a process must observe the key principles of the TFEU Treaty. Although the reform of the procurement regime introduces more flexibility, placing an emphasis on the importance of competition for procurement contracts. Hence, such provisions have been transposed into Lithuanian nation law. Pursuant to Article 35 (5) of the PPL, if the additional information concerning the procurement documents has been requested within reasonable time limits, the public contracting authority shall provide it to all the suppliers maximum 6 days before the deadline for the submission of tenders.

8 Competitive procedure with negotiation and competitive dialogue

This chapter will discuss the reasons for the application of the competitive procedure with negotiation and competitive dialogue. Procedures will be discussed together because the reasons for their use are identical, which raises a question whether there is a need to have two procedures and in turn which procedure is the preferred one. The answer will be provided at the end of the section when all arguments and grounds for use of these procedures have been discussed and elaborated upon. These two procedures are also based on a two-stage approach and the process is exactly the same as that of a restricted procedure, which was discussed in the previous section. Therefore, the only difference is that during

414 Ibid.
415 Ibid.
416 Article 56 (3) of the Directive 2014/24/EU.

these procedures negotiations are allowed and these procedures could be applied only if the specific requirements are met. Therefore, the author will not discuss the process of two-stage approach in this section but rather focus on the specific requirements that are needed in order to apply these procedures.

Recital 42 of the Directive 2014/24/EU States that public contracting authorities have additional flexibility when it comes to choosing a procurement procedure, which includes negotiations. The circumstances for the use of these two procedures are laid down in Article 26 (4) of the Directive 2014/24/EU. The first is that the needs of the public contracting authority cannot be satisfied without adapting the solutions that are already available. The assumption is that the public contracting authority knows its needs cannot be met by off-the-shelf solutions and that means the product does not exist on the market without it being modified or adapting to the requirements of the public procurement authority.

Secondly, the needs of the authority are based on design or innovative solutions. This includes for example, the design of works or additional parts of the building that are not standard or where such works, services and supplies include innovative elements. However, it is not clear if the provisions cover all construction works of an existing design and it does not clarify what kind of percentage has to correspond to design and innovation[417].

Thirdly, the contract should be negotiated as a result of specific requirements arising from the nature, complexity or legal and financial issues or as a result of the risks accompanying them.[418] Given the latitude promised by the recitals, this seems contradictory and lacking in proportionality. These conditions mainly deal with situations where the negotiations are indeed indispensable. Such negotiations are needed to obtain the best value for their money. During the competitive procedure with negotiation, negotiations are held with the tenderers during the procurement process and meanwhile, during the competitive dialogue negotiations take place during the different stages of the process.

Another reason is found in the circumstances where the technical specifications cannot be specified with sufficient precision.[419] The technical requirements must include the characteristics required for works, goods and services (such

---

417 Sue Arrowsmith, The law of public and utilities procurement, par. 8.21, 2014.

418 http://ec.europa.eu/growth/content/simplifying-rules-contracting-authorities-ensure-better-quality-and-value-money-0_en (27.05.2018).

419 Article 135 of the Commission Delegated Regulation (EU) 2015/2462, of 30 October 2015 amending Delegated Regulation (EU) No 1268/2012 on the rules of application of Regulation (EU, Euratom) No 966/2012 of the European Parliament and of the Council on the financial rules applicable to the general budget of the Union.

as quality, performance, safety or dimensions as well as terminology-related requirements, symbols, tests and testing methods etc.) so that they are expressed in such a manner that will ensure they comply with the purpose intended by the public contracting authority. These are all distinct grounds for use of the procedures – that is, only one of these grounds needs to be satisfied for the application of these.

The recitals[420] provide some specific examples of the types of projects where the use of the competitive procedure with negotiation or competitive dialogue is purposeful. These are: innovative projects; integrated transport infrastructure projects; large computer networks/major ICT projects; projects involving complex and structured financing; non-standard buildings or works based on design or innovative solutions; services or supplies that require adaptation or design efforts; and complex purchases such as sophisticated products and intellectual services, for example some consultancy, architectural or engineering solutions. This list is obviously not exhaustive.[421]

There is a possibility to award contracts based on initial contracts without the need to negotiate if the public contracting authority has included these provisions in the contract notice.[422] In such cases, the negotiated procedure is almost the same as the restricted procedure, the only difference being that in the restricted procedure five short-listed candidates have to be invited to the second stage of the procurement whereas the negotiated procedure requires minimum three candidates to be invited to the next stage.[423] It is questionable why there are specific requirements that must be met in order to opt for a negotiated procedure with publication. The author is of the opinion that such requirements are not adequate to the process of such a procedure.

The aim of the procurement reform in 2014 was to simplify procedures and to provide more flexibility for the public contracting authorities and suppliers. Hence, the reform did not simplify the application of procedures and even introduced an additional innovation partnership procedure. Following the arguments above and similarities between these two procedures, the author would like to suggest these two procedures including restricted procedure to be merged and proposes the following wording for a new procedure: "competitive procedure".

---

420 Recital 42 and 43 of the Directive 2014/24/EU.
421 Ibid.
422 Article 29 (4) of the Directive 2014/24/EU.
423 Article 65 (2) of the Directive 2014/24/EU.

Public contracting authorities may apply a competitive procedure either with negotiation or without negotiation or use a competitive dialogue in cases where its use is related to the subject matter of the public contract.[424] Accordingly, the restricted procedure, competitive procedure with negotiation and competitive dialogue could be merged into a single procedure without establishing such a complex process for each one of them individually. In addition, the author believes that all procedures should be applied equally without having any restriction. This approach has already been set out in the Directive 2014/25/EU[425].

8.1 Provisions in Germany

In Germany, as in Lithuania, the procedure of competitive dialogue is hardly ever used. According to the statistics of 2017, Germany did not apply any competitive dialogue procedure over the year. On the contrary, the negotiated procedure with publication[426] was applied in 14 % out of the total available procurement procedures[427]. One of the arguments as to why it is not used is that the competitive dialogue is too complex and time consuming. Public contracting authorities also have very little knowledge on how to apply this procedure in practice.

The competitive procedure with negotiation is described in detail in § 17 VgV. To be able to apply the competitive procedure with negotiation, the public procurement authorities should comply with one of the specific requirements outlined in § 14 (3) VgV.

The competitive procedure with negotiation differs from the open or restricted procedure in that the nature of the services require negotiations in the call for tenders. After the deadline to submit the proposals, the process is different from open and restricted procedures. The public contracting authority engages in a dynamic process of negotiations with the suppliers involved. The negotiations shall not result in a change of the scope of main requirements which were purchased. In this context, negotiations refer to the dialogue the public contracting authority and potential suppliers are engaged in to discuss the contract until it is clear to the parties how these services should be provided. Negotiations are completed by signing an agreement with the successful supplier, which is the one that is able to provide the best value for money. The negotiation process may take place in stages. Negotiated procedures must respect the key principles of

---

424 Article 44 of the Directive 2014/25/EU.

425 Ibid.

426 This procedure today is called competitive procedure with negotiation.

427 https://opentender.eu/de/dashboards/market-analysis (05.07.2018).

public procurement law, namely the principles of competition, transparency and non-discrimination.

The competitive dialogue procedure is defined in § 119 (6) GWB and § 18 VgV. The competitive dialogue is applied only if the conditions pursuant to § 14 (3) VgV are met. In other words, the public procurement authority has not in itself the know-how to describe the supply of services. The competitive dialogue is aimed at finding a solution with selected tenderers, i.e. to determine how to meet the needs of the contracting entity, and how to do it in the best possible way. During this stage all tenderers involved must be treated equally and be provided with the same information. Due to many difficult requirements linked to the design or implementation of the project, this type of procurement procedure is applied only for particularly complex contracts in question. Mainly such a procedure is applied for the Public-Private Partnership projects[428].

The new provision is introduced in § 38 (4) VgV. According to § 38 (4) VgV, with the exception of supreme federal authorities, the public contracting authority in a restricted procedure or a negotiated procedure is permitted not to publish a contract notice if the information notice published previously included certain required information. Such requirements are not set out in the Directive 2014/24/EU.

8.2 Provisions in Lithuania

The statistics shows that Lithuania rarely, if ever, applies the competitive dialogue procedure and the competitive procedure with negotiation is used in only 5 % of total cases of procurement procedures.[429] It is regrettable that Lithuania does not take advantage of using these two procurement methods and by extension have better outcomes in the procurement processes. In the author's view, application of these procedures requires time, knowledge and effort.

The provision of the competitive dialogue is defined in Articles 66 and 67 of the Public Procurement Law. The competitive dialogue could be applied only if specific requirements are met, in accordance with Article 62 (1) of the Public Procurement Law.[430] A competitive dialogue procedure is to be conducted in the

---

428 Michael Burnett, Competitive Dialogue and Negotiated Procedures, A practical Guide, 2nd edition, 2015, p. 70. https://www.eipa.eu/wp-content/uploads/2018/01/CompetitiveDialogue2015_complete.pdf (31.05.2018).

429 http://vpt.lrv.lt/lt/statistika-ir-analize/ketvirtines-ir-metines-ataskaitos-1 (05.07.2018).

430 Sue Arrowsmith and Steeen Treumer, Competitive dialogue in EU procurement, 2012, p. 449.

following stages. First, the public contracting authority issues the contract notice. After all applications have been submitted, the public contracting authority assesses the qualification criteria, short-list the candidates and sends them an invitation to start the competitive dialogue in order to clarify and select the means that best correspond to the needs of the public contracting authority[431].

During the competitive dialogue the short-listed candidates and the public contracting authority may discuss different aspects of the tender. However, the dialogue procedure must be carried out in compliance with the principles of transparency and equal treatment as well as with confidentiality requirements laid down in the technical specifications. For a consistent and equal access to information, all suppliers must be treated equally. The ongoing dialogue must also be recorded in the minutes, which must be signed by the chair of the meeting and members of the public procurement committee. The dialogue shall continue until the public contracting authority can pick one or more customised solutions. In the competitive dialogue, the public contracting authority may also define the following stages in order to reduce the number of solutions to be consulted in the course of the procedure.

Pursuant to Article 69 of the Public Procurement Law, in the final stage of the dialogue and having informed the participants thereof, the public contracting authority asks them to submit their final proposals based on the solution or solutions proposed and defined during the dialogue. The public contracting authority must inform all the participants of the completed procedure and request the ones whose solutions were short-listed to put forward a proposal containing all the elements necessary for the performance of the project.

Furthermore, the author will briefly review the conditions to apply the competitive procedure with negotiation. Article 62 of the Public Procurement Law sets out the main circumstances to use the competitive procedure with negotiation. Furthermore, the process for conducting negotiations is outlined in Article 63 of the Public Procurement Law. Negotiations are defined in a broad sense as a process of communication between partners for different purposes and positions towards reaching a mutually satisfactory solution. Public contracting authorities have to publish a contract notice that outlines the requirements for the competitive procedure with negotiation. Only the tenderers that meet the requirements of the public contracting authority are invited to submit a proposal. When planning to conclude the negotiations the public contracting authority shall set the

431 Ibid.

deadline for the submission of the final offers and shall inform the remainder of the participants of the results.

To sum up, it must be said that the requirements of a competitive procedure with negotiation and competitive dialogue have been successfully transposed into the national law of Lithuania.

9 Negotiated procedure without publication

This procedure is considered to be exceptional because the contract notice is not published and can be used only if other procedures are not applicable. Article 32 of the Directive 2014/24/EU lays down a list of exceptions, which should be justified in order to apply this particular procedure. According to Recital 46, urgency needs have to be duly substantiated.[432] The exceptions cannot be applied based on the urgency or short time schedule of the delivery.

As a general comment, an exception is only permitted in exceptional circumstances where the criteria of one of the listed exceptions in Article 32 apply and must be interpreted narrowly. In addition, it has to be noted that Article 32 requires that the specifications that form the basis for the decision whether a contract can be awarded directly to one supplier have to be drafted lawfully (i.e. based on objective, non-discriminatory criteria, in particular without artificially narrowing down the specifications to the capabilities of only one supplier)[433].

It is worth mentioning that in most cases the contract is directly awarded because of additional deliveries where a change of supplier would result in incompatibility or disproportionate technical difficulties[434]. Such justification could be applied if deliveries would result in deterioration of service levels, difficulties in operation, difficulties in maintenance, deterioration in cost-efficiency, or would lead to disproportionate deterioration in value for money.

In this procedure the public contracting authority approaches the suitable candidates of its own choice. A direct award procedure needs to be registered as any other procurement procedure. The contract award must be based on an offer that should be properly evaluated and, if needed, negotiated.

---

432 Lisa Chever, John Moore, Negotiated Procedures Overrated? Evidence from France Questions the Commission's Approach in the Latest Procurement Reform, 2012, p. 228.

433 Pedro Telles and Luke Butler, Award procedures in the new public procurement directive, in European Procurement Law Series, Vol 6 Djof Publishing, 2014, p. 131.

434 Article 32 (3) (b) of the Directive 2014/24/EU.

In the Lithuanian and German law these provisions have been successful transposed.

According to Article 72 of the Public Procurement Law in Lithuania, the negotiated procedure without publication can only be conducted if it is permitted by the Public Procurement Office. The law also lists specific exceptions for the contracts, the value of which is below the EU threshold, namely:

1. goods and services acquired for the funds of the budget of representation;
2. museum exhibits, documents from archives and libraries, subscribed newspapers and magazines;
3. goods from the State reserve fund;
4. licences to use library documents or data (information) bases;
5. training and conference services for judges, prosecutors, professional military personnel, civil servants and (or) employment-contract-based staff of the public contracting authority;
6. non-material (intellectual) services of expert commissions, committees, council members, as well as of experts they hire and of experts necessary to perform the control of the activity of the State institutions;
7. services of expert evaluation for the activity of science and study institutions, scientific and artistic activity, studies, as well as of the applications of science and study institutions, which are necessary to obtain the permission to organise studies and study-related activities;
8. goods which are produced exceptionally for purposes of the research, experiments, studies or experimental development, and which are labelled exclusively as goods designated for the purposes of research;
9. financial services, services of determining the credit rating and provision of financial information, which are necessary to perform the State treasury functions;
10. passenger transportation, accommodation services and other secondment-related services, when they are purchased from the direct service provider.

The negotiated procedure without publication is stipulated in § 101 (50) GWB in Germany. The contacting authority can approach the suppliers of its own choice and negotiate the terms and conditions of the contract or the price. In § 14 (4) (1–9) VgV are listed main requirements for application of negotiated procedure without publication that were transposed from the Directive 2014/24/EU.

10 Innovation partnership

The new Directive 2014/24/EU introduces a new procedure called the innovation partnership. The availability of the new provisions may also involve complex contracts. The introduction of an innovation partnership may not only help to overcome the existing challenges, but also contribute to achieving the objective of a smart, sustainable and inclusive growth that the Europe 2020 strategy extensively focuses on. The application of the innovation partnership procedure may have challenges on its own. The aim of this section is to identify and discuss these challenges.

Recital 49 of the Directive 2014/24/EU provides a definition of the innovation partnership: this new procedure should enable public contracting authorities to start a long-term innovation partnership for the development and acquisition of a new, innovative product, service or works on the condition that such product, service or works can be delivered to required performance levels and costs[435]. The innovation partnership should be designed in such a way that it can lead to the desired outcome, promoting the development of an innovative product without a negative impact on the market. Innovation partnerships should not be used by public contracting authorities in ways that would impede, restrict or negatively affect the competition.[436]

Article 31 of the Directive 2014/24/EU lays down the guidelines for conducting this new procedure. It can be emphasised, first, that this is not a typical procedure but a partnership. The name of the new procedure, including the reference to partnership rather than procedure in its title, indicates the emergence of fundamental characteristics when purchasing innovation not necessarily found elsewhere, especially regarding the need for a close cooperation between public contracting authorities and economic operators during the innovation process that occurs in the contract execution phase.[437]

The innovation partnership encompasses three different phases. First, the conduct of an innovation partnership award procedure to choose the possible supplier that will participate in the innovation phase under the contract awarded

---

435 Recital 49 of the Directive 2014/24/EU.

436 Andreas Neun, Wolfram Krohn, Marc Gabriel, Handbuch Vergaberecht, Gesamtdarstellung und Kommentierung zu Vergaben nach GWB, VgV, SektVO, VSVgV, KonzVgV, VOB/A, UVgO, VOL/A, VO(EG) 1370, SGB V, AEUV, 2. Auflage 2017, p. 301.

437 Marta Andrecka, Innovation partnership in the new public procurement regime – a shift of focus from procedural to contractual issues? P.P.L.R. 2015, Issue 2, p. 18–31.

at the end of that procedure. The second phase is the innovation process itself, following the award of the contract under the Directive, when the contract in underway. The third stage encompasses the actual placing of orders to acquire the result of the innovation phase, which took place simultaneously with the execution phase of the contract concluded between the public contracting authority and selected partners. It must be emphasised that the criterion to award the partnership must always be the most economically advantageous tender, which is the most efficient criterion for assessing tenders regarding innovative solutions.

The new partnership procedure is mostly applied in the EU Member States with highly advanced public administrations and high preferences in terms of innovations, such as the Nordic countries, Sweden, Denmark, Finland, the Netherlands, Germany, the UK and Luxembourg. According to the recent innovation scoreboard of 2017, these countries are the European innovation leaders.[438] Although this data refers only to private sector innovation, it may be an important indicator of which Member States will seek to innovate through public procurement, as it indicates which cultures are rooted in the development and purchase of innovation. It can be argued that soft law will be important to promote use of the innovation partnership in countries less familiar with innovation.

10.1 Provisions in Germany

It has to be noted that there are no statistics regarding the application of this procedure. Hence, the procedure is very new and most likely to be applied soon in Germany. Germany is one of the leaders in the innovation sector and therefore, Germany has good knowledge in innovation solutions and the application of the new technologies.

The innovation partnership procedure is set out in § 119 (7) GWB and 2016 § 19 VgV[439]. The contracting entity may enter into an innovation partnership to engage in public procurement that aims to develop an innovative supply or service, followed by the acquisition thereof. The innovation partnership process also takes place in several stages. After publishing the contract notice the suppliers may submit their applications to participate in the process. During the innovation partnership stages of research and innovation process

438 Innovation Union Scoreboard 2017, available at: https://ec.europa.eu/growth/industry/innovation/facts-figures/scoreboards_en (08.08.2018).

439 Martin Burgi und Meinrad Dreher: Beck'scher Vergaberechtskommentar Band 1: Gesetz gegen Wettbewerbsbeschränkungen - GWB - 4. Teil, 3 Auflage 2017, p. 583.

contacting authority may negotiate with tenderers. The supplier that best meets all requirements of the public contracting authority will be awarded the contract.

10.2 Provisions in Lithuania

According to the scoreboard statistics of 2017 Lithuania is considered as a moderate innovator.[440] In 2014 the minister of the economics issued a decree to develop innovative procurement in Lithuania[441]. The guidelines on innovative procurement have been designed to encourage public contracting authorities, within the existing legal system for public procurement, to acquire higher quality goods, services or works that would improve the quality of public services and/or the performance of public contracting authorities, at the same time stimulating the innovation demand in the market[442].

Accordingly, the author believes that these guidelines will help the Lithuanian public procurement authorities to apply an innovation partnership procedure which is established in Article 72 of the Public Procurement Law. The innovation partnership can take place in stages. The public contracting authority simultaneously and in writing asks the chosen candidates to submit initial proposals which may contain stages of research and innovation projects. In accordance with Article 24 of the Public Procurement Law, the negotiations with each supplier on their initial and subsequent proposals take place to achieve the best possible result according to the requirements laid down in procurement documents.

11 Conclusions

The new Directive 2014/24/EU establishes the following six procedures: open, restricted, competitive procedure with negotiation and without it, competitive dialogue and innovation partnership. The general procurement procedures are open and restricted procedures, while the specific procedures include a competitive procedure with negotiation and without, competitive dialogue and innovation partnership. Public procurement authorities may apply specific procedures

440 Innovation Union Scoreboard 2017, available at: https://ec.europa.eu/docsroom/documents/30690 (08.08.2017).

441 Decree of the Minister of the Economy on the approval of innovative public procurement guidelines, 29 December 2014. http://eimin.lrv.lt/uploads/eimin/documents/files/Inovaciijos/LR%20Ukmin%20isakymas%20del%20inovatyviujju%20pirkimu%20gairiu_14-12-29.pdf (07.08.2017).

442 European Commission notice, Guidance on Innovation Procurement, C(2018) 3051, 15.05.2018.

only to a limited extent; hence, the Directive 2014/24/EU envisages certain specified conditions.

The new Directive 2014/24/EU aims to improve flexibility and increase simplification in the application of new procedures. However, it must be acknowledged that, in fact, the reform did not simplify the application of public procurement procedures but rather added one more procedure: innovation partnership. The author analysed in detail all available public procurement procedures established in the Directive 2014/24/EU and their transposition into the nation law of Lithuania and Germany. Germany and Lithuania successfully transposed all procurement procedures established in the Directive 2014/24/EU.

In the author's opinion, the application of current procedures should be further simplified to ensure more flexibility that would increase procurement's efficiency and transparency. Following the arguments discussed above and the similarities between restricted procedure, competitive procedure with negotiation and competitive dialogue, the author would like to suggest these three procedures be merged and proposes the following definition for a new procedure: "competitive procedure". Public contracting authorities may opt for a competitive procedure with negotiation or without negotiation. Restricted procedure has the same meaning as the competitive procedure with negotiations and the competitive procedure with negotiations has the same meaning as a competitive dialogue procedure. Such approach would be in line with the GPA agreement[443], which defines only three procedures: open, selective and limited tendering. The selective tendering is similar to the restricted procedure, limited tendering is similar to the negotiated procedure without publication. Negotiations can be applied in any procedure, if required or by the choice of the public contracting authority[444]. A long time ago the GPA agreement was the basis for the establishment of the EU public procurement directives. Therefore, the major reforms in the EU have developed cumbersome procurement procedures, which are not effective today and require simplification. Therefore, three procedures as discussed above could be merged to establish more simplified procedures. It seems that the restricted procedure, competitive procedure with negotiation and competitive dialogue could be combined in one single procedure without establishing such an exhaustive process for each one of them. In addition, in the author's view all procedures should be applied

443 Article IV (4) GPA.

444 Article XII GPA.

equally without having any restrictions. Such an approach is already defined in the Directive 2014/25/EU.[445] Specific conditions which limit application of these procedures (competitive procedure with negotiation and competitive dialogue) create a huge barrier for public contracting authorities, therefore they decide mainly to apply standard procedures such as open procedure in most cases. Negotiations should be also applied in any procedure, if required similar to the GPA agreement, therefore the name of the negotiated procedure without publication author would rename it into "limited procedure" similar to the provisions of Article IV (4) of the GPA agreement.

The overall effect of the modifications proposed in Directive 2014/24/EU should be assessed for the application of the procedures in practice and the impact of these changes on how capable the public contracting authorities are to ensure value for money by means of transparent and competitive procurement. In that sense, the impact of the new legislative provisions will, as at present, depend on the competence of public contracting authorities and in particular, on their level of competence in the dialogue/negotiation phase of the award procedure.

Finally, the author would suggest to introduce the following simplified procedures: open procedure, competitive procedure (two-stage approach), innovation partnership and limited procedure, which would be similar to the procedures defined in the GPA agreement.

The apple pie chart below provides further details of the procurement procedures applied in Germany and Lithuania in 2017 and also justifies the need to simplify the application of procedures, because mainly only one open procedure is applied. Lithuania applied open procedure 90 % out of total 2,104 procedures[446] and Germany applied open procedure 80 % out of total 19,076 procedures[447] among all available procedures. It is to be concluded that both countries mainly apply open procedure and have difficulties in applying other available procedures, which are difficult to understand and have certain restrictions.

445 Article 44 of the Directive 2014/25/EU.

446 http://vpt.lrv.lt/lt/statistika-ir-analize/ketvirtines-ir-metines-ataskaitos-1 (05.07.2018).

447 https://opentender.eu/de/dashboards/market-analysis (05.07.2018).

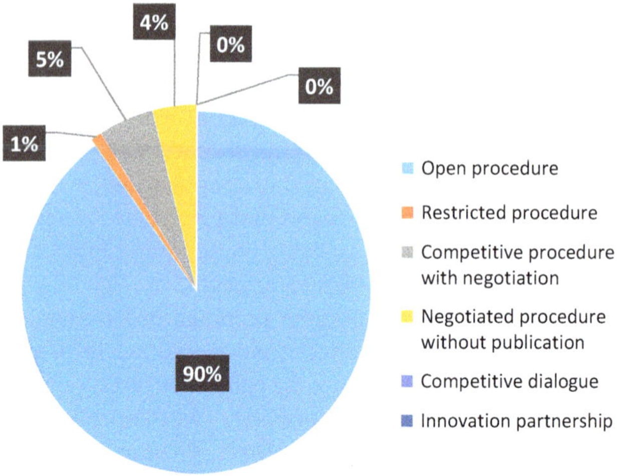

Chart 4: Percentage of public procurement procedures applied in Lithuania in 2017.

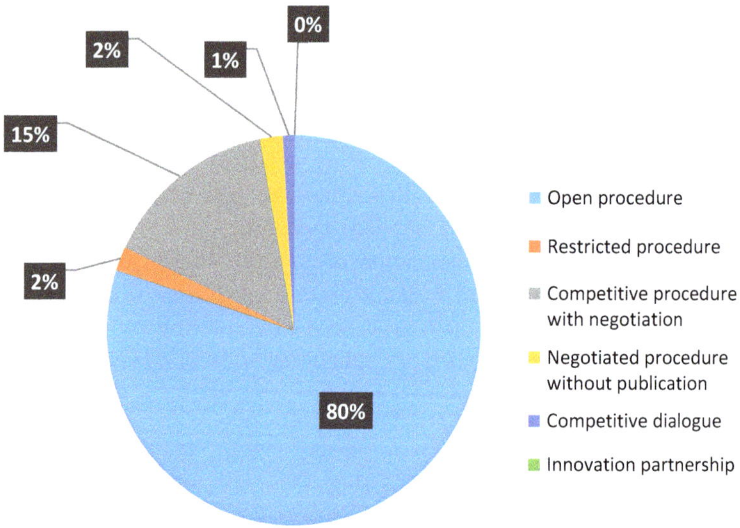

Chart 5: Percentage of public procurement procedures applied in Germany in 2017.

IV Key weaknesses of the EU procurement framework

1 Wider application of competitive procedure with negotiation

When revising public procurement directives in 2004, goals such as rule simplification and assurance of bigger legal certainty particularly while implementing negotiated procedures were set. Unfortunately, as of yet, it has not been possible to achieve these goals. The decisions of the CJEU have partially helped to explain unanswered legal questions. When reviewing any rules of the EU, it is essential to take into consideration the goals of the public procurement procedure streamlining the rationalisation and strictly respect the objectives.[448]

Non-compliance with public procurement rules is one of the most common errors cited in the budget approval reports[449], therefore, it is vital to come up with solutions that would simplify the rules, ensure optimal use of resources and seek transparency. In order to overcome these challenges, one of the options would be to apply wider competitive procedure with negotiation. The competitive procedure with negotiation contains a great extent of flexibility as it limits the supply chain. For this reason, the use of the said procedure is restricted.

On the grounds of the application in practice concerning competitive procedure with negotiation, it can be stated that negotiations, as an exceptional means of awarding public contracts, are used relatively rarely compare to statistics below.[450]

In countries with many years of experience and established tradition in public procurement, negotiations are used even less often. Examples of this include Germany where negotiations accounted for only 15 % of all procurement.[451]

Based on the best practices of Member States in the EU, it would be purposeful to update the existing public procurement legislation with more flexible procurement measures and procedures. Currently, there is a great variation between how Member States use different procedures in public procurement.

448 European Parliament Resolution of 25 October 2011 on the modernisation of public procurement.

449 http://www.lsdp.lt/lt/naujienos/2188-z-balcytis-ragina-europos-komisija-tobulinti-es-viesuju-pirkimu-sistema.html (05.06.2017).

450 Aušrinė Mincienė, Public Procurement by Direct Agreement: Application Problems; http://www.verslobanga.lt/lt/patark.full/4aa40d7784723.1; (05.06.2017).

451 Ibid.

Therefore, it is appropriate to give Member States the right to refrain from or restrict the application of certain procedures set out in this Directive.

The relatively rare practical use of the competitive procedure with negotiation in the European Union calls for widening the scope of this procedure's application. The practical relevance of applying competitive procedure with negotiation could be increased if it were applied under the same conditions as the open or restricted tendering procedure.[452] Public contracting authorities may, from the outset, provide for at least some minimal conditions for the procedure and written document order for any tenderer as it is foreseen in the private procurement rules.[453]

Below is a summarised apple pie chart representing the percentage of public procurement procedures used in Member States in 2017 out of total 125,625 procedures[454]. It shows that Member States applied only 7 % of competitive procedure with negotiation among all procedures. The analysis of the data in the table, unfortunately, shows that the role of the competitive procedure with negotiation is much lower when compared to other forms of public procurement and highlights why it is important to create more opportunities and favourable conditions for public contracting authorities to use these procedures on a more regular basis.

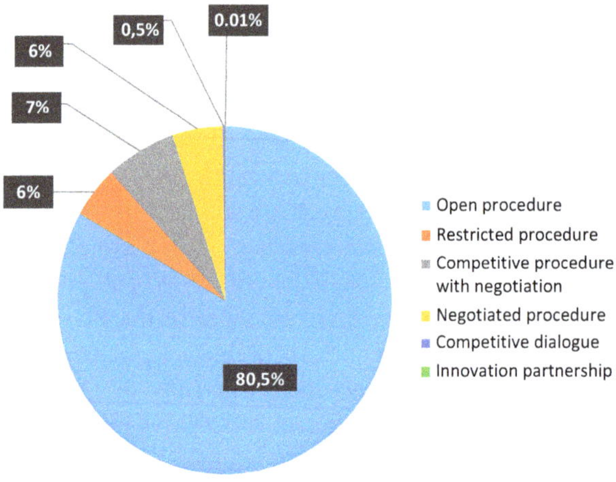

Chart 6: Percentage of public procurement procedures applied in the EU in 2017.

452 Totis Kotsonis. Green Paper on the modernisation of EU public procurement policy: Towards a more efficient European procurement market, Public Procurement Law Review, 2011, 3, NA51–58, p. 2.

453 European Parliament Resolution of 25 October 2011 on modernisation of public procurement.

454 https://opentender.eu/all/dashboards/market-analysis (05.07.2018).

2 Administrative burden reduction opportunities

One of the toughest to overcome challenges in the area of public procurement is the alleviation of the administrative burden. Although the respective EU legislation regulates common rules and procedures of public procurement, Member States still find it challenging to apply the laws properly, in particular those that concern the application of administrative rules to ensure these provisions are fully met.

Firstly, the emphasis should be placed on reducing the amount of bureaucracy involved in the process, a way to simplify public procurement procedures and increase flexibility of respective procedural rules.[455] Furthermore, it would be highly useful to apply specific methods, data, and technologies for suppliers instead of applying overly detailed technical specifications and, in this way, create better conditions for candidates.[456]

One way to reduce the administrative burden is by assessing the equivalence criteria in advance and giving suppliers an opportunity to submit the missing documents later, because not all participants have equal opportunities to provide all the relevant documents in due time.[457] Such provisions are already included in the Directive 2014/24/EU; however, they are not yet applied in practice.

Many authors are in favour of implementing the electronic registration system at the national level of Member States. The establishment of such a system would facilitate the work of the public contracting authorities. In order to alleviate the administrative burden, there is a need to set a time-limit during which a supplier is assessed as complying with the requirements, as the information they provided would be stored in a created system or programme. In addition, a more precise definition of the concept of equivalent measures in technical

455 Rosemary Boyle, The EU procurement green paper on the modernisation of EU public procurement policy: A personal response, Public procurement law review, 2011, 5, NA171–184, p. 2.

456 Opinion of the European Parliament, Industry, Research and Energy Committee of 19 July 2011 on Modernisation of Public Procurement, p. 3.

457 Joost van Iersel, Miguel Angel Cabra de Luna. Green Paper on the modernisation of EU public procurement policy. Towards a more efficient European Procurement Market, 13 July 2011, p. 7.

specifications and the establishment of clear-cut criteria would also help to reduce the bureaucracy.[458]

Having assessed their extraordinary significance and benefits, the standardised systems should be implemented in most Member States. Reducing the amount of administrative work would help suppliers involved in procurement to cut down the costs and facilitate the strict European public procurement rules,[459] and therefore improve public procurement efficiency, transparency and cost-effectiveness.

3 Better participation opportunities for SMEs in public procurement

Cutting down the administrative costs would allow SMEs to easier participate in the EU tenders. It is important to keep in mind the different capacities and levels of experience of different companies and also that they operate differently and choose their own operating strategies.[460]

Today SMEs are one of the European development pillars and, therefore, over the last few years a great emphasis has been placed on improving their opportunities to take part in public procurement, which would help to secure employment, sustainable development, innovation and economic growth. It is therefore necessary to ensure that public procurement procedures are fair and respectful of competition rules.

Already in 2008, the Commission adopted the "Small Business Act"[461] initiative in order to improve the overall political approach to entrepreneurship in the policy-making process, from adoption of the rules to the public service, once and for all establishing the principle "think small first", and to

---

458 http://www.ukmin.lt/lt/veikla/veiklos_sritys/viesieji-pirkimai/naujienos/zalioji_knyga_del_pirkimu.pdf, p. 13; (05.06.2017).

459 European Parliament resolution of 25 October 2011 on modernisation of public procurement.

460 Professional Association of Lawyers Soloveičikas, Markauskas, Aviža, Bagdanskis. The Study of Improvement and Development Strategy for Lithuanian Public Procurement System, 14 August 2007, p. 192.

461 Report from the Commission to the Council and the European Parliament, minimising regulatory burden for SMEs, adapting EU regulation to the needs of micro-enterprises, 2011, p. 2. http://ec.europa.eu/governance/better_regulation/documents/minimizing_burden_sme_EN.pdf; (05.06.2017).

promote the growth of SMEs helping them tackle the remaining development problems.[462] In particular, the document highlights the need to adapt the State policy measures to SME needs: to ensure an increased participation of SMEs in public procurement and to distribute the State aid funds to SMEs more appropriately.

In addition to this, public contracting authorities often require participants to present guarantees confirming the financial situation, insurance and performance, which often lead SMEs to obstacles while submitting the documents. Today it is particularly difficult to get the financial resources and, therefore, public contracting authorities, instead of requiring guarantee documents, should avoid qualification requirements, which are disproportionate with respect to the financial criteria.[463]

What is even more important is that in introducing flexible and user-friendly solutions Member States should avoid generating new obstacles for SMEs and consider their interests in order to improve their access to public procurement procedures and increase procedural transparency, particularly in the interest of smaller public contracting authorities. In order to promote awareness, the modernisation of 'Tenders Electronic Daily' (TED) website should be considered to increase its appeal and user-friendliness and make it easier to access.[464]

In order to promote SMEs participation in public procurement tenders, it would be beneficial to eliminate improperly limiting criteria, such as, requirements for a certain turnover or having been awarded similar contracts.[465] The company turnover should instead be respective of the particular nature of the contract.

A number of authors have acknowledged that one of the ways to promote SMEs participation in public procurement tenders is to divide public procurement into

---

462 Communication from the Commission to the Council, the European Parliament, the European Economic and Social Committee and the Committee of the Regions – "Think Small First" – A "Small Business Act" for Europe, p. 11. http://eurlex.europa.eu/LexUriServ/LexUriServ.do?uri=CELEX:52008DC0394:en:NOT; (05.06.2017).

463 Joost van Iersel, Miguel Angel Cabra de Luna. Green Paper on the modernisation of EU public procurement policy. Towards a more efficient European Procurement Market, 13 July 2011, p. 10.

464 European Parliament Resolution of 25 October 2011 on modernisation of public procurement, p. 6.

465 Nicola Dimitri, Gustavo Piga, Giancarlo Spagnolo. Handbook of procurement, UK, 2006, p. 33.

stages, and whenever possible put the 'apply or explain' principle[466] into practice which requires to follow the rules and ensures a better visibility of opportunities for SMEs and a greater access to them.[467] It is complicated for SMEs to have broad administrative resources so it would be important to keep minimum requirements and, in this way, provide simplified, equal and fair conditions for all businesses participating in public procurement.

It is promising that the Commission has made a number of efforts to assess the added value of SMEs in public procurement procedures. It is also worth mentioning that public contracting authorities should be motivated to divide contracts into subcontracts so that SMEs would have higher possibilities to take part in the race. In addition, the issues on SME turnover restrictions are addressed and a possibility for direct payment to subcontractors for public contracting authorities is foreseen. There is no doubt that extensive case law will be issued in this field in order to clarify a number of questions which are new to a lot of public procurement participants.

Statistical analysis shows that in public procurement, which exceeds the thresholds in the EU, SMEs represent a particularly small number.

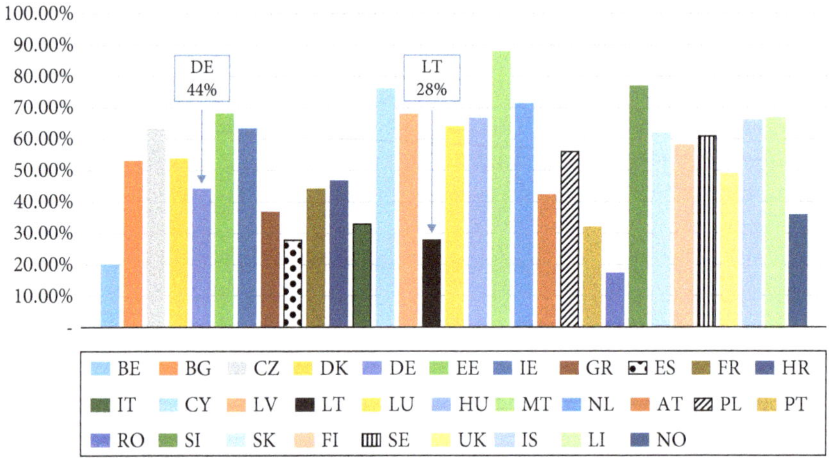

Chart 7: SME contractors in the EU Member States in 2017. The EU Scoreboard 2017. http://ec.europa.eu/internal_market/scoreboard/performance_per_policy_area/public_procurement/index_en.htm (07.06.2018).

466 Ibid.

467 Rosemary Boyle. EU procurement green paper on the modernisation of EU public procurement policy: a personal response, P.P.L.R., 2011, 5, NA171–184, p. 8.

The chart results show an increased role of SMEs in public procurement compare to years before 2017, which leads to expecting a further growth in SMEs weight in public procurement. Lithuania awarded 28 % contracts to SMEs and Germany 44 % contracts to SMEs of all contracts together in 2017.

4 The criteria of the most economically advantageous tender

The objectives of the reform that was proposed in 2014 were first referred to in the first Green Paper on public procurement in the European Union in 1996.[468] At the time, the aim was to pursue the same goals: to improve SMEs access to public procurement policy, to address social and environmental protection policy objectives by awarding the most economically advantageous tender and to ensure greater transparency.[469]

Public contracting authorities have to award contracts taking into account the objective criteria and ensuring that the principles of transparency, non-discrimination and equal rights are met and tenders are assessed adhering to the fair competition principle. Therefore, Article 67 of the Directive 2014/24/EU allows for the application of two criteria: "the lowest price" and "the most economically advantageous tender", which determine the winning contract.

It is worth noting that many experts believe the price should not have been included in the Directive 2014/24/EU. The most economically advantageous tender criterion should outweigh the price criterion during public procurement procedures to help to reduce life cycle costs.

It is at the public contracting authority's discretion to determine the most economically advantageous cost method through the life cycle. Product life cycle costs cover all stages, from the acquisition of raw materials to the final disposal of production resources (for example, development, production, transporting, use, maintenance, disposal etc.). It is necessary to adopt common methodologies at the EU level based on a specific calculation of the life cycle costs of products or services, and their use should be compulsory.[470]

468 The green paper, public procurement in the European Union: exploring the way forward, 1996 November 27, http://europa.eu/documentation/official-docs/green-papers/index_en.htm (07.06.2018).

469 Simon Evers Hjelmborg, Peter Stig Jakobsen, Sune Troels Poulsen. Public procurement law, the EU Directive on public contracts, 2006, Denemark, p. 52.

470 Ibid.

To award the most economically advantageous tender public contracting authorities must determine the criteria that are relevant to the subject matter[471] of the contract. These criteria could be: quality, technical merit, aesthetic and functional characteristics, all-user accessibility and environmental characteristics, design, price and other costs, as well as the life cycle cost methodology.[472]

Public contracting authorities frequently award the contract on the basis of the lowest price criterion because their budget to purchase goods for a longer period is limited, but the key point is that they lack practical knowledge, they fail to properly assess the price and quality of the goods acquired throughout their entire life cycle.[473]

A worthy example is Scandinavian countries that have successfully applied the principle of life-cycle costs for decades.[474] Meanwhile, in the Eastern countries, including Lithuania, this principle has not been given enough significance. Therefore, when selecting the successful tenderer, public contracting authorities should, as often as possible, evaluate the price of the offered goods throughout their life cycle, while taking into account the circumstances, such as a certain rise in the price of electricity, water, gas and other energy in the future, resulting in an inefficient product becoming even more expensive. It is also appropriate to take into consideration European Council conclusions of 4 February 2011[475], which promote the inclusion of energy efficiency standards in public procurement across the EU from 1 January 2012.[476]

Furthermore, it is advisable for the public contracting authorities to be able to assess their operational, social and environmental risks. Taking this into account, it would be significant to introduce eco-responsible public procurement information centres in the individual Member States. The establishment of

---

471 Article 67 (3) of the Directive 2014/24/EU.

472 Totis Kotsonis, Green paper on the modernisation of EU public procurement policy: Towards a more efficient European procurement market, Public Procurement Law Review, 2011, 3, NA51–58, p. 4.

473 Professional Association of Lawyers Soloveičikas, Markauskas, Aviža, Bagdanskis. The Study of Improvement and Development Strategy for Lithuanian Public Procurement System, 14 August 2007, p. 192.

474 Professional Association of Lawyers Soloveičikas, Markauskas, Aviža, Bagdanskis. The Study of Improvement and Development Strategy for Lithuanian Public Procurement System, 14 August 2007, p. 244.

475 The conclusions of the European Council meeting of 4 February 2011.

476 Opinion of the European Parliament, Industry, Research and Energy Committee of 19 July 2011 on Modernisation of Public Procurement, p. 5.

socially responsible public procurement practice and legal advice to Member States would be beneficial.[477]

To conclude, it might be said that public contracting authorities should show concern for other policy objectives, at the same time ensuring the principles of non-discrimination and transparency are respected. This would help to ensure a level competition for the European enterprises. For the sustainable public procurement to be feasible, the criterion of the lowest price should be applied rarely. The criterion of the most economically advantageous proposals should lead to social, economic and innovative products and services[478], also always being aware of their life-cycle costs. This would significantly reduce the environmental damage caused by production and consumers.

5 Promoting innovation in public procurement

A successful procurement process requires more focus to be placed on the sustainability of public procurement. Therefore, it is important to create favourable conditions for promoting and including technology and innovation into the various stages of public procurement procedures[479].

The term "innovation" is interpreted in different ways. Some researchers argue that it is a transfer of new ideas to a product or demand, a new or improved process in production, and distribution or, in general, a new public service.[480] Others consider buying innovative goods, services or processes as innovation as well.[481]

It is important to note that the new procedure for innovation partnership[482] should inspire the development of new innovative products, works and services. However, there is still a lack of guidelines and references as to how this procedure should be applied, and only few Member States are able to use these opportunities[483].

477 The European Parliament, the Employment and Social Affairs Committee's opinion of 18 July 2011 on modernisation of public procurement, p. 4.

478 Roberto Caranta, Martin Trybus, The law of green and social procurement in Europe, Denmark, 2010, p. 59.

479 OECD public governance review, public procurement for innovation, 2017, p. 19.

480 Expert group report, Public procurement for research and innovation, developing procurement practices favourable to R&D and innovation, 2005, p. 5.

481 Professional Association of Lawyers Soloveičikas, Markauskas, Aviža, Bagdanskis. The Study of Improvement and Development Strategy for Lithuanian Public Procurement System, 14 August 2007, p. 220.

482 Ibid.

483 Max Rolfstam, Public procurement of innovation, 2008, p. 5.

In 2018, the European Commission prepared a guide on how to use innovative solutions. The guide offers cases of good practice, on the basis of which it would be easier to reconcile innovative needs of public contracting authorities and suppliers.[484] In addition to this, the guide provides suggestions on how to promote innovations in public procurement. For example, before announcing a tender it is necessary to carry out a public market research, pre-announce the innovative needs and let suppliers bring forward their innovative solutions prior to the tender.[485] Unfortunately, these guidelines have been difficult to establish in practice, therefore further actions were taken.

Innovations-related objectives were also included in the Commission's Strategy 2020.[486] One of the highlights in the European Commission´s strategy for the EU development up to 2020 is to increase the competitive edge and sustainable growth through the promotion of science, technology and innovations. This strategy offers the vision of the European economy for the next decade and points out three priority areas of which public procurement must be the driving power to promote innovation, energy consumption and efficiency.[487]

Despite established strategy goals, the Member States fail to take full advantage of measures that promote innovation in public procurement. The implementation and promotion of innovation must be at the heart of European Union´s economy to ensure competitiveness and welfare growth.

In response to the Green Paper survey[488], the majority of answers called for a significant contribution of public procurement in promoting innovation and novelty. In addition, a great deal of contributors advocated the need for informational campaigns in the field of research and innovation because a significant number of stakeholders involved in public procurement still feel there is a lack of information in the field. The dissemination of information would help to achieve high-level research results. In addition, standards play a key role in business, especially in the SME industry. It is important to establish a balance between

---

484 Commission notice, Guidance on Innovation Procurement. https://ec.europa.eu/digital-single-market/en/news/commission-notice-guidance-innovation-procurement-published (07.06.2018).

485 Ibid.

486 Ibid.

487 Ibid.

488 European Commission, Green paper on the modernisation of EU public procurement policy, towards a more efficient European Procurement Market, 2011, p. 16.

educational institutions, users of deployed standards, civil society and business partners.[489]

Another key factor in promoting innovation is the deployment of standards and their appropriate use in public procurement procedures.[490] It is important to develop regularly updated standards linked to environmental and social criteria and ensure their availability to public contracting authorities while preparing tenders. There should be provided an access to the existing guidelines, rules, and how to evaluate eligible tenders against the standards, such as non-discriminatory and open standards in ICT and environmental matters. The introduction of new standards would help public procurement organisations achieve their desired goals in an efficient and transparent manner. Thus, the development of standards, innovation and research must be seen as a key measure for the Member States in creating new jobs and improving quality of life.[491]

The analysis of published arguments and the Commission's proposals lead to the conclusion that innovations in public procurement would play an important role in improving the quality and efficiency of public services in order to take advantage of the unused innovation potential across the Europe in the best possible way.

This raises a question as to why public contracting authorities make so small an effort to innovate. There are a few reasons for that. Firstly, public contracting authorities are not willing to make risky decisions, they lack the knowledge and skills necessary for successful public procurement in the area of new technologies and innovations. Secondly, there is a clear-cut need to align political goals with those of public procurement.[492] Public procurement in all relevant services (such as education and skill development, product and service markets, financial

---

489 European Parliament resolution of 24 May 2007 on putting knowledge into practice: A broad-based innovation strategy for Europe, p. 7.

490 Communication from the Commission to the Council, the European Parliament and the European Economic and Social Committee of 11 March 2008 "Towards an increased contribution from standardisation to innovation in Europe", p. 4.

491 Communication from the Commission to the European Parliament, the Council, the European Economic and Social Committee and the Committee of the Regions of 6 October 2010. Europe 2020 Flagship Initiative Innovation Union, p. 10, COM(2010) 546.

492 Ibid.

markets, labour market, entrepreneurship and business environment, industry policy, cohesion, spatial planning, infrastructure and ICT etc.) at all levels must be developed and executed on the basis of an integrated and coherent system.[493] It is essential to prioritise core funding solutions in such areas as resource efficiency, climate change, health, ageing and, above all, to seek innovative ways to address the problems through innovations.

Another setback preventing the development of innovations is the lack of human resources and funds in many Member States, especially the ones in the Eastern Europe including Lithuania.[494] The Member States are still not sufficiently aware of existing options to fund projects that promote innovation. In 2011 the European Commission announced a call for proposals amounting to 15 million EUROS to promote innovative solutions in procurement with the purpose to improve the cooperation between the Member States. So far public procurement accounts for about 2 % of the total of cross-border procurement. Therefore, the said initiative would increase the possibilities for the Member States to enter public procurement procedures in other countries across the EU and, what is even more important, reach the main target of creating and implementing innovative techniques that would facilitate economic development, the EU competitiveness and sustainable job creation.[495]

In order to bring forward innovative solutions based on good practice, Member States have to collaborate when submitting their applications. The new Member States, including Lithuania, rarely take advantage of the opportunity to bid or to cooperate with other Member States due to insufficient human resources.

These challenges could be overcome through prior consultations and sharing of good practices in innovative procurement with other Member States, in particular with Nordic countries, Great Britain, the Netherlands, Germany and Belgium, which are the most advanced States when it comes to innovative public procurement.

However, standards must be kept up-to-date in light of the latest and most dynamic technologies. A constructive system of standardisation is key in strengthening the EU's role in both European and global standards especially as Asian countries are very keen on imposing their standards on Europe.[496]

493 Ibid.

494 OECD public governance review, public procurement for innovation, 2017, p. 127.

495 European Parliament amendments (1–210) of 7 July 2011 to the report on the resolution on the modernisation of public procurement.

496 Ibid.

6 Pre-commercial procurement

The pre-commercial procurement is a key source for the funding of R&D in the field of high technology and innovation, as well as a major factor in contributing to the competitiveness of the economy.[497] Innovations in the EU may be particularly generated by the development of pre-commercial procurement, which also improves the quality and efficiency of public services.

Both the buyer of R&D services and the supplier share the risks and benefits that come from the development of innovative solutions in pre-commercial procurement.[498] The European Parliament resolution[499] on promoting pre-commercial procurement advises on methods to boost innovation in European research and development. Moreover, the resolution discusses how an improved access to pre-commercial procurement can contribute to the competitive development of research and technology. It is important to foresee the best way to share the benefits of risk-taking in pre-commercial procurement through research and development services and through the benefits of intellectual property rights. The resolution also provides instances of how public contracting authorities can acquire innovative products, in line with the procurement directives and the provisions of the State.

R&D services may refer to looking for solutions, to their design, and the development of prototypes. R&D services can also limit the creation of the first batch of products and services, the production at the testing stage to show the test results and that the product or service is suitable for the output or supply in required quantities that meet quality standards.[500] In any case, R&D does not cover commercially targeted products intended for production, supply or development in wholesale quantities or those intended to expand the commercial market and which fully cover the costs of R&D and facilitate the improvement of service supply integration.[501] It must be acknowledged that so far the

497 European Parliament's Resolution of 1 January 2009 on pre-commercial procurement. Driving innovation to ensure sustainable high-quality public services in Europe.

498 http://eimin.lrv.lt/lt/veiklos-sritys/viesuju-pirkimu-politika/darnieji-inovatyvus-ir-ikiprekybiniai-viesieji-pirkimai/ikiprekybiniai-viesieji-pirkimai (08.06.2017).

499 Ibid.

500 Ibid.

501 In this case, the Procurement Directives are not applicable (see Article 16 (f) of the Directive 2004/18/EC and Article 24 (e) of Directive 2004/17/EC). These exemptions only apply to public R&D service contracts but not to R&D supply or works.

pre-commercial procurement approach has not been fully put into practice in the Member States.

Public contracting authorities are encouraged to propose and support innovations and start implementing and applying them[502]. Unfortunately, many public contracting authorities, due to their lack of human resources and the nature of the structure, are not suitable for pre-commercial procurement.

To encourage public contracting authorities to innovate there are measures and funds at the EU level put in place to enable them to launch pilot innovative procurement projects. The following countries have already successfully developed projects and recommendations for innovative public procurement and are ready to implement them: Great Britain, Norway, the Netherlands, Germany, Austria and Sweden. In this area, the most advanced countries that have implemented the greatest number of pre-commercial procurement projects are as follows: Great Britain, the Netherlands and Belgium. Unfortunately, many of the new Member States including Lithuania have so far only developed strategies for the application and implementation of pre-commercial procurement.

In many cases, large enterprises are awarded contracts to implement high-tech based projects. One country that is very advanced in innovative procurement is the United States. It spends at least $49 billion per year on pre-commercial procurement.[503] This figure is 20 times more than in Europe and it is almost half of the total of investments into technological research and development in the USA. In addition, the States themselves invest large quantities in biotechnology and nanotechnology. This is why pre-commercial procurement should be a top priority when implementing cutting-edge technologies and at the same time acquiring as much practical knowledge as possible to outperform other Member States.[504]

Europe has a huge potential for innovation yet it has not been taken full advantage of, thus it is important to adopt a flexible strategy for the suppliers to use and implement comprehensive strategies in innovation. The pre-commercial procurement requires highly specific skills and knowledge in addition to a qualified staff. Unfortunately, many Member States lack skilled staff with the said competences that could develop training programmes, cooperate with other Member States and submit proposals to win a tender. Purchasing innovative products requires technological know-how. This is why it is necessary to build

---

502 Ibid.

503 Ibid.

504 European Parliament's Resolution of 27 January 2009 on pre-commercial procurement. Driving innovation to ensure sustainable high-quality public services in Europe.

on good practices in pre-commercial procurement and exchange skills and latest achievements with other Member States.

To this day, many Member States have faced major challenges when implementing pre-commercial procurement. It is expected that public contracting authorities will help and improve the overall quality and efficiency of public services by means of constructive solutions, which currently face the challenge of insufficient number of well-developed products and services on the market.

One of the ways to promote pre-commercial procurement is to provide SMEs with better opportunities to enter procurement transactions. It is necessary to involve SMEs in the resale of products, services or works to other suppliers so that pre-commercial procurement would also support the "Think Small First" principle.[505]

The pre-commercial procurement plays a very important role in improving the quality of services, works or products and at the same time helps to secure a more sustainable innovation and technology system across the European Union. It is therefore necessary to develop cross-border networks, share good practices and, above all, properly coordinate and implement pre-commercial public projects, which would involve foreign suppliers.[506]

To properly follow the examples of the pre-commercial procurement required the Commission to adopt guidelines for an efficient implementation of innovative public procurement within the legal framework of public procurement. Such guides were issued to local and regional authorities this year[507] so they could successfully follow best practices. It is in small towns that the required expertise is mostly found to be lacking.

7 The need for professionalism among public contracting authorities staff

In order to promote innovation in public procurement it is necessary to select properly skilled staff and ensure their respective training and improvement of qualifications. So far, there has been no discussion on the need of professionalism of public contracting authorities neither in the directives on procurement nor in the Green Paper on the modernisation of EU public procurement policy.[508]

505 Ibid.

506 Max Rolfstam. Public procurement as an innovation policy toll: The role of institutions. Journal Science and Public Policy, 36/5, June 2009, p. 358.

507 Guidance for public authorities on public procurement of innovation, 2017; Commission notice, Guidance on innovation procurement, 2018.

508 Ibid.

Only Article 81of the Directive 2014/24/EU refers to the composition of the jury, which should have certain professional skills. However, no further specific references, guidelines or explanations are given regarding professional skills, required knowledge and ways to exchange good practices with other Member States.

A large number of respondents in the Green Paper considered the lack of skilled and competent staff to be an obstacle preventing progress in public procurement. Member States should be interested in providing training for specialised staff and developing their skills within their own structures. There is a need to cooperate with other industries to stimulate experienced managers' enrolment in public procurement.

Staff qualifications between Member States vary, therefore, it is important to develop training programmes for buyers (particularly at local and regional levels) to help them prepare for negotiations, conclude successful contracts and exchange good practices.[509] In addition, each Member State has its own public procurement culture. In order to achieve greater transparency, it is necessary to coordinate the objectives of public procurement policy in each country.

What is of most importance is that the risk management approach is properly implemented at all hierarchical levels of the public contracting authority, from the highest to the lowest level. Before launching any procurement procedures and announcing a tender, public contracting authorities should be well aware of the offer on the market. Therefore, it is necessary that the staff collects all the relevant information and duly communicates it to suppliers and specialists.[510]

The Commission's proposal suggests that Member States should be required to set up service centres that would provide legal and economic advice, guidance, organise training and support in establishing and implementing procurement procedures.[511] The author can only hope that this new initiative will help Member States to work together in sharing their experience. Similar centre is already established in Germany to promote innovative procurement and exchange best practises[512]. It would be a great opportunity for many Member States including Lithuania to exchange best practices and database of innovative procurement across the Europe.

509 Ibid.
510 Ibid.
511 Ibid.
512 OECD public governance review, public procurement for innovation, 2017, p. 115.

8 Conclusions

To summarise, key weaknesses were discussed and solutions were proposed. In conclusion, it can be said that a wider use of the competitive procedure with negotiation would contribute to promoting investments and sustainable solutions, provided that certain conditions are met.

In order to deal with challenges such as internal market failure, which SMEs face along the life cycle, SMEs should take better advantage of the opportunities stemming from the State aid, while Member States should support the setting up of new enterprises and encourage SMEs to take part in procurement procedures more frequently. Smaller businesses are often unaware of future opportunities and are afraid of bureaucratic burdens. Furthermore, public contracting authorities tend to conclude the contracts with large companies, which are more familiar with tenders than with those which are new. This would help to ensure a level of competition for European enterprises.

Another challenge that the Member States are facing is the application of the right award criteria. The criterion of the lowest price should be supplemented by the criterion of the most economically advantageous proposal.

Furthermore, to promote new technologies, Member States would need to become more involved in the field of modern joint technologies, which would encourage the design of new products and services. At the same time, introducing new technologies also promotes policies for setting of standards. For example, the well-developed telecommunications system and GSM standards have contributed to the development of a dynamic European mobile phone network.[513]

At the EU level, public contracting authorities should take shared responsibility in ensuring the exchange of any specific information and best practices as well as actively promoting a cultural exchange in innovative public procurement across the Europe. For this purpose all Member States should establish a set of rules regarding the public procurement to acquire innovation services.

513 European Commission's Green Paper of 9 February 2011 "From Challenges to Opportunities: Towards a Common Strategic Framework for EU Research and Innovation Funding".

V Enforcement of the EU public procurement rules in Lithuanian legislation

1 EU provisions

The regulation of legal relations arising from public procurement is of paramount importance for the EU legislation aimed at harmonising and improving the Member States legal systems.

Public procurement regulation at the EU level is being strengthened, since the focus on the competition in the field of public procurement has increased, creating a need to establish more effective transparency and non-discrimination measures. In order to achieve tangible results, effective and efficient remedies system had to be established. The EU has adopted specific directives to regulate procurement remedies:

1) Council Directive 89/665/EEC of 21 December 1989 on the coordination of the laws, regulations and administrative provisions relating to the application of review procedures to the award of public supply and public works contracts.
2) Council Directive 92/13/EEC of 25 February 1992 coordinating the laws, regulations and administrative provisions relating to the application of Community rules on the procurement procedures of entities operating in the water, energy, transport and telecommunications sectors.
3) Directive 2007/66/EC of the European Parliament and of the Council of 11 December 2007 amending Council Directives 89/665/EEC and 92/13/EEC with regard to improving the effectiveness of review procedures concerning the award of public contracts.

These directives provide uniform standards for the legal remedies system set up by the Member States. Following the schematic analysis of directives, from an institutional point of view, directives provide similar model of the system of dispute resolution as the UNCITRAL Model Law[514] and the GPA[515]:

514 United Nations Commission on International Trade Law (UNCITRAL), Procurement of Goods, Construction and Services, 1994.

515 The revised Government Procurement Agreement (GPA) of the World Trade Organisation (WTO), 2012.

1) in particular, it is proposed that the review of decisions to be addressed to the public contracting authorities first;
2) provides for an administrative review procedure by non-judicial nature authorities, which would be subject to similar requirements as the courts;
3) a judicial review procedure.

It should be noted that Article 2 (9) of the Directive 2007/66/EC defines that in any case the final instance of the dispute should be the court or authority that would be considered as a court, i.e. would meet all requirements of the courts. Such provisions provide more flexibility in the implementation of directives in the national legal system of the Member States of the EU.

Following the analysis of the UNCITRAL, GPA and the EU directives shows that there is a number of dispute resolution models:

1. A two-stage model:
   1.1. Pre-litigation procedure that is carried out primarily through the same public contracting authority and then by the administrative review body (independent of the judiciary in line with relevant standards) as the forum for dispute resolution or a court of last instance for the settlement of disputes[516];
   1.2. Pre-litigation review procedure to be carried out first by the administrative review body which is independent from the judiciary body, and then by the court as a last dispute forum.[517]
2. The three-stage model, which includes: 1) the pre-litigation procedure for dispute carried out by the same public contracting authority, 2) an independent body of the appeal against the decisions of the public contracting authority, 3) the court[518].

The major innovations were introduced by amending Directive 2007/66/EC. The Directive introduced a mandatory standstill period for contracts falling within the scope of procurement Directives 2014/23/EC or 2014/24/EC for at least 15 calendar days between the decision to award contract and the conclusion of the

516 Article 54, United Nations Commission on International Trade Law (UNCITRAL), Procurement of Goods, Construction and Services, 1994.

517 Specialised independent administrative bodies whose competence is sometimes referred to as "quasi-judicial", Chapter V, (4), United Nations Commission on International Trade Law (UNCITRAL), Procurement of Goods, Construction and Services, 1994.

518 Article XYIII, GPA Agreement.

contract. If fax or electronic means are used, the standstill period is reduced to at least 10 calendar days.[519]

In order to ensure the proportionality of the sanctions applied, the Member States may grant the body responsible for review procedures the possibility of not jeopardising the contract or of recognising some or all of its temporal effects, when the exceptional circumstances relating to a general case concerned require certain overriding reasons relating to a general interest to be respected. In those cases, alternative penalties must be applied instead.[520]

2 Evolution of legal regulation of public procurement disputes in Lithuania

The first legal act adopted in Lithuania on public procurement was the Regulations of State Order of the Republic of Lithuania[521]. Provisions on disputes regarding the decision of the parties of public procurement were inevitably set as early as in the first legal acts that regulate these relationships because the risk of a dispute is rather high in this area. Chapter III of the Regulations of State Order contained provisions that provided for liability failure to carry out State order, whereas Chapter IV contained the settlement procedure for disputes over State order. This legal act stipulated that in case losses were incurred due to the failure to execute State order, the guilty party was obliged to compensate not only the losses, but also the loss of profit. If the State order was not carried out due to the fault of the party that was awarded the contract (the supplier), it had to pay a penalty to State budget of Lithuania together with the compensation for losses and lost profit. Internal disputes between the parties of this relationship over the acceptance of an order and the conditions of its performance were settled by the Government of the Republic of Lithuania. This legal act was a post-Soviet relict in Lithuania when physically there was no time for the design of legal acts regulating this area at the time the independence was restored.

519 Directive 2007/66/EC, Recitals 4, 5, 6; Directive 89/665/EEC, Article 2a; Directive 92/13/EEC, Article 2a.

520 Directive 2007/66/EC, Recital 22; Directive 89/665/EEC, Article 2d (3) Directive 92/13/EEC, Article 2d (3).

521 Lietuvos Respublikos Vyriausybės 1991 m. lapkričio 26 d. nutarimas Nr. 489 "Dėl Lietuvos Respublikos valstybinio užsakymo nuostatų" (Vyriausybės žinios, 1992, Nr. 5–90).

Later dates show an improvement of the Regulations of State Order[522]. A penalty for the avoidance to conclude the contract of State order was introduced and the executing party had to pay a penalty of 25 % of the value of the order, which was recovered to the budget of the Republic of Lithuania according to the claims of the contractors, i.e. ministries, State agencies or municipalities, which they brought in the court or in the arbitrage depending on which authority had to be addressed. The above-mentioned legal act also provided for disputes between contractors and suppliers over the award and execution of the contract of State order to be settled by the court or the arbitrage on the basis of their competence.

As independence was restored, another resolution of the Government of the Republic of Lithuania under the title "On Procedure of Procurement of Goods (Services) in Budgetary Institutions"[523] was applied along with the Regulations of State Order; however, it did not contain special provisions regulating dispute settlement.

Another resolution on public procurement of the Government of Lithuania, "On Regulations of Tender of State Order, Regulations of Contract of State Order, and Approval of Methodology of Loss Assessment due to Failure to Comply with Obligations of State Order"[524] was approved in 1992. However, this legal act only regulated contractual relationships and disputes between suppliers and public contracting authorities but not disputes over procedures of public procurement.

A new stage of the design of the public procurement system in Lithuania began with the Provisional Rules of State Procurement[525]. As the restoration of the independent State of Lithuania was announced on 11 March 1990, the bureaucratic apparatus was unstructured, deconcentrated and with no clear competence of institutions and no practical separation of executive and legislative powers,

---

522 Lietuvos Respublikos Vyriausybės 1991 m. balandžio 15 d. nutarimas Nr. 139 "Dėl Lietuvos Respublikos valstybinio užsakymo nuostatų pakeitimo ir papildymo". Valstybės žinios. 1991, Nr. 13–356.

523 Lietuvos Respublikos Vyriausybės 1992 m. gegužės 15 d. nutarimas Nr. 355 "Dėl prekių (paslaugų) įsigijimo tvarkos biudžetinėse įstaigose". Valstybės žinios, 1992, Nr. 20–604.

524 Lietuvos Respublikos Vyriausybės 1992 m. birželio 9 d. nutarimas Nr. 444 "Dėl Valstybinio užsakymo konkurso nuostatų, Valstybinio užsakymo sutarties nuostatų, Valstybinio užsakymo įsipareigojimų nevykdymo nuostolių įvertinimo metodikos patvirtinimo". Valstybės žinios. 1992, Nr. 24–716.114.

525 Lietuvos Respublikos Vyriausybės 1995 m. balandžio 12 d. nutarimas Nr. 510 "Dėl valstybinio pirkimo laikinųjų taisyklių patvirtinimo". Valstybės žinios. 1995, Nr. 33–778.

therefore, the first legal act to regulate the execution of public procurement was approved by the resolution of the Lithuanian Republic Government. This resolution contained general legal provisions on procurement procedures and their course (announcing information about procurement, evaluating applications, determining the winner and concluding the contract); it also regulated an unannounced procurement procedure.

It can be concluded that the first provisions of settling public procurement disputes were also approved by this resolution (the rudiments of legal regulation of public procurement dispute settling). Article 31 of the Provisional Rules of State Procurement provided for disputes between the public contracting authority and suppliers that participated in the procurement tender shall be settled by operation of law, and as long as the dispute is not settled, no procurement contract shall be awarded based on the tender results. Although it was a blanket provision and made a reference to general procedures of dispute settling, it also determined one of the important guarantees for the actual effectiveness of public procurement disputes, namely, the prohibition to award the contract as long as the dispute is not settled. Certainly, one general principal related to public procurement disputes cannot be considered a separate legal institution per se and its application often caused more damage than benefit (dispute initiation could clearly be used as a tool for unfair competition, since judicial proceedings regarding the dispute in the broad sense could take a very long period of time during which the public contracting authority was utterly unable to award a contract to the winner).

A concise regulation of the general process of public procurement presented in the Provisional Rules of State Procurement did not form the background for the creation of effective public procurement system, therefore, its development in the Republic of Lithuania has more links with the year 1996 when the country took a more Western viewpoint and thus there were incentives to conduct public procurement in a more transparent manner and to spend tax payers' money in a more appropriate way. It should be noted that during the evolution of the public procurement system in the Republic of Lithuania, the Provisional Rules of State Procurement left an important mark as the concepts and the methods of procurement used in historically, are now used in the current regulation. The Seimas of Lithuania adopted the Law on Public Procurement on 13August 1996[526], which formed the background for more effective and transparent public procurement and provided for the establishment and competence of an institution to control

526 Lietuvos Respublikos viešųjų pirkimų įstatymas. Žin., 1996, Nr. 84–2000.

public procurement, as well as having determined the procedure of dispute settlement in public procurement as a prerequisite for the effective enforcement of supplier rights.

The 1996 Law on Public Procurement[527] consolidated the obligatory pre-litigation procedures for the first time, which had a feature that no longer exists. A public procurement dispute is perceived as a disagreement between the public contracting authority which organised the public procurement and the supplier regarding the decision taken by the public contracting authority, thus, pre-litigation procedures of the dispute currently involve precisely these two parties (i.e., pre-litigation procedures are pursued between the public contracting authority and the supplier). Meanwhile, regulation of the time stipulated that the claim against the decisions of the public contracting authority is filed to the newly established authority that controlled the public procurement – Public Procurement Office. It was also established that the claim could be lodged only by the supplier who was officially awarded with the public procurement documents; therefore, this period featured an artificial and currently unacceptable restriction of subjects who had the right to lodge a claim.

Unlike the Provisional Rules of State Procurement[528], the Law on Public Procurement of 1996[529] provided for the suspension of public procurement procedures not until the dispute is settled altogether, but rather only until the dispute regarding the decision of the public contracting authority is examined in the Public Procurement Office. Although such a procedure of dispute settlement might indeed be effective, its regulation at the time had several significant gaps. The first gap is Article 38(1) of the Law on Public Procurement of 1996[530] that established that public procurement procedures may not be suspended provided the appeal is not motivated properly or the supplier or the public contracting authority may incur losses because of such a suspension. Such conditions are faulty not only because the evaluative criteria might be broadly interpreted (motivated appeal, possible losses), but also because it is only possible to state whether the supplier's claim is motivated (substantiated) or not after it has been examined.

527 Ibid.

528 Lietuvos Respublikos Vyriausybės 1995 m. balandžio 12 d. nutarimas Nr. 510 "Dėl valstybinio pirkimo laikinųjų taisyklių patvirtinimo". Valstybės žinios. 1995, Nr. 33–778.

529 Lietuvos Respublikos viešųjų pirkimų įstatymas. Žin., 1996, Nr. 84–2000.

530 Ibid.

The second gap of this regulation pertains to Article 38(2), which stated that the decision regarding the suspension of public procurement procedures is taken by the Public Procurement Office where the claim was lodged. Based on Article 36(2) of the then applicable Law on Public Procurement, the claim was to be filed directly to the Public Procurement Office within 10 days from becoming aware of the decision of the public contracting authority, therefore, with regard to the additional time allotted to adopt the decision on the suspension of procurement procedures and introduce the public contracting authority to this decision, there was a possibility for situations where the procedures are ended altogether by the time they are suspended, i.e. the public procurement contract is awarded. It should be noted that the appeal to the court regarding the decision of the Public Procurement Office could be filed only by the supplier, therefore, the decision made by the public contracting authority was final and of a binding nature. This is not a very fair aspect bearing in mind that in this case it was the third party that examined the dispute between the supplier and the public contracting authority.

Another interesting provision which is different from the current legal regulation was Article 36(3) of the Law on Public Procurement of 1996[531], which meant that the supplier could not lodge a claim against the decisions of the public contracting authority over the selection of a procurement method and over the decision to reject all the proposals from suppliers. It should be noted that by rejecting all proposals, the public contracting authority would essentially terminate the procurement procedure; therefore, it may be considered that the protection of the suppliers' interests that were affected due to the decision of the public contracting authority to suspend procurement procedures was essentially insufficient. It is to be noted that this was not an occasional gap in legal regulation; it pertained to Article 10 of the Law on Public Procurement of 1996[532] that provided for the right of the public contracting authority to reject all proposals put forward by suppliers at once, therefore, it was a mechanism that was designed by legislators on purpose.

Another important update on the examination of public procurement disputes was the Law of 3 June 1999 No VIII-1210[533] that replaced the Law on Public Procurement of the Republic of Lithuania (hereinafter referred to as the Law on Public Procurement of 1999). The Law on Public Procurement acquired

531 Ibid.

532 Ibid.

533 Lietuvos Respublikos viešųjų pirkimų įstatymas. Žin., 1996, Nr. 84-2000; 1999, Nr. 56-1809.

a new form with this legal act and key changes of public procurement dispute examination procedure were made. Shortcomings in the public procurement dispute examination procedures, in terms of the effectiveness of the protection of suppliers' violated interests that were present in the Law on Public Procurement of 1996, were eliminated; however, it is evident that this was regulation specific to that time.

The Law on Public Procurement of 1999[534] provided for a twofold stage of pre-litigation procedures. If the supplier did not agree with the decision of the public contracting authority it could file a claim to it. However, the compulsory part of the pre-litigation procedures was filing a claim to the Public Procurement Office. This claim could be filed by the supplier independently from submitting or not submitting a claim to the public contracting authority. Both lodging a claim to the public contracting authority or to the Public Procurement Office would suspend procurement procedures immediately, which would later on be renewed after the claim was examined, or by the approval of the Public Procurement Office in case the public contracting authority or the supplier would suffer bigger losses because of the suspension of procurement procedures than the supplier who filed the claim. This version of the law also established an interesting procedure of reviewing claim in the Public Procurement Office. Claims lodged by suppliers were examined by an independent committee of public procurement dispute examination. For the examination of each claim an independent committee of public procurement dispute was formed containing 3 members who were selected by the supplier that filed the claim, the public contracting authority and the Public Procurement Office from the list approved by the Public Procurement Office. These were compulsory pre-litigation procedures and both the supplier and the public contracting authority could file an appeal to the court against the decision of the committee. It was a considerable change as the version of the Law on Public Procurement of 1996[535] stipulated that only the supplier may appeal against the decision of the Public Procurement Office.

The enforcement of the Law on Public Procurement of 1999[536] was concise since Lithuania was preparing for its accession to the European Union, and the Law of 3 December 2002 No IX-1217[537] replaced the Law on Public Procurement

534 Ibid.

535 Lietuvos Respublikos viešųjų pirkimų įstatymas Žin., 1996, Nr. 84–2000.

536 Lietuvos Respublikos viešųjų pirkimų įstatymas Žin., 1996, Nr. 84–2000; 1999, Nr. 56–1809.

537 Lietuvos Respublikos viešųjų pirkimų įstatymas Žin., 1996, Nr. 84–2000; 2002, Nr. 118–5296.

of the Republic of Lithuania (hereinafter referred to as the Law on Public Procurement of 2002). With this law, legal regulation of public procurement was harmonised with the Council Directive 92/50/EEC[538], the Council Directive 93/36/EEC[539], the Council Directive 93/37/EEC[540] and other European Union legal acts related to public procurement.

This legal act established the legal regulation of public procurement disputes that is largely enforced nowadays. According to this regulation, pre-litigation procedures cover filing a claim to the public contracting authority, and should the suppliers disagree with the results of the claim review, they can bring an action to court. It should be noted that pre-litigation procedures stipulated by the Law on Public Procurement of 2002[541] were not compulsory, and the supplier reserved the right to start the proceedings in the court without filing a claim to the public contracting authority. This aspect changed with the adoption of Law of 22 December 2005 No X-471[542] to replace the Law on Public Procurement of the Republic of Lithuania, when pre-litigation procedures became compulsory. This law harmonised the Law on Public Procurement with the Directive 2004/17/EC[543] and the Directive 2004/18/EC[544].

A significant change that left a trace in the evolution of public procurement dispute examination in the Republic of Lithuania was the Law of 11 February 2010 No XI-678[545] on updating and amending Articles 2, 6, 7, 8, 10, 13, 15, 18, 22, 23, 24, 31, 32, 39, 41, 54, 58, 78, 85, 89, 90, 91, 92, 93, 94, 95, 96, 97, as well as the title of chapter and annex of the law on Public Procurement of the Republic of Lithuania. It further updated the Law concerning Articles 21–1, 94–1, 95–1, 95–2 and repealing Articles 98, 99, 100. With this version of the Law on Public Procurement the possibility to apply alternative sanctions among the protection

---

538 Ibid.

539 Ibid.

540 Ibid.

541 Lietuvos Respublikos viešųjų pirkimų įstatymas Žin., 1996, Nr. 84–2000; 2002, Nr. 118–5296.

542 Lietuvos Respublikos viešųjų pirkimų įstatymas Žin., 1996, Nr. 84–2000; 2006, Nr. 4–102.

543 Ibid.

544 Ibid.

545 Lietuvos Respublikos viešųjų pirkimų įstatymo 2, 6, 7, 8, 10, 13, 15, 18, 22, 23, 24, 31, 32, 39, 41, 54, 58, 78, 85, 89, 90, 91, 92, 93, 94, 95, 96, 97 straipsnių, V skyriaus pavadinimo ir priedo pakeitimo ir papildymo, Įstatymo papildymo 21–1, 94–1, 95–1, 95–2 straipsniais ir 98, 99, 100 straipsnių pripažinimo netekusiais galios įstatymas. Žin., 2010, Nr. 25–1174.

measures of violated interests of suppliers was introduced, the procedure of conciliation was eliminated, the procedure to establish the size of material damage was outlined and lastly, the rules and cases of nullification of contracts were regulated.

A positive aspect of the judicial dispute settlement evolution in the Republic of Lithuania should also be stressed. Until 10 November 2011 public procurement cases were heard in courts in line with the general judicial procedures of disputes, however, in practice such handling of public procurement cases was insufficiently expeditious, the hearing of individual cases could take several years. These reasons were a stimulus to the development of special rules of judicial procedures that were applied only to public procurement cases, therefore, the Code of Civil Procedure was supplemented with a separate chapter[546] that regulated shorter terms of preparation to hear the case, shorter time periods on the substance of the claim, additional requirements set for procedural documents of such cases and lastly, provisional protection measures that were to be applied particularly for public procurement cases were also indicated. According to the statistics[547] provided by the Public Procurement Office, one can see that as of 2012 the duration of judicial proceedings reduced by half According to the data available, in 2009, 2010 and 2011 the average duration of hearing public procurement cases in courts was 216, 223 and 193 days respectively, whereas in 2012 and 2013 it was 115 and 119 days. This proves that goals set out by the new legal regulation were met and had a positive influence on the total duration and speed of the judicial proceedings.

In addition, one of the significant changes as of 10 November 2011 was that the Code of Civil Procedure[548] stipulated a stamp duty exclusively applied to public procurement cases. Unlike other changes, this one resulted not from the need of speedy procedures, but from the legitimacy of the need to protect the rights of suppliers with a vested interest. In public procurement the legal relationship is established between many suppliers and one public contracting authority, and there can only be one winner (except for the cases when the public procurement is carried out for awarding a framework contract to several suppliers), therefore, this particular aspect means that the decision of the public contracting authority

546 Lietuvos Respublikos civilinio proceso kodekso pakeitimo ir papildymo įstatymas. Žin., 2011, Nr. 85-4126.

547 Viešųjų pirkimų bylų nagrinėjimo teismuose trukmės nustatymas, 2013.

548 Lietuvos Respublikos civilinio proceso kodekso pakeitimo ir papildymo įstatymas. Žin., 2011, Nr. 85-4126.

to determine one supplier inevitably affects the interests of other suppliers who have lost the tender. However, one might ask whether their interests were violated because of the lack of their competitiveness or because the public contracting authority violated legal provisions and public procurement principles. A stamp duty of one hundred Litas that was applied until 10 November 2011 as a tool to enforce judicial protection of rights but was insufficient for the suppliers to assess the legitimacy of actions brought by them in courts. Therefore, as of 10 November 2011 the stamp duty was raised tenfold (to one thousand Litas), which was supposed to reduce the number of unfounded claims.

In summary, it can be stated that a stable protection system of public procurement disputes and damaged rights in Lithuania was established by 2005 when Lithuania was actively getting ready for the accession to the European Union. Such key changes at the time were influenced by the goal to consolidate fair and competitive opportunities for foreign suppliers when participating in public procurement. Therefore, among other goals in public procurement, it was important to consolidate in the national legal acts effective procedures for reviewing the decisions of the public contracting authority and their general criteria, as well as to ensure the compliance with the European Union legal requirements when awarding public procurement contracts. Though subsequent improvements of the Law on Public Procurement and its harmonisation with the European Union law led to constantly improved and supplemented protection measures of violated suppliers' rights, the fundamental rules of the current public procurement dispute institution were not set until 2005. Up to this period the changes of legal regulation of public procurement disputes were rather chaotic when the regulation was essentially being changed and the balance of rights and obligations would be distorted to the extreme in terms of benefit either to suppliers or to the public contracting authority.

The final changes of the institution of public procurement dispute settlement were made on 2 May 2017 by the Law No XIII-327[549] to amend the Law on Public Procurement. The new version of the Law on Public Procurement was adopted in order to transpose Directive 2014/24/EU of the European Parliament and of the Council of 26 February 2014 on public procurement[550]. Although a number of significant changes were made with the transposition of the Directive's

549 Lietuvos Respublikos viešųjų pirkimų įstatymas. Žin., 1996, Nr. 84–2000; TAR, 2017–05–04, Nr. 2017–07550.

550 Ibid.

provisions to national law, from a systematic point of view, the institution of legal regulation of public procurement disputes did not undergo any key changes.

Quite the opposite, the majority of changes were actually determined by the interpretation of the national case law in terms of the rules of application of the relevant legislation. Therefore, when changes were being made, these rules were consolidated in the law itself, i.e. the liability of experts who take part in public procurement procedures and who act as persons with specialist knowledge was determined, and it was also set that the claims with the same subject-matter are not re-examined and the institution of the compensation for the damages was improved. An interesting change that warrants attention was the establishment of a new measure of suppliers' rights protection, i.e. the right to bring an action against the decision of the public contracting authority to terminate the public procurement contract due to substantial infringement of the contract. Suppliers already enjoyed this right as a remedy before as it was specified by general fundamental constitutional rights. However, such a choice of legislators opens the door to a broader discussion about the goal of this measure in protecting suppliers' rights and its influence on the general perception of the process of public procurement.

Currently, the main legislation which regulates public procurement is concentrated in Chapter 7 of the Law on Public Procurement[551] and Chapter 21^1 of the Code of Civil Procedure[552]. Protection measures of suppliers' rights that were infringed during public procurement (pre-litigation procedures, the extent to which the damages can be awarded, annulling the public procurement contract, alternative sanctions) are regulated in the Law on Public Procurement (material law), whereas the Code of Civil Procedure provides for the dispute proceedings that are closely related and applied specifically to such disputes (procedural law).

It should be noted that among material legal acts, the Law on Public Procurement establishes legal regulation that sometimes provides for procedural legal acts related to dispute settlement, such as Article 106 (3–4) of the Law on Public Procurement, wherein not only possible alternative sanctions are indicated, but also the duty of the court to take all significant aspects into account, such as the gravity of the infringement, the behaviour of the public contracting authority which all have to be motivated in the court's ruling; or, for instance, Article 101(2) of the Law on Public Procurement that has a blanket provision on the right of suppliers to ask for the application of provisional protection

551 Ibid.

552 Lietuvos Respublikos civilinio proceso kodeksas. Žin., 2002, Nr. 36-1340.

measures in public procurement disputes. Such legislation in terms of its nature is more related to the procedural law and judicial process; therefore, in terms of enacting the law, it could be established in the very Code of Civil Procedure, however, such legal regulation does not have any major influence on the application of protection measures of suppliers' rights.

3 The system of remedies for suppliers in the Republic of Lithuania

The system of remedies for suppliers refers to the totality of the institutional and procedural preventive means to ensure the transparent and fair procedures of public procurement, as established by law. The system of remedies for suppliers under Lithuanian law includes the following means: pre-litigation procedures, suppliers' right to effective judicial protection to annul any of the public contracting authority's decisions that infringe the Law on Public Procurement, compensation for damages, interim measures, and termination of the contract due to a major violation deemed unfounded. The remedies also include the right of the court to apply alternative sanctions and the EU law infringement proceedings. The wide range of procedural elements leads to the conclusion that Lithuanian law extensively covers the settlement of disputes in public procurement and, in this respect, complies with the general standards of the EU legislation. However, it is worth noting that it is the practical application of these instruments and its contribution to the procedural review and ensuring remedies that are of key importance.

Lithuania applies the approach of judicial review of public contracting authorities, together with a mandatory stage of the pre-litigation investigation. The effective enforcement of remedies for aggrieved bidders is an important precondition for fair and real public procurement legislation as well as the bidders' trust in the procurement system as a guarantee of fair competition[553]. With this in mind, the analysis of the remedies for suppliers in the Republic of Lithuania will be based not only on the examination of legislative regulations but also on the analysis of the efficiency of their practical enforcement. It must be noted that the up-to-date legal regulation enforcing Directive 2014/24/EU of the European Parliament and of the Council of 26 February 2014 on public procurement came

553 Trybus Martin, Improving the Efficiency of Public Procurement Systems in the Context of the European Union Enlargement Process. See the link below: http://citeseerx.ist.psu.edu/viewdoc/download;jsessionid=D59784085737B5996852A94F4987B49D?doi=10.1.1.612.1406&rep=rep1&type=pdf.

into force only on 1 July 2017, therefore there is no case-law regarding its specific application as of yet, but has been stated the main remedies remain the same and previous court practices and interpretations are relevant in this analysis.

3.1 Judicial disputes in public procurement following the legislation of the Republic of Lithuania

Article 101(1) of the Law on Public Procurement[554] stipulates that if a supplier determines that a public contracting authority has not complied with the requirements of this Law or has unreasonably terminated the contract, would consider it a material breach of the procurement contract that has violated or will violate his legitimate interests. Thus, he may in accordance with the procedure established in this chapter, apply to the district court, as a court of first instance, for the annulment or amendment of decisions of the public contracting authority that does not comply with the requirements of this law; compensation for damage, nullification of the procurement contract or framework contract, the application of alternative sanctions in accordance with Article 106 (1) of this Law or the termination of the purchase contract due to a major violation deemed unfounded. Paragraph 2 of this Article stipulates that a supplier may refer to court so that interim protection measures are applied in accordance with the procedure set in the Code of the Civil Procedure of the Republic of Lithuania.

There are four different cases in terms of enforcing suppliers' access to justice:

1) Filing a claim with the public contracting authority, the supplier has the right to bring a lawsuit before court within 10 days (in case of simplified procedures within 5 working days) after the dispatch to suppliers of a written notice of the decision taken by the public contracting authority; where such a notice is not sent electronically; within 15 days after its dispatch to suppliers.
2) Where the public contracting authority fails, within the specified time limit, to examine a claim filed, the supplier shall have the right to file a request or bring a lawsuit before court within 15 days from the day on which the public contracting authority ought to have given a written notice of the decision taken to the supplier who has filed the claim, interested candidates and tenderers.

554 Lietuvos Respublikos viešųjų pirkimų įstatymas. Žin., 1996, Nr. 84-2000; TAR, 2017-05-04, Nr. 2017-07550.

3) A supplier shall have the right to bring a lawsuit for nullification of a public contract or preliminary contract within 6 months from the date the public contract was awarded.
4) Where the supplier believes the public contracting authority has unlawfully terminated the contract due to a major contract violation, it shall refer to court within 30 days after the termination of the contract.

It must be noted that despite the fact that Lithuanian law provides for mandatory pre-litigation procedure, this procedure is only applied prior to the award of the contract, i.e. pre-litigation procedures apply only in cases specified in points 1 and 2. In cases laid down in points 3 and 4, pre-litigation does not constitute a condition to exercise the right to bring an action and it is not compulsory to initiate an extra-judicial settlement.

The analysis of Article 105 of the Law on Public Procurement[555] shows that cases of lawsuits referred to in Paragraphs 1 and 2 cover situations where the supplier files a claim against the public contracting authority's decisions in the course of procurement procedures prior to the award of the contract and their right to do so has not been impeded. If the supplier is able to prove that the public contracting authority has impeded their right to refer to court and file a claim against the decision of the public contracting authority, the claim is subject to a 6 month limitation period. Thus, the limitation period of 6 months applies in cases where the public contracting authority does not announce a tender (even though obliged), does not apply a deferral period, has not suspended public procurement procedures, has not notified a purchase by means of a dynamic purchasing system or an electronic auction, or has performed other imperative violations of legal norms that has resulted in the supplier having no access to remedies and concluding a public procurement contract.

3.2 Litigation efficiency and volumes

The procedural aspect of litigation in public procurement is regulated by Chapter 21 of the Code of the Civil Procedure. As has already been pointed out by the author, the amendments introduced in the 2011 Code have already had a positive effect on the procedural efficiency of litigation. The table below shows that statistically, the said amendments have reduced the average length

555 Ibid.

of court proceedings by half. The amendments have reduced preparation time for the case for both parties, have set specific time limits (the preparation for trial should be completed no later than 30 days from the application day, and the decision must be taken no later than 60 days from the day of the court adjudication) to set priorities of public procurement cases in courts and lastly, have adopted the method of suspending the adjudication for plea repair only if the corrections cannot be made after accepting the plea and within the time limit set for the preparation for trial. These kinds of amendments, uncommon in other types of cases, allow public procurement disputes to be settled in a more efficient and prioritised manner. As a result, in order for cases to be solved in such an expedited manner, which would not adversely affect the decision quality, judges have started to receive specialised training on public procurement cases.

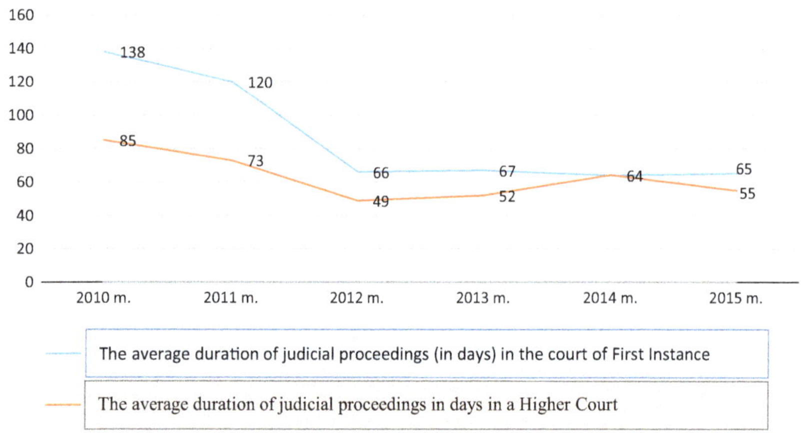

Chart 8: The duration of judicial proceedings (in days) in the Court of First Instance and Higher Courts in the Republic of Lithuania. Average duration of public procurement trials in courts in 2015. Public Procurement Office. See the link below: http://vpt.lrv.lt/uploads/vpt/documents/files/Vie%C5%A1%C5%B3j%C5%B3%20pirkim%C5%B3%20byl%C5%B3%20nagrin%C4%97jimas%20teismuose%202015%20m.pdf (02.05.2018).

Although, as we can see, the problem of lengthy judicial proceedings has been solved, no decisions have been taken to reduce the number of court cases. The chart below shows the variation in the number of public procurement cases in courts, which is unfavourable especially due to the currently increasing number of public-procurement-related cases.

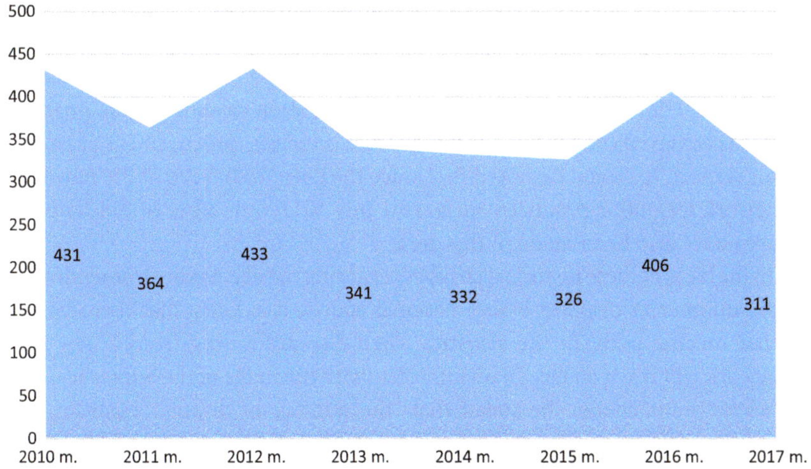

Chart 9: The number of cases received by the Court of First Instance in 2010 – 2017. The text quotes the official statistics of Lithuanian Courts. See the link below: http://www.teismai.lt/lt/visuomenei-ir-ziniasklaidai/statistika/106 (01.05.2017). http://vpt.lrv.lt/uploads/vpt/documents/files/Pirkimu_stebesenos_ataskaita_2017_m.pdf (01.05.2017).

The statistical data shows that during the period in question, the number of new judicial proceedings fluctuated inconsistently. The turning point was 2012 when the number of new claims increased significantly. This was the result of the above-mentioned amendment of 11 February 2010[556] that led to major changes in the regulation of dispute review procedures and amendments of the Law on Public Procurement of 23 December 2010[557], which came into force as of 1 January 2012, and, in many respects, modified the legal regulation of procedures that were previously in place. These amendments have led to a significant change in volumes of initiated litigation. Therefore, statistical fluctuations

556 Lietuvos Respublikos viešųjų pirkimų įstatymo 2, 4, 6, 8, 9, 10, 18, 19, 20, 21, 22, 23, 24, 25, 27, 33, 37, 38, 40, 41, 56, 57, 71, 73, 81, 82, 83, 85, 86, 91, 92, 94, 95–1, 97 straipsnių, V skyriaus pavadinimo, 1, 2, 4 priedėlių ir priedo pakeitimo ir papildymo įstatymas. Žin., 2011, Nr. 2–36.

557 Lietuvos Respublikos viešųjų pirkimų įstatymo 2, 6, 7, 8, 10, 13, 15, 18, 22, 23, 24, 31, 32, 39, 41, 54, 58, 78, 85, 89, 90, 91, 92, 93, 94, 95, 96, 97 straipsnių, V skyriaus pavadinimo ir priedo pakeitimo ir papildymo, Įstatymo papildymo 21–1, 94–1, 95–1, 95–2 straipsniais ir 98, 99, 100 straipsnių pripažinimo netekusiais galios įstatymas.Žin., 2010, Nr. 25–1174.

have not been accidental and clearly demonstrate the impact of the new regulation in public procurement legislation on the number of dispute trials. Later, we can witness that until 2016, when there was a slight increase in filed claims, some stabilisation in the number of initiated litigation cases in public procurement was achieved (on average, 156 new cases on public procurement per year). In this respect, it should be noted that since the entry into force of the new legal framework for public procurement as of 1 July 2017, a number of fundamental changes have also been made in this area.

On the basis of these historical changes regarding the effect of such amendments on the number of disputes before national courts, it is likely that there will be another turning point in the statistics when disputes arising from a new legal framework will reach courts. In an interview with the judge of the Supreme Court of Lithuania Rudėnaitė, she stated that "the number of disputes regarding the application of the most economically advantageous proposal criteria will increase".

So far, the majority of public procurement tenders have been based on the lowest price criterion, but the criterion of the most economically advantageous proposal, which according to the new framework will have to be applied to 30 % of public procurement procedures, is way more complicated for both the public contracting authorities in determining tender requirements and courts in deciding whether the criteria have been applied correctly.[558] Sigita Vaitukaitytė, Head of the Prevention and Purchase Contract Supervision Department under the Public Procurement Office, also confirms that with the adoption of the new law on public procurement, the number of disputes in court will increase. She believes that for some time there will be a lack of well-defined practices in applying certain new provisions[559]. It should be noted that, as mentioned before, as of 1 July 2017, the legal framework for public procurement has changed significantly, but the instrument of litigation in public procurement has received little review, without major modifications or improvements.

Assuming the volumes of judicial and pre-judicial trials regarding public procurement in Lithuania will only increase and bearing in mind the historical statistics on the current litigation procedures it is unlikely that the arising challenges will be responded to. As has already been mentioned, the system for reviewing decisions of public contracting authorities is guaranteed in order to ensure public procurement principles are enforced, the law on public procurement is actually and

558 Viešųjų pirkimų reforma: kas pajėgus užtikrinti skaidrumą? Teismai.lt. 2017, Nr. 1 (25).

559 Ibid.

properly applied but it is also a bureaucratic procedural burden that results in delays in public procurement procedures and increased workloads for judicial authorities.

3.3 Pre-litigation procedures in public procurement

The legislation in Lithuania provides for mandatory pre-litigation procedures, including filing a claim with a public contracting authority regarding the decision adopted by it. Pre-litigation procedures in public procurement are regulated by Articles 101–103 of the Law on Public Procurement. Article 101(3) provides for that in order for the supplier to challenge decisions or actions taken by the public contracting authority before awarding the contract or preliminary contract, the supplier must first file a claim with the public contracting authority in writing (by fax, electronic means or by certified post or appropriate carrier service with delivery receipt). This provision refers not to the supplier's right to file a claim, but the obligatory nature of the pre-litigation procedure and the form of its implementation. Therefore, in order to exercise their right to judicial protection, suppliers must first resort to pre-litigation procedures.

As the pre-litigation procedure is the first stage in reviewing decisions of public contracting authorities, on the basis of which other remedies may be applied, Courts of the Republic of Lithuania, in their practice, emphasise that the effectiveness of review procedures should not be limited to the judicial stage of settling disputes. The obligation of the public contracting authority to ensure the effectiveness of review procedures arises from its obligation to address the claims of suppliers. The public contracting authority, in line with its competence and available means must take the necessary actions to ensure effective protection of aggrieved supplier rights. Therefore, the public contracting authority must also ensure supplier's access to review procedures is not formal but appropriately implemented[560]. If applied properly, this procedure will be the foundation of the fundamental principles of public procurement: transparency, equal treatment, mutual recognition and non-discrimination. Thus, fair competition and rivalry between suppliers does not only depend on the correct application of public procurement laws but also on the guarantee their rights will be protected.

Article 102 of the Law on Public Procurement[561] stipulates that suppliers have the right to file a claim with the public contracting authority, lodge a request

560 Lietuvos Aukščiausiojo Teismo 2011 m. kovo 21 d. nutartis civilinėje byloje Nr. 3K-3-119/2011.

561 Lietuvos Respublikos viešųjų pirkimų įstatymas. Žin., 1996, Nr. 84–2000; TAR, 2017-05-04, Nr. 2017-07550.

or bring an action before the court (except an action for nullification of procurement contract or preliminary contract or an action for recognition of the contract to be terminated unreasonably) within 10 days (in case of simplified procedures within 5 working days) after dispatch to suppliers of a written notice of the public contracting authority of the decision adopted by it. Where such a notice is not sent electronically; within 15 days after its dispatch to suppliers or within 10 days (in case of simplified procedures within 5 working days) from the day the public contracting authority has announced its decision, unless the Law on Public Procurement requires the public contracting authority to inform suppliers of its decisions in writing. Indeed, these mandatory time limits effectively ensure the expediency of public procurement dispute settlements; however, the author doubts they are sufficient in all cases.

3.4 Different and mandatory time limits of pre-litigation procedures

It is important to mention that with the Law on Public Procurement the legislature of Lithuania has consolidated common procedures and rules of conducting the public procurement including action review procedures and excluding certain differences in regulation, for instance, different time limits and specific regulation of aspects of procedure for low value procurement review irrespective of the value of the public procurement contract. Therefore, one could argue that disputes that originate from the application of the Law on Public Procurement can be related to the same material basis (subject matter of the dispute) in terms of its nature and content. The same situation also pertains to the procedures of dispute examination, i.e. the procedures are the same whatever the procurement value (except for the case of low value procurement), it is only the time limits that differ.

A question can be raised as to whether such a separation of dispute review procedures is well-founded and by extension, justifies the aim to shorten simplified procedures, thus allowing for the statement that the concept of simplified public procurement could essentially be replaced by the concept of accelerated public procurement in Lithuanian national law. In some cases a public procurement dispute arises over public or simplified procurement from the same basis. Why then would the chances to protect supplier rights be more constrained timewise in the case of simplified procurement? In order to put forward a motivated and well-founded claim, the supplier needs to analyse the competitor's product, to address the public contracting authority in order to get acquainted with the winner's proposal, to work together with lawyers and to evaluate the legal basis and its legitimacy; in the case of missing certain information, to address the public contracting authority for answers, and to perform various other actions.

Completing this to-do list may take quite some time, therefore, 5 working days for filing a claim in the case of simplified procurement may be too little. The key problem being that the above-mentioned set of actions is substantially the same for both simplified and international procurement, therefore, different regulation in terms of time limits for the right to protect one's rights raises doubts. This separation is logically based on the assumption that simplified procurement contains no competition on the international level; rather, it is only the local market that suppliers compete in. However, in the opinion of the author, this should not be considered a significant argument for establishing different time limits for the enforcement of this right, because:

1) In broad terms, the subsequent procedures of public procurement dispute examination (e.g. judicial dispute hearing) are already identical (with the exception of the time limit of instituting proceedings before the court), i.e. all established procedural time limits and procedures concur irrespective of the procurement value;
2) Usually the same local market players participate in both international and simplified public procurement.

It would be logical to make the separation with regard to who is likely to participate in public procurement only. In this case, however, the principle of equality of treatment would definitely be affected. Therefore, it can be stated that different time limits for the enforcement of rights protection with respect to the value of public procurement are not well-founded.

With respect to Article 103(1) of the Law on Public Procurement, the public contracting authority is obliged to examine only those claims that were received until the day of awarding the procurement contract or preliminary contract and were submitted in line with the above mentioned time limits of filing claims. It is this legal regulation that reveals the mandatory nature of time limits of filing a claim.

When interpreting the application of these provisions, national courts emphasised that mandatory time limits of filing claims can be applied only for such actions of the public contracting authority infringing the interests of public procurement participants that were established or appear before the end of these time limits. One must take into account the time that the supplier had to file a claim before the end of the mandatory time limit, because time limits that are too short are also incompatible with the effective protection of rights[562]. Time limits for reviewing the decisions of the public contracting authority should not

---

562 Lietuvos Aukščiausiojo Teismo 2011 m. balandžio 5 d. nutartis civilinėje byloje Nr. 3K-3-158/2011.

be established and applied in such a way that suppliers could not use them practically or that it would be very difficult for them to do so[563]. Moreover, the court of appeal concluded in one of the cases that with respect to the shortness of the time limit to file a claim (five days), the provision of the appeal procedure according to which the public contracting authority cannot look into the claims of the suppliers that were filed beyond this time limit (until the procurement contract is not awarded) and that suppliers who missed this deadline are unconditionally deprived of the right to judicial proceedings of infringed rights, could make it too difficult for suppliers to take advantage of rights provided to them by the Law on Public Procurement and would not be in line with the principle of effectiveness of review procedures.

A claim filed by the supplier and examined after awarding a public procurement contract would not affect other suppliers' interests and would not contradict the principle of equal treatment[564]. With respect to the case law of the courts of appeal and according to legislation the time limits have features of mandatory time limits, their application is not unconditional and depends on the decision of the public contracting authority. Therefore, if the public contracting authority receives a claim beyond the time limits of filing a claim indicated in Article 102 of the Law on Public Procurement[565], it can still examine the claim, and the limitation period for that supplier is re-opened.

4 Problem of the claim "on the same subject matter"

Article 103 (1) of the Law on Public Procurement[566] establishes that there is no obligation to examine claims that are re-filed against the same decision or action of the public contracting authority. It should be noted that this provision is new and applies only to the version of the Law on Public Procurement of 1 July 2017. On the one hand, this rule solves a practical problem when the supplier re-files the claim on the same subject matter to the public contracting authority. However, it presupposes a different type of a dispute, i.e. in those cases when the supplier and the public contracting authority perceive the material

563 Lietuvos Aukščiausiojo Teismo 2010 m. balandžio 6 d. nutartis civilinėje byloje Nr. 3K-3-150/2010.

564 Lietuvos Aukščiausiojo Teismo 2009 m. vasario 9 d. nutartis civilinėje byloje Nr. 3K-3-35/2009.

565 Lietuvos Respublikos viešųjų pirkimų įstatymas. Žin., 1996, Nr. 84–2000; TAR, 2017–05–04, Nr. 2017–07550.

566 Ibid.

aspect of the dispute differently. In the opinion of the supplier, it will file a claim on a different subject matter, whereas the public contracting authority will treat it as a claim on the same subject matter as the previous one. This issue has an important practical meaning for determining the date from which the limitation period should be calculated to bring an action before the court. The law provides for the situation when the claim is not examined, however, and it does not additionally regulate anything in this case: it is not clear whether the public contracting authority, which has made the decision of not looking into the claim because it was filed on the same subject matter, is obliged to inform the supplier about this decision, and when doing so, what legal consequences may follow.

As interpreted by courts in their case law, since the law does not provide for the method of calculating the time limits of filing a claim, further improvements should be made. When the public contracting authority does not analyse the claim, in terms of the content and legal consequences, it can be comparable to a situation when the demands of the supplier were not satisfied or partially satisfied having analysed their claim, and, therefore, the beginning of the time limit should be the day when the supplier finds out or is supposed to find out about the refusal to examine the claim[567]. This practice has always been applied and currently is not amended; however, it is questionable whether it can be applied to interpret the new Law on Public Procurement without additional interpretation.

The new provision leads to two problems with its application. "Is not obliged to examine" linguistically presupposes that the public contracting authority, upon the receipt of such a claim, is not going to analyse it whatsoever, including the fact of its receipt, i.e. subject to the assessment of the public contracting authority, it may not respond to the supplier altogether or, in other words, not examine the received document in the procurement procedure. In such a situation, the limitation period of the supplier's claim would be calculated according to Article 102 (2) of the Law on Public Procurement that stipulates if the public contracting authority does not examine the claim within a given time frame, the supplier has the right to file a request or a claim before a court within 15 days of the day when the public contracting authority had to in writing inform the claimant, as well as candidates and tenderers concerned about its decision.

However, the key issue is the calculation of the beginning of the limitation period and the part of the dispute to which it applies. The problem is that when the public contracting authority treats the claim as re-filed and does not analyse

567 Lietuvos Aukščiausiojo Teismo Civilinių bylų skyriaus 2012 m. balandžio 18 d. nutartis civilinėje byloje Nr. 3K-3-170/2012.

it, irrespective of this decision and information about it, a basis for a new dispute between the public contracting authority and the supplier occurs, i.e., the dispute over the repeated nature of the claim. For example, the supplier files the second claim against the decision of the public contracting authority in its determining of the winning bid, however, the factual reason for the infringement is indicated as in the first claim (another supplier was announced the winner because he was not removed from procurement procedures when there were grounds for such a removal) so could be disputed as a repeated/duplicate refiled claim.

A question can be raised as to whether the supplier is going to be able to enforce his right to judicial proceedings (will not miss the deadline of the limitation period for instituting proceedings) against the decision of the public contracting authority to recognise the qualification of the supplier, when the public contracting authority treats the claim as re-filed (because its subject matter is the decision of the public contracting authority against which the claim was already filed before). On the one hand, we cannot refer to an assumption that the aim of re-filing the claim is to delay public procurement procedures because the supplier is most likely going to present new arguments, explanations and motives in this claim, whereas the public contracting authority will not look into the claim merely because of the same decision that the supplier is filing a claim against.

Therefore, courts have a duty to interpret the guidelines of application of this provision on refusal to analyse the claim on the grounds that it is re-filed; whether in situations where a re-filed claim is supplemented with new arguments, the supplier, with the goal of pre-litigation procedures, acquires valid expectations regarding the outcome of the dispute, the limitation period should be divided into the limitation period for the initial (genuine) dispute and the dispute over re-filing the claim.

5 Discretion of the public contracting authority as a factor for dispute

If we look at the very beginning of the dispute on public procurement, in the opinion of the author, it focuses on the discretion of the public contracting authority that is stipulated by the Law on Public Procurement. For example, Article 57(1) of the Law on Public Procurement[568] establishes that the public contracting authority requires the supplier to justify the prices or costs of goods,

568 Ibid.

services, works or their constituent parts indicated in the proposal if they appear abnormally low. The prices or costs of goods, services, works or their constituent parts in all cases shall be considered as abnormally low if they are 30 or more percent lower than the average prices and costs indicated by other suppliers whose proposals were not rejected for other reasons and whose bids do not exceed the amounts of procurement established and registered in the documents prepared by the public contracting authority before the procurement procedure. The hypothesis in this legal provision already contains the wording "if they appear abnormally low" and indicates the cases when the price would always be considered abnormally low. However, the public contracting authority also has the right to declare the price indicated in the proposal abnormally low in other undefined cases. Declaring the price abnormally low per se does not have any legal consequences for the supplier, however, the obligation that arises to justify the price may lead to the removal of the supplier from the procurement procedures.

Therefore, the second medium for the dispute to occur arises from the legal regulation that was previously in force, i.e. "the discretion of the public contracting authority is manifested through the application of the assessment procedure of abnormally low price, when the public contracting authority has a discretion to decide on the acceptability of justification for abnormally low price given by each supplier."[569] Should the supplier fail to provide proper justification, it is removed from the procurement procedures and therefore, with no clarity as to what proper justification is or with the public contracting authority's right itself to declare the price abnormally low, in the context of application of this article alone, there are two threats for a dispute with the public contracting authority that arise.

The discretion of the public contracting authority during the public procurement is generally perceived as its right to select the procurement method, to lay down procurement conditions, to set out requirements for suppliers and the object of procurement within the framework of legal acts and case law. This discretion is partially determined by rights of the public contracting authority that are established in legal acts (for instance, Article 33 (2), Article 42 (2), Article 85 (2) etc. of the Law on Public Procurement). On the other hand, its discretion may also result from vague or ambiguous legal regulation or from insufficiently

569 Deividas Soloveicikas, Neįprastai mažos kainos koncepcijos taikymo ypatumai pagal Europos Sąjungos ir Lietuvos viešųjų pirkimų teisę//Teisė. – Vilnius, 2008, Nr. 67, p. 7–23. ISSN 1392-1274.

developed case law. With the absence of a clear model of behaviour in certain situations, the public contracting authority has the possibility to solve problems in two ways. This problem is especially relevant after each major reorganisation of the public procurement system when certain legal acts are supplemented with new provisions.

The discretion of decisions made by the public contracting authority in terms of legal consequences can have a twofold influence on public procurement participants: on the interests of one particular supplier or on contrary interests of several suppliers. This is reflected through the contrary interests of suppliers during the public procurement, i.e. interests of a certain supplier in the public procurement can be influenced both in cases when the decision is favourable to suppliers or when it is favourable to their competitors. There are no two winners in public procurement, therefore, each supplier is actually interested in the decisions which are made regarding the winner. Due to such a situation, the complexity of rulings and the possibility of judicial proceedings have increased in pre-litigation procedures.

The discretion of the public contracting authority can be evidenced from the application of the institution of grounding suppliers' removal or of the institution of qualification assessment (for example, what time frame could be given by the public contracting authority for suppliers to clarify the documents that prove their compliance to qualification requirements, or how the public contracting authority will solve a situation when the supplier only partially clarifies the documents related to qualification requirements). If it comes to other stages of assessment of proposals, the discretion of the public contracting authority can clearly be manifested during the assessment of economic efficiency (which is sometimes determined according to rather subjective criteria) or in selecting the criteria for economic efficiency in general; it can also be manifested in selecting qualification requirements of public procurement. All these factors have a direct influence on the competitiveness of suppliers as well as on the outcome of public procurement.

In terms of the assessment of the discretion provided to the public contracting authority by law, it has been stated a number of times in the case law that, "legal regulation of public procurement aims at avoiding situations where the public contracting authority has unlimited discretion"[570]. The right of discretion

570 Lietuvos Aukščiausiojo Teismo Civilinių bylų skyriaus 2010 m. gegužės 4 d. nutartis civilinėje byloje Nr. 3K-3-126/2010.

provided to the public contracting authority by the Law on Public Procurement is based on the inability to apply all public procurement aspects for any procurement or the object of procurement for any situation that can emerge during public procurement. Therefore, it often stands as a guideline on which one can make an assessment whether the public contracting authority has overstepped the discretion provided to it by law.

However, the key problem remains in situations of decisions of the public contracting authority which occur namely because of vague or insufficient legal regulation and vague application of legislation, because in such cases there are no obvious guidelines which can be referred to by the supplier or the public contracting authority in order to accurately assess the background and motives of decisions made, as well as to determine their legitimacy and validity.

In very rare cases the dispute between the public contracting authority and the supplier can arise in a situation that is legally regulated in a clear manner, however, the dispute is more likely to occur in a situation where the public contracting authority has discretion provided to it by law, and the dispute is most likely in a situation where discretion is manifested in cases of vague and insufficient regulation. In 2010, the Ministry of Economy of Lithuania stated in its report that the most frequent reasons of infringements in public procurement are related to the lack of qualification of specialists who organise public procurement, absence of their training and methodological material.

Other reasons include too frequent changes in legal acts regulating public procurement and shortage of information about the changes, vague provisions of the Law on Public Procurement and its bylaws that allow for a different interpretation, irregular and contradictory case law of interpretation and application of the Law on Public Procurement[571]. Some of these reasons remain one of the most frequent factors that determine infringements in public procurement, because even nowadays, with the current version of the Law on Public Procurement, it is again interpreted and applied in a partially vague manner.

571 Lietuvos Respublikos ūkio ministerija. "Projekto "Viešųjų pirkimų ginčų nagrinėjimo sistemos tobulinimas" ataskaita". 2011. Prieiga per internetą: http://eimin.lrv.lt/uploads/eimin/documents/files/Viesieji%20pirkimai/VPGNS[1].pdf (2014.01.07).

6 Information exchange between the supplier and the public contracting authority during pre-litigation procedures

Article 103 (2) of the Law on Public Procurement[572] establishes the rule of the deferral period so that the public contracting authority cannot award a contract or a framework contract earlier than 10 days (in case of simplified procedures, earlier than 5 working days) after dispatch of a written notice by the public contracting authority, informing the claiming supplier, candidates and tenderers concerned of its decision, and if such a notice is not sent electronically, earlier than 15 days. In all cases, upon receipt of a claim, the public contracting authority has to immediately suspend the procurement procedure until the claim has been investigated and a decision has been taken. Article 103 (3) of the Law on Public Procurement[573] establishes the procedure of the claim examination that requires the public contracting authority to investigate the claim, make a justified decision and notify the claiming supplier and candidates and tenderers concerned about it, as well as about any changes in previously communicated procedure deadlines. The notification should be in writing and within 6 working days from the receipt of the claim. In the analysis of these terms it should be noted that the public contracting authority must justify its decision, i.e. the decision has to be substantiated from the factual and judicial point of view, and deliver it to the claiming supplier, as well as candidates and tenderers concerned. However, the scope of the response to the claiming supplier and candidates concerned may be generally different. The courts have based this on different party interests in the result of the claim examination.

Nevertheless, it has also been acknowledged that in certain cases other tenderers may want to learn the motives in the claim and this right might be enforced through other means established by the Law on Public Procurement. The courts have stated that the public contracting authority must communicate its justified response to the claim only to the supplier that has filed the claim, whereas other tenderers have to be informed of the result of the claim investigation (its rejection or acceptance) and the subsequent course of the procedure. Other tenderers have access to the claim and the justified response on the grounds of other provisions of the Law on Public Procurement, if they submit a separate request to the public contracting authority to be informed of the claim, and under the condition that the claim or the response to it (or part thereof)

572 Lietuvos Respublikos viešųjų pirkimų įstatymas. 1996, Nr. 84–2000; TAR, 2017-05-04, Nr. 2017-07550.

573 Ibid.

shall not violate the respective economic entity's right to the protection of confidential information[574].

Reviewing the regulation of pre-litigation procedures in public procurement by law and assuming that one of the common reasons of disputes between the supplier and the public contracting authority is the latter's discretion in adopting decisions in the course of procurement, it is clear that one challenging aspect is the communication between the supplier and the public contracting authority. Often in disputes arising from civil matters it is the communication and collaboration between parties that play an important role in finding a mutually beneficial solution before referring to litigation procedures in court. In public procurement, the goals of the supplier are indeed different from the goals of the public contracting authority but they are also characterised by the aspect of mutual benefit, which is common in civil matters, i.e. even if the goals differ they are beneficial to both parties. Mutual benefit, as long as it remains within the limits of transparent and fair procedures, which are to be ensured by the public contracting authority, may help when settling disputes in public procurement. However, mutual benefit can only be achieved through a successful and comprehensive communication between parties interested in receiving maximum benefits.

Article 58 (1) of the Law on Public Procurement defines that the public contracting authority shall, in writing, inform the candidates and tenderers concerned (except cases when the contract is verbal) within 5 working days of the decision taken to determine the successful tender that will result in the conclusion of a procurement contract or preliminary contract; or of the decision to allow them to participate in a dynamic purchase system; shall provide a summary of the relevant information referred to in Paragraph 2 that has not yet been submitted during the procurement procedure; shall determine the ranking of tenders, the successful tender and the exact deferral period. Another example is Article 55 (7) of the Law on Public Procurement[575] stating that if the public contracting authority assesses the bids on the basis of the price/cost and quality ratio and technical characteristics of its choice are not subject to qualitative assessment, the public contracting authority must first check and evaluate the

574 Lietuvos Aukščiausiojo Teismo 2016 m. kovo 30 d. nutartis civilinėje byloje Nr. 3K-3-177-916/2016.

575 Lietuvos Respublikos viešųjų pirkimų įstatymas. 1996, Nr. 84–2000; TAR, 2017–05–04, Nr. 2017–07550.

technical data of the bids and only then, having informed the tenderers of the results obtained, perform an overall assessment of the bid taking into account the price.

These examples show that the public contracting authority, when informing suppliers of its significant decisions, is not obligated to share its motives, specific reasons or explanations thereof. The public contracting authority must provide reasons for its decision only in response to a claim filed by a supplier.

The author has already analysed that pre-litigation procedures only cover the filing of a claim with the public contracting authority. Therefore, the next stage of the public contracting authority decision review is to refer to court. It is to be noted that the supplier, opposed to the public contracting authority's decision, will only learn the true reasons that have been argued after receiving the response to his claims, so that the only way he can submit his objections, without the risk of exceeding the deadline to bring an action, is in court. And this is for a reason; in Article 423 (3) of the Code of the Civil Procedure[576] it is only a requirement that the plea should coincide with the factual circumstances that were the basis of the claim filed during pre-litigation proceedings, except the cases where the plaintiff was not able to indicate these circumstances when filing his claim. The current model of pre-litigation procedures in terms of the reason submission can be generally illustrated by the figure below.

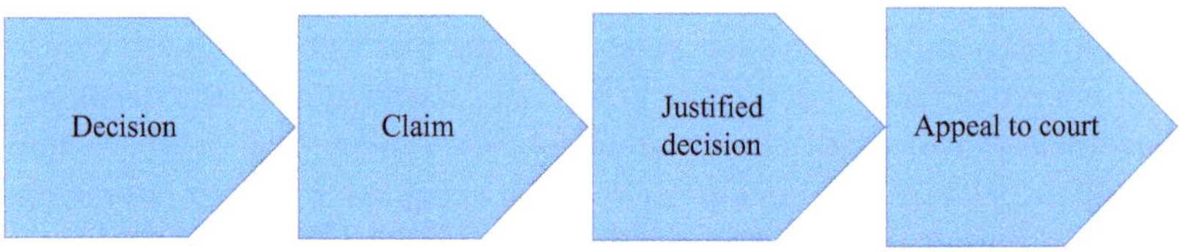

Chart 10: Dispute settlement in terms of the reasons presented by the public contracting authority.

It means that more specific supplier reasons and their legal basis will be established when bringing an action to court and initiating legal proceedings. The analysis offers sufficient evidence that there is a lack of communication between the supplier and the public contracting authority in public procurement procedures and it is caused by the legal regulation of pre-litigation procedures.

576 Lietuvos Respublikos civilinio proceso kodeksas. Žin., 2002, Nr. 36–1340.

The author believes the procedures would be more efficient and would provide better possibilities to settle disputes out of court, if the public contracting authority disclosed its true and legal basis for making a decision before the supplier has submitted a claim. This would reveal both, the content of a discretely adopted decision and the clarification of the legal rules followed by the public contracting authority. If the supplier rejects the explanation, it will allow the supplier to file a better-reasoned claim with more accurate factual and legal allegations. This would enable the dispute to be settled from an improved perspective before appealing to courts.

There are a few alternatives to solve this issue. The first is that each decision by the public contracting authority should be accompanied by extensive reasons. This solution, however, would generate an excessive bureaucratic burden in cases where no supplier has the intention to challenge the decision by the public contracting authority and all of them agree with it without a further explanation. To avoid conflicts with the general efficiency of procurement procedures, a more appealing solution would be to establish the right of the supplier who has a doubt regarding the public contracting authority's decision to receive an explanation of its reasons before filing a claim. This would allow the supplier to receive a detailed justification of the public contracting authority's decision in cases where he so wishes; and the public procurement procedure would not be overloaded with excessive tasks in situations where they are not required.

In addition, the proposed solution (the right to address the public contracting authority for a detailed explanation of the decision made) could be related (although for the desired objective it is not necessary) with time limits assigned for the supplier's claim to remedies, i.e. the claim could be filed only if, during a reasonable period of time (for example, 3 working days) after the public contracting authority's decision announcement, at least one supplier has exercised his right to receive to the reasons behind the public contracting authority's decision. The proposed solution is shown in the figure below.

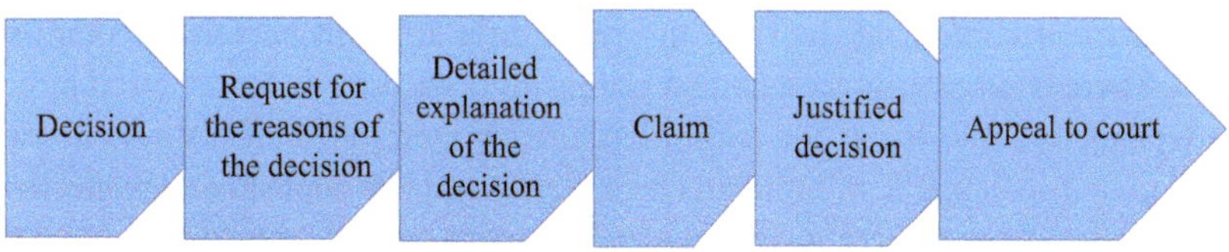

Chart 11: Proposed model for dispute settlement in terms of the reasons presented by the public contracting authority

7 Review of the decision by the same entity

The analysis of pre-litigation procedures as regulated by the Law on Public Procurement has revealed another complicated issue. Article 19 (1) stipulates that in order to carry out public procurement procedures the public contracting authority must set up a Procurement Commission (for low value procurement procedures or renewed supplier bidding under a preliminary contract setting up of such a commission is optional), which will be assigned certain tasks and given full competence to carry them out. A systematic analysis of the Law on Public Procurement shows that all provisions on public procedures and their enforcement refer to the public contracting authority as the entity in charge of purchasing through procurement procedures. Similarly, in pre-litigation procedures, which are an element of public procurement procedures, determined by specific circumstances (filing of a claim), the entity in charge of reviewing the claims is again the public contracting authority. Although the Law on Public Procurement does not include any provisions that would suggest a different commission should be in charge of examining claims in the course of public procurement, such distribution of rights and duties within an organisation is not prohibited but rather optional.

The Public Procurement Commission, in charge of procurement procedures from the start to the end, having made a decision will not be willing to change it solely on the basis of a claim received, unless the violation is accurately stated. Therefore, if the supplier is not able to identify specific violations (due to the lack of information as well as ambiguous legal regulation), the Public Procurement Commission will continue to stand by its decision. It should be noted that the claim receipt and review procedures are similar to an administrative complaint procedure as it is the public contracting authority that adopts a decision with legal consequences, however, in the case of an administrative complaint, Article 14 (4) of the Law on Public Administration prohibits forwarding of the complaint to the administrative entity, its unit or transferring it to the official, civil servant or employee whose actions have been reported.

Therefore, a similar principle could be implemented in the context of public procurement conferring the right to review on a different person or commission. There is no ground to state that claims must necessarily be reviewed by an independent authority, as the author has already mentioned such a system was in place in the Republic of Lithuania before 2002 and was abolished as ineffective and excessively bureaucratic. Perhaps in the current times of information society such a system would be efficient and its previous failure was the result of inadequate regulation and more limited possibilities to use information technology for a continuous, transparent and efficient settling of disputes in public procurement. Nevertheless, a more appealing approach in terms of bureaucracy and financial resources is to assign the review of supplier claims to other entities.

As pointed out by the author, a number of disputes arise from the discretion of the public contracting authority, established by the Law on Public Procurement and common in various procurement procedures. The right to choose, albeit within the limits set by law, is the result of an opinion on a particular factual situation and the legal regulation applicable to it. Therefore, an obligatory transfer of the public contracting authority's decision examination to a different entity than the one that has made it – a Public Procurement Commission – would improve the efficiency of pre-litigation procedures and increase the trust in the public contracting authority's decision. The supplier would know that the arguments laid down in the claim would be reviewed by an entity other than the decision-adopting commission and its members.

8 Conclusions and suggestions

In summary, it can be stated that the legislation of Lithuania adequately regulates the decision review system of the public contracting authority, which gives suppliers real possibilities to defend their infringed rights. However, the recent increase in the number of disputes brought before courts, which is believed to continue to grow largely due to the recent amendments in legal regulations of public procurement, should lead to the consideration of how to improve the benefits and efficiency of dispute settlement procedures. It is not the regulation of dispute settlement that causes the main issues, but its failure to settle a dispute still during the public procurement procedure, allowing parties to debate their positions by communicating through pre-litigation procedures and increasing suppliers' trust in the decisions of the public contracting authority. The regulation of pre-litigation procedures should help in ensuring the trust in the public contracting authority's decision. Bearing this in mind and in order to ensure a more thorough dispute settlement through pre-litigation procedures, the following changes in the Law on Public Procurement[577] are suggested:

1. Amendment of Article 19 so that it reads as follows:

   "Article 19. Public Procurement Commission, Claim Examination Commission, Experts, Observers.

577 Lietuvos Respublikos viešųjų pirkimų įstatymas. 1996, Nr. 84–2000; TAR, 2017–05–04, Nr. 2017–07550.

1. For the procurement procedures (except for the procurement procedures provided for in Article 103 of this Law) the public contracting authority must set up a Public Procurement Commission (hereinafter referred to as the Commission) (for low value procurement procedures or renewed supplier bidding under a preliminary contract setting up of such a commission is optional), assign its tasks and give it full competence to carry them out. If the public contracting authority contracts a different entity to take charge of the procurement procedures, these actions are performed by the latter. The Commission shall operate under the labour regulations approved by the public contracting authority that set it up, reporting only to it and only performing its written assignments and obligations.
2. To examine claims under Chapter 7 of this Law, the public contracting authority must set up a Claim Examination Commission, assign its tasks and give it full competence to successfully carry them out. The Claim Examination Commission shall be set up by order of the head of the public contracting authority, comprising of at least 3 natural persons – the Chairperson and two Members. Members of the Claim Examination Commission shall not be persons who at the time of the decision were acting as members of the Commission whose decision has been reported in the claim. Employees of a different authority than the one that has set up the Claim Examination Commission may also be appointed members of this Commission. The public contracting authority that has set up the Claim Examination Commission shall have the right to invite experts – specialists on the subject – to provide consultations on an issue that requires specific knowledge or evaluation.
3. The Commission shall be set up by order (decree) of the head of the public contracting authority, comprising at least 3 natural persons – the Chairperson and at least 2 Members of the Commission (hereinafter referred to as Commission Member(s)). Commission Members may not be employees of the public contracting authority that has set up the Commission. The public contracting authority that has set up the Commission shall have the right to invite experts – specialists on the subject – to provide consultations on an issue that requires specific knowledge or evaluation.
4. The Chairperson of the Commission shall be the Head of the public contracting authority or an employee of the public contracting authority or an affiliated public contracting authority as authorised by the Head of the public contracting authority. When appointing Members of the Commission or the Claim Examination Commission, it is necessary to

consider their economic, technical and legal expertise and the knowledge of this Law as well as other legislation on procurement regulation. Members of the Commission and Claim Examination Commission may only be persons of good repute. Meetings and decisions of the Commission are only legitimate when the meeting is attended by more than half of the Commission Members and all the Members if the Commission comprises 3 persons.

5. The public contracting authority that has set up the Commission may invite representatives of The Member State and municipal institutions to attend the meetings as observers (hereinafter referred to as the Observers) if they have an issued authorisation by the institution they represent.
6. The Commission shall operate from the moment it has been set up and assigned tasks until the decision to dissolve it or from the moment it has been assigned written tasks by the public contracting authority until the completion of all tasks assigned or until the decision to suspend the procurement procedures. The Claim Examination Commission shall operate from the moment it has been set up and assigned tasks until the decision to dissolve it or until the completion of all tasks assigned.
   The Commission and the Claim Examination Commission shall adopt decisions at the meetings by a simple majority vote, voting by open ballot. The only voting options allowed shall be "for" or "against" the proposed decision. In the event of a tie, the Chairperson of the Commission shall have a casting vote. The Commission and the Claim Examination Commission's decisions shall be recorded in the minutes. The minutes shall specify the reasons of the decision, give explanations and the separate opinion of each Member. The minutes shall be signed by all the Members present at the meeting.
7. Meetings of the Commission may take place through the means of the Central Public Procurement Information System.

2. Complement the Law with Article 101[1] which reads as follows:

Time limits for filing a claim with the public contracting authority, lodging an application or bringing an action to court.

1. Before filing a claim with the public contracting authority under Article 102 of this Law, the supplier has the right to request the public contracting authority to provide detailed reasons for its decision.
2. After a supplier has requested the public contracting authority to provide detailed reasons for its decision, the public contracting authority shall submit them to the respective supplier, the interested candidates and tenderers within 3 working days from the receipt of the inquiry.

3. For the purposes of the information referred to in Paragraph 2 of this Article, the public contracting authority shall disclose the legal basis of its decision, circumstances and reasons leading to it. In providing information, the public contracting authority shall ensure the protection of the information referred to in Article 20 of this Law.
4. The inquiry referred to in this Article and the public contracting authority's response to it, shall not affect the calculation of the time limits for filing a claim, specified in Article 102 of this Law."

VI Enforcement of the EU public procurement rules in German legislation

This chapter of the thesis is based on legal protection system in Germany. It will first examine how the legal protection options above and below the thresholds are designed and how the subjective rights are structured to protect the tenderers. The focus will be given to the fourth part of the GWB[578] – the standardised review procedure. Particular attention will be devoted to the relevant legal remedies below the thresholds whether the principles of equal treatment, and transparency could be also effectively enforced.

1 History

After many years of criticism of the German procurement rules and various proceedings before the Court of Justice, in which the Court held the Federal Republic of Germany to have failed[579] to implement the EU Procurement directives adequately, the Act Amending Procurement Law was adopted in 1998[580]. Until this Act entered into force as of January 1, 1999 and conferred individual rights on tenderers with respect to the application of procurement law, including the right to obtain interim measures and to have unlawful decisions set aside (the so-called primary legal protection), the only genuine remedy tenderers had in cases of infringement of procurement law was the possibility to obtain damages on the basis of the general rules and principles of German civil law. Thus, in Germany the development of the main principles governing the possibilities for tenderers to obtain damages with respect to unlawful procurement actions to a large extent took place before the procurement directives had been implemented properly and so to speak occurred outside the scope of EU procurement law.

The introduction of efficient primary legal protection for tenderers through the Act Amending Procurement Law, ensuring them actionable rights to interim measures in procurement procedures and having unlawful procurement decisions set aside, has reduced the importance of the possibility to claim

578 Act against Restrains on Competition (GWB), 2016.

579 Cases C-433/03, *Commission v Germany*, 1995, E.C.R. I-2303; C-253/95, *Commission v Germany* [1996] E.C.R. I-2423 and Case C-54/96, *Dorsch Consult* [1997] E.C.R. I-496.

580 *Gesetz zur Änderung der Rechtsgrundlagen für die Vergabe öffentlicher Aufträge* (Vergaberechtsänderungsgesetz – VgRÄG) vom 26. August 1998 BGB.

damages against a public contracting authority that has breached the procurement rules. The adoption of the Act Amending Procurement Law led to the implementation of the Act against restraints on competition (GWB)[581], which was recently updated in 2016. These provisions define review mechanism, which are in line with the European Directive 2007/66/EC.[582] The recent transposition of the rules led to the unified German Remedies system.

Nevertheless, claims for damages for infringement of procurement law will still be brought before the German courts and damages both as compensation of the costs of participating in the procurement procedure and of loss of profit can be awarded under certain circumstances. In the following discussion, various types of actions for damages that may be available to tenderers against the public contracting authority for the breach of procurement law are introduced. In this context, the conditions for the award of damages and the rules on the burden of proof are outlined, and the kind of damages that can be obtained is described. It should be noted that in all cases concerning claims for damages disregarding the legal basis on which they are brought, jurisdiction belongs to the ordinary civil courts, and not to the special review bodies, i.e. the Procurement Tribunals, that were introduced with the Act Amending Procurement Law to decide on the primary legal protection of tenderers. However, if a Public Procurement Tribunal or the Higher Regional Court has granted a valid decision on the question, whether an infringement of procurement law has taken place or not, the decision is binding on the court that is later dealing with the question of damages with respect to the same procurement action. The remedies system in Germany is divided into two stages: 1. the legal protection above the EU thresholds, 2. the legal protection below EU thresholds.

2 Remedies system above the thresholds

The German primary legal protection is established for public contracts only above the EU thresholds. The legal capacity of a tenderer depends essentially on whether, in the case of a procurement procedure, the contract value exceeds the

---

581 Act against Restraints on Competition (GWB) – Part 4, in the version of the Act on the Modernisation of Public Procurement Law [*Vergaberechtsmodernisierungsgesetz* - VergRModG] of 17 February 2015, Federal Law Gazette I of 23 February 2016, p. 203.

582 Directive 2007/66/EC of the European Parliament and of the Council of 11 December 2007 amending Council Directives 89/665/EEC and 92/13/EEC with regard to improving the effectiveness of review procedures concerning the award of public contracts.

EU thresholds or not. The primary legal protection means that it is possible to address the claim against the award decision and aims to get the contract or to prevent a competitor from getting it. This means that the tenderer is in a position to address a claim directly against the final award decision and seek the damages. The following section describes the German remedies system exceeding these thresholds[583]. The legal protection for contracts with values above the EU thresholds is regulated in § 155 GWB and is in accordance with § 135(2) GWB and limited to the time before the claim is awarded[584].

2.1 Obligation to submit a claim to the public contracting authority

According to the intentions of the legislator such obligation is required to prevent the initiation of unnecessary review procedures and tactical speculation with procurement errors to delay the awarding of contracts. The public contracting authority receives via the complaint the possibility to recognise a possible mistake and to correct it. § 160 (3) GWB contains admissibility requirements for review. The infringement of the rules only arise if the public contracting authority has already (at least supposedly) breached public procurement rules. The fact that the infringement of the procurement rules is foreseen in the future is not yet to be reprimanded[585]. It is questionable how to deal with a situation in which the receipt of the claim by the public contracting authority cannot be clarified with sufficient certainty. In accordance with the principles of material burden of proof in such cases the applicant has the burden of proof[586].

Given the tight deadlines according to§ 134 GWB, it is not yet the 10-day deadline for submitting the claim to the public contracting authority that is in the interest of effective primary legal protection, however if the deadline is missed it would lead to the inadmissibility of the review procedure. The public contracting authority reserves the right to remedy the situation during the ongoing review procedure. As a rule, the tenderer is therefore well advised to give the public contracting authority sufficient time to comment on a review procedure (and

583 See the paragraph 5.5 of this dissertation with regard to the question of when a contract value exceeds the EU threshold.

584 § 135 GWB, "the claim should be submitted within 30 calendar days after the public contracting authority informs the affected candidates and tenderers concerning the conclusion of the contract, but at the latest six months after conclusion of the contract. If the award notice is published din the OJEU than the claim should be submitted within 30 calendar days after the publication".

585 OLG Düsseldorf Beschluss vom 30.06.2011, VII-Verg 25/11.

586 Vergabekammer des Bundes vom 05.11.2012 - VK 3-120/12.

thus also to rethink its previous course of action and if necessary to reverse it), which are relevant to the question of "if" and "how" for the subsequent review procedure. On the other hand, the public contracting authorities do not so seldom take the opportunity to eliminate an infringement of public procurement rules or at least make clarifications that may already be of help to the signing contractor. However, there is no obligation on the public contracting authority to respond to a complaint. In order to comply with the obligation to object § 160 (3) GWB provisions, the tenderer, candidate or party concerned must, from an objective point of view, firstly, prove that an infringement of public procurement rules exist and, secondly, the complainant expects the public contracting authority to abolish the violation of the rules.[587]

Both elements are indispensable components of the complaint and whether a letter contains these two explanatory elements is to be determined by interpretation in accordance with § 133, 157 BGB[588]. If the tenderer declares objections without using legal assistance, this must be taken into account when interpreting the statement.[589]

2.2 First instance review

2.2.1 Competence of the Public Procurement Tribunal

The German system defines a two-stage process[590] for the judicial review. The public procurement tribunals are considered as the first instance judicial review body, which are established at State and federal levels[591]. The Federal Government has established the public procurement tribunals responsible for its territory at the Federal Cartel Office, while the Lands have designated the relevant public procurement tribunals in their territory.

587 Andreas Neun, Wolfram Krohn, Marc Gabriel, Handbuch Vergaberecht, Gesamtdarstellung und Kommentierung zu Vergaben nach GWB, VgV, SektVO, VSVgV, KonzVgV, VOB/A, UVgO, VOL/A, VO(EG) 1370, SGB V, AEUV, 2. Auflage 2017, p. 1243.

588 Das Bürgerliche Gesetzbuch (BGB), Auslegung von Willenserklärungen§ 133, 157 BGB, 2002.

589 OLG Düsseldorf Beschluss vom 07.12.2011, Verg 81/11.

590 Horn/Hofmann: Nachprüfungsverfahren, von Martin Burgi und Meinrad Dreher: Beck'scher Vergaberechtskommentar Band 1: Gesetz gegen Wettbewerbsbeschränkungen - GWB - 4. Teil, 3 Auflage 2017, p. 1297.

591 § 159 GWB of 23 February 2016.

The decisions of public procurement tribunals could be appealed at the higher regional courts, which are considered as the second instance of the review body.

The legal protection is granted only under certain circumstances[592]. The public procurement tribunals are responsible for the fulfilment of the provisions under § 97(6) GWB. According to § 155 GWB, all suppliers whose rights were breached are entitled to apply for a review of public procurement rules. Suppliers must state that they have been harmed by the alleged infringement of public procurement rules. Finally, there must also be a general interest in legal protection. The Federal Constitutional Court has confirmed that the public procurement tribunals grant access to the primary legal protection[593]. The public procurement tribunals have extensive powers.

According to § 158 GWB, the public procurement tribunals are administrative authorities and not courts. The decisions taken by the public procurement tribunals are in accordance with § 168 (3) GWB and are based on an administrative act. In that regard, the legislator has mixed classical elements of administrative law. This requires a careful determination of the applicable procedural law (VwVfG etc.)[594], but does not entail the intervention of administrative court as a consequence. According to § 171 GWB on the decision of the public procurement tribunal, the immediate appeal could be filed to the higher regional court and not to the administrative court for annulment or obligation for damage[595].

An application may be submitted by any undertaking that has an interest in the award of the contract, alleging infringement of its rights in the procurement procedure by failure to comply with public procurement rules and shows that the alleged breach has caused damage pursuant to § 160 (2) GWB. The infringement of public procurement rules may also consist of unlawful failure to tender for the award of a contract. Any person who has been prevented from submitting a tender by virtue of the alleged infringement may also submit applications.

In addition, compliance with the alleged condition is compulsory for a request for a review pursuant to § 160 (3) GWB. This is inadmissible in so far as the applicant has received a positive finding in the award procedure for the breach of public procurement rules and has not been informed by the public contracting

592 Andreas Neun, Wolfram Krohn, Marc Gabriel, Handbuch Vergaberecht, Gesamtdarstellung und Kommentierung zu Vergaben nach GWB, VgV, SektVO, VSVgV, KonzVgV, VOB/A, UVgO, VOL/A, VO(EG) 1370, SGB V, AEUV, 2. Auflage 2017, p. 1229.

593 BVerfG, Beschluss von 29.07.2004, Aktenzeichen:2 BvR 2248/03.

594 §§ 9, 49 Verwaltungsverfahrensgesetz (VwVfG), 23. Januar 2003.

595 Martin Burgi, Vergaberecht, 2018, p. 223.

authority within 10 days (§ 160(3) GWB). If the error declared is apparent in the contract notice or in the procurement documents, it must be submitted to the public contracting authority at the latest by the deadline specified in the contract notice or the public contracting authority's application.

An application for review shall also be inadmissible in so far as more than 15 calendar days have elapsed after receipt of the notification by the public contracting authority that a complaint is not intended to be withdrawn pursuant to § 160 (3) (4) GWB. If an applicant is forced to file an early complaint within 15 calendar days and decides quickly to submit an application for a review during the procurement procedure or during the procurement evaluation, the requirements for the submission of an application must be accordingly met. In this case the applicant cannot successfully argue that the violation of public procurement provisions infringes his rights because it is still completely uncertain whether the applicant will possibly be awarded the contract after the standstill period despite the continuation of the procedure[596]. The higher regional court of Düsseldorf has declared that "the intention of the legislature is to allow an applicant to lodge a claim for a review as soon as possible provided he proves reasonable grounds for admissibility and justification of an application, which could prove that the applicant is entitled to the contract award"[597].

The complaint may be made in writing. Once the complaint has been lodged, the tenderer may submit a written request for a review to the public procurement tribunal without further delay. The legal award of the contract is only triggered by the transmission of the request for a review in text form to the public contracting authority.

Unless the application is manifestly inadmissible or unfounded, the Public Procurement Tribunal informs the public contracting authority of the request for a review in text form. After having received the information from the public contracting authority, the latter must not award the contract prior to a decision of the Public Procurement Tribunal and the expiry of the time limit for filing the immediate complaint to the Higher Regional Court pursuant to § 169 (1) GWB.

---

596 Andreas Neun, Wolfram Krohn, Marc Gabriel, Handbuch Vergaberecht, Gesamtdarstellung und Kommentierung zu Vergaben nach GWB, VgV, SektVO, VSVgV, KonzVgV, VOB/A, UVgO, VOL/A, VO(EG) 1370, SGB V, AEUV, 2. Auflage 2017, p. 1246.

597 OLG Düsseldorf, Beschluss von 04.03.2010.

2.2.2 *Identification of facts and decision of Public Procurement Tribunal*

When submitting a request for a review to the public contracting authority, the Public Procurement Tribunal at the same time requests the procurement files. The public contracting authority makes reference to the business case. The Public Procurement Tribunal then determines the facts relevant to the decision. For this purpose, the Public Procurement Tribunal has extensive investigative powers and is fully independent and consists of three members pursuant to § 157 GWB[598]. The members of the Tribunal are appointed for the term of five years. It should be also pointed out that the members of the Public Procurement Tribunal are civil servants under the obligation to carry out official orders of their supervision and to follow general guidance and statutory provisions.[599]

The involved parties may, on request, inspect the files of Public Procurement Tribunals or send copies, extracts or copies thereof by post at their own costs. The Public Procurement Tribunal may refuse access to documents in so far as this is necessary for important reasons, in particular for the protection of commercial secrets pursuant to § 165 (2) GWB.[600]

In practice, however, the secrecy protection is extremely extended. The public contracting authorities may ask the tenderers to block off certain specific parts of the offer. In practice usually an entire offer could be blocked, as the bidders already have a confidentiality interest in the scope and prices. Thus, the inspection is limited to the documentation of the public contracting authority and general information about the offers of the respective bidders. The decisions of the Public Procurement Tribunal will in principle be taken after an oral hearing. However, they may be dispensed with if the application is inadmissible or manifestly unfounded or if all the parties concerned agree pursuant to § 166 GWB.

The Public Procurement Tribunal takes its decision on the request within a period of five weeks and States the reasons on which it is based. This period may exceptionally be extended by reasoned decision of the Chairman pursuant to § 167 (1) GWB.

The Public Procurement Tribunal decides whether the applicant is in breach of his rights and takes the appropriate measures to eliminate the infringement

598 Horn/Hofmann: Nachprüfungsverfahren, von Martin Burgi und Meinrad Dreher: Beck'scher Vergaberechtskommentar Band 1: Gesetz gegen Wettbewerbsbeschränkungen - GWB - 4. Teil, 3 Auflage 2017, p. 1350.

599 § 35 (3) BeamtStG, vom 17.06.2008.

600 OLG Düsseldorf, Beschluss von 12.01.2009.

and prevent damage to the interests concerned pursuant to § 168 (1) GWB. The applicant may decide to lodge an appeal to the Higher Regional Court.

2.3 Second instance review

An immediate appeal against the decision of the Public Procurement Tribunal is admissible pursuant to § 171 GWB. The parties submit the decision in writing within a period of two weeks from the date of notification of the decision to the appeal court referred to in the letter of appeal. A specific legal protection is to prevent from awarding a contract to the competitor.

The appeal has suspensive effect on the decision of the Public Procurement Tribunal for a period of two weeks after the expiry of the time limit for appeal. The appeal court may, at the request of the complainant, extend the suspensive effect until the decision on the appeal is taken, if the Public Procurement Tribunal has refused the application for review (§ 173 GWB).

If the court considers the complaint to be well-founded, it abrogates the decision of the Public Procurement Tribunal. It decides either on the substance of the case (as a rule) or obliges the Public Procurement Tribunal to take a new decision on the merits of the case, taking into account the interpretation of the case law.

If the unsuccessful applicants succeed in submitting applications for review on time, then the public contracting authority would be prohibited from awarding the contract pursuant to § 169 GWB, and the principle "pacta sunt servanda" would be imposed.[601] It is the most serious breach of public procurement provisions when the contract is awarded without applying the standstill period. The Remedies Directive 2007/66/EC[602] contains specific requirements, namely the standstill period under Article 2 and the duty of the Member States to ensure that these requirements are met.

In some cases the German law is not in conformity with the European case law. The Public Procurement Tribunal of Northern Bavaria[603] took the view that bidders are not entitled to challenge the decision by the public contracting authority to cancel an award procedure. Although the bidder expressly referred

601 Martin Burgi, Vergaberecht, 2018, p. 229.

602 Ibid and 92/13/EEC with regard to improving the effectiveness of review procedures concerning the award of public contracts.

603 Vergabekammer Nordbayern, Beschluss vom 28.10.2002 (ref. 320.VK-3194-33/02). http://www.regierung.mittelfranken.bayern.de/aufg_abt/abt2/Vergabe/33_02a.pdf (14.04.2018).

to case C-92/00[604], the Public Procurement Tribunal did not give a hearing and rejected the application because of alleged inadmissibility. The Public Procurement Tribunal held that the decision of the CJEU in case C-92/00 had to be transposed into national law first. Without such transposition, a cancellation could – according to the Public Procurement Tribunal – not be subject to review.

2.4 Contracts that have already been concluded

According to § 169 (3) GWB the Public Procurement Tribunal upon specific application can also intervene in the procurement procedure if any rights of the applicant are jeopardised under § 97 (6) GWB. The wording "intervention in the procurement procedure" is to be understood as non-technical. Finding a contract ineffective, according to § 135 (2) GWB, would need to be proved. The claimant is entitled to claim for damages if he succeeds. If the Public Procurement Tribunal in the decision under § 169 (3) GWB expresses its views that the main outcome of the claim depends entirely on the applicant, the claimant may therefore no longer put greater importance to the additional provisional measures because he must reckon with claims for damages pursuant to § 180 (3) GWB.

2.5 Preliminary ruling procedure pursuant to Article 267 TFEU

According to Article 267 TFEU national courts can initiate a procedure for a preliminary ruling if there is a question of relevance with regard to the interpretation or validity of European law and if there is no judicial remedy under national law.

National judges decide on how a specific rule of European law is to be interpreted. It is then the task of the judge at the national level to apply the interpretation of European law as rendered by the CJEU to the specific case and, if necessary, to "correctly" construe the national rule in accordance with the interpretation provided by the CJEU[605].

Unlike the Public Procurement Tribunals, the Higher Regional Courts in accordance with Article 267 (3) TFEU have the duty to submit it to the CJEU,

---

604 Case C-92/00, *Hospital Ingenieure Krankenhaustechnik Planungs-Gesellschaft mbH (HI) v Stadt Wien*, 2002, ECR I-05553.

605 Wiebke Dettmers, The preliminary ruling procedure pursuant to Article 267 TFEU, http://www.ejtn.eu/Documents/About%20EJTN/Administrative%20Law%202016/AD201605%20Preliminary%20Ruling%20ERA%2019-20%20Sept/DETTMERS_The_Preliminary_Ruling_Procedure_2016.pdf (14.04.2018).

because the decision of the Higher Regional Court in the specific case can no longer be challenged with domestic remedies.

2.6 Secondary legal protection

For awards below and above the thresholds, there is the so-called secondary legal protection in addition to a prohibition of the award contracts, which deals with damages. In any case, before the ordinary courts up to the Federal Court of Justice, this legal protection also has a much greater significance than the primary one. This certainly applies without restriction to claims for damages by tenderers. On the other hand, there is hardly any case law on possible claims for damages from public procurement authorities. In particular, the case law of the Federal Court of Justice on the consequences of a delay in subsequent review procedures has significantly increased the importance of possible claims for compensation against unsuccessful claimants.

2.7 Civil claims

Where claims for damages are made in respect of an infringement of public procurement law before the ordinary courts, they are bound by final decisions taken by the Public Procurement Tribunals and the Higher Regional Courts on the award procedure in question pursuant to § 179(1) GWB.

Companies that abuse the means of redress need to claim damages from the opposing party and other parties concerned under § 180 GWB. In particular:

(1) obtain the suspension or further suspension of the award procedure by means of false information which has been provided deliberately or as a result of serious negligence,
(2) request the review with a view to obstructing the procurement process or causing damage to competitors, or
(3) make an application with the intention of later withdrawing against money or other benefits.

2.8 Costs

For official acts of the Public Procurement Board, costs (fees and expenses) are collected to cover the administrative burden. As a general rule, the fee should be no less than EUR 2,500 and should not exceed EUR 50,000. The costs of the procedure must be borne in principle by the party (s) subject to the procedure (§ 182(3) GWB). A fee is payable for review procedures. The minimum fee is

EUR 2,500. If an application is submitted, an advance payment of that amount is paid, if and in so far as the application is successful.

2.9 Statistics of the review procedures

Currently, there are 21 Public Procurement Tribunals and 16 Higher Regional Courts established in Germany[606]. The Federal Ministry of Economics in Germany publishes annually the statistics on the figures and results of the review procedures received and completed[607]. The results below are provided for the year 2016[608].

Public Procurement Tribunals completed 880 procedures, which corresponds exactly to the number of applications received. The number of applications has slightly increased compared to the year 2015 (864 applications). In 61.5 % of the cases, the applications were withdrawn or the decisions were made in favour of the procurement authority, which is slightly above the average. Applicants were successful in 15.9 % of the procedures. The number of extensions of the decision deadline reaches a new number of 57.5 %. However, this is mainly due to the fact that the Public Procurement Tribunal of Rheinland has extended the decision-making period 200 times for 60 proceedings. In terms of the number of undelivered decisions, the Public Procurement Tribunal of Berlin is back in the lead with 13 decisions out of a total 42 applications.

The Higher Regional Courts received 180 applications of which 154 were successfully completed[609]. Applicants were successful in 21.4 % of the procedures, whereas 37.7 % of cases were rejected and the rest were withdrawn. Germany is a leading European country in terms of court proceedings due to the remarkable quality of lawyers, for example in the United Kingdom (as of 2009) only 20 proceedings were initiated during the year.[610] The reasons for such an unequal distribution of the legal protection requests at a substantially identical legal framework

---

606 http://www.vergabe.de/nachpruefungsinstanzen/ (04.04.2018).

607 Statistische Meldungen über Vergabenachprüfungsverfahren gem. § 129a GWB, The annual report for 2016 could be looked under https://www.bmwi.de/Redaktion/DE/Downloads/G/gesamtuebersicht-vergabekammern.pdf?__blob=publicationFile&v=11 (04.04.2018).

608 http://www.forum-vergabe.de/news-detail/statistiken-der-nachpruefungsverfahren-2016-veroeffentlicht-6806/ (04.04.2018).

609 http://www.forum-vergabe.de/fileadmin/user_upload/Downloads/2016_OLG_Statistiken_Nachpruefungsverfahren.pdf (04.04.2018).

610 The Higher Court and the Sheriff Court, see Martin Trybus, Enforcement of the EU Public Procurement Rules, 2011, p. 201.

at the material and procedural level can only be speculated. Obviously, the willingness to act against a procurement authority and market competitors is more pronounced in Germany than in other legal cultures where the motto "Do not bite the hand that feeds you" is more widespread.[611]

2.10 Enforcement of decisions

Judgements made by the Public Procurement Tribunals are enforceable according to § 168(3) GWB. Appropriate means for penalties are defined in § 9 (1) VwVG. The penalties are defined up to a frame of magnitude given the volume of claims in hand. Pursuant to § 11 (3) VwVG penalty payments of up to EUR 25,000 could be imposed. Thereafter, Public Procurement Tribunals can also enforce further interim measures it has taken on behalf of the Federal Government and the States the measures pursuant to § 86a (2) GWB also apply accordingly.

The enforcement of judgements of the Higher Tribunal Courts is stipulated in § 178 GWB and takes place according to the regulations of the ZPO[612]. According to § § 704 –888 ZPO, the penalty payments of up to EUR 25,000 could be imposed. This can also be carried out several times, if necessary.

3 Public procurement protection below the thresholds

The largest number of procurement procedures in Germany does not exceed the EU thresholds. As many as 90 % of all public procurement procedures in Germany are awarded below the EU thresholds. These funds must be used as effectively as possible with low procedural costs and the most economical results possible. At present, there are many controversial discussions as to whether effective legal protection is guaranteed below the EU thresholds.

Also, in the course of the introduction of the UVgO no review procedure was provided. Only occasionally have federal States introduced a legal protection procedure for national contracts with certain order values (for example, Saxony, Thuringia).

Unless public contracts reach the relevant EU thresholds, the fourth part of the GWB is inapplicable. This also implies the inapplicability of the provisions on the review procedure pursuant to § 160 GWB, which ensures an effective primary legal protection of the bidder for the lower thresholds. However, the effective legal protection before the Public Procurement Tribunals is only available

---

611 Zivilprozessordnung (ZPO), 2005.

612 § § 704 –888 ZPO.

to tenderers in proceedings above the EU thresholds. In the case of errors in the tendering procedure above and below the thresholds, disadvantaged bidders have so far always been referred to the claim for damages in secondary legal protection, which is difficult to enforce and to prove. This gap in primary legal protection in public procurement has diverse discussions among experts.

According to the VgV a legislator does not want to guarantee a primary protection of bidding rights in procurement procedures below the thresholds[613]. Following the decision of the Federal Constitutional Court of 2006[614] it is widely recognised in the literature and jurisprudence today that primary legal protection below the thresholds must be granted.

Due to lack of clear legislative requirements, however, it is still controversial, which rights under the general legal protection are covered. Namely, how to enforce these rights and which jurisdiction is competent for such procedures. These questions have been the subject of scientific arguments and regularly lead to inconsistent and unforeseeable answers for bidders.

3.1 Administrative law

The opinion in the literature is that the award of the contract consists of a two-step approach[615]. The procedure until the award of the contract is then considered as an independent procedure; it is the consideration of the award of the contract and thus the following one is the signature of the contract. Only after the contract award decision the private law is considered. In this constellation, the two-step theory applies to public-law contract and private-law contract.[616]

First of all, the question arises as to when a public dispute within the meaning of the § 40 (1) (1) VwGO[617] is present. The classification of a dispute as public law is in principle, by virtue of the nature, based on the legal relationship. If this legal relationship – on the basis of an overall assessment of all the standards to be taken into account in the context of the claim and thus the litigation – is considered to be public, the resulting dispute is public law and this is to be decided by

613 OLG Saarbrücken, Beschluss vom 29.04.2003; OLG Brandenburg, Beschluss vom 17.12.2007; OLG Düsseldorf, Beschluss vom 15.10.2008; OLG Stuttgart, Beschluss vom 11.04.2002.

614 BVerfG, Beschluss vom 13.06.2006.

615 BVerwG, Beschluss vom 02.05.2007.

616 Martin Burgi, Vergaberecht, 2018, p. 235; Martin Burgi, NVwZ 2007, 737 (737 ff.).

617 Kopp/Schenke, VwGO, Verwaltungsgerichtsordnung Kommentar, 16 Auflage, 2009, p. 133.

the administrative courts[618]. The classification as a public-law or private-law is discussed in various theories. The Subordination theory defines that the nature of the provisions of public law is established through a subordinate relationship between State and its citizens. According to the theory of special law, a provision of public law is considered, if at least one party exclusively carries a public interest[619].

The public law remedy in accordance with § 40 paragraph (1) (1) VwGO is only applied if a public law dispute of non-constitutional nature is given. This can only be determined by the nature of the legal relationship from which the claim is derived.

Basically, one can assume that the action of the state is immediate or indirectly always serves the interest in the performance of public duties[620]. For a public interest as an administrative purpose States in addition, the provisions of § 6 (1) HGrG[621] and § 55 BHO[622] set the objectives of economical procurement.

As a result, even with a consistent separation between procurement arrangements and contractual arrangements it cannot be clearly assigned to the public law. Thus, even if the public-law nature of the award procedure is recognised, the procedure is influenced by private law elements.[623]

3.2 Civil law

It is disputed whether the procurement protection in Germany before the civil or administrative courts can be requested. A widespread and, in particular, historically developed view[624] is that the award of public contracts belongs to the private law. The tenderer's bid is an acceptance, which leads directly to the conclusion of the contract[625], which is characterised under the private law.

In addition, the Federal Administrative Court confirmed, by the judgement of 2007[626], that below-threshold procurement law disputes should be handled

618 Sodan/Ziekow, Verwaltungsgerichtsordnung, 5 Auflage, 2018, Rn. 266.

619 Rennert, in Eyermann, Verwaltungsgerichtsordnung, 14 Auflage, 2014, Rn. 49.

620 Carsten Hormann, VergabeR 2007, Heft 4, p. 431.

621 Gesetz über die Grundsätze des Haushaltsrechts des Bundes und der Länder (Haushaltsgrundsätzegesetz - HGrG), 1969.

622 Bundeshaushaltsordnung (BHO), 1969.

623 Carsten Hormann, VergabeR 2007, Heft 4, S. 433.

624 BVerwG, Beschluss vom 08.03.1962, VIII C 160/60; BVerwG, Beschluss vom 13.03.1970.

625 OLG Naumburg, Beschluss vom 23.12.2004.

626 BVerwG, Beschluss vom 02.05.2007.

through the ordinary proceedings. In the court view, the award of public service contracts belongs to the private law, in the same way as the procurement procedure prior to the conclusion of the contract, which is also a private law relationship, or awarding the contract to one of the tenderers as a matter of routine. Public procurement must be regarded as a single transaction that belongs to private law as a whole.[627]

In the literature, this development was welcomed as "the end of legal confusion"[628] and probably contributed to a certain simplification of the complex legal protection system below the thresholds. However, so far there has been no uniform line to the scope and range of legal protection within the ordinary jurisdiction and the case law remains inconsistent. Moreover, the affirmation of the civil procedure is very difficult for tenderers to enforce their rights.

The Munich Regional Administrative Court has also outlined the possibility of primary legal protection even in procurement procedures below the thresholds in a judgement of 18.04.2012.[629] The court saw the need to review procurement procedures and to prohibit the award. The court justified by stating that, according to Article 3 GG[630], even in the award procedure below the EU thresholds an effective protection of the bidder had to be guaranteed.

This should not apply to every decision, but at least in the cases were the principle of equal treatment is breached. This is the case when the public contracting authority deviates from an earlier practice without a substantive reason. If such a serious mistake has been made by the public contracting authority, the tenderer should have the possibility to stop the award and have it judicially reviewed. The tenderer is not entitled to submit the claim to the Public Procurement Tribunals, as they are only competent for procedures above the EU thresholds, so that in such cases a legal claim will be brought before the civil courts. In accordance with §§ 935 ff. ZPO[631], the court must then make a decision as to what extent the legal protection of the tenderer is to be applied. In the event of a manifest error

627 BVerwGE 129, 9, 13 f.; VG Leipzig, Beschluss vom 06.09.2005.

628 Wolfram Krohn, NZBau 2007, S. 493.

629 LG München I, Beschluss vom 18.04.12, 11 O 7897/12.

630 It follows from Article 3 of the Basic Law, that below-threshold procurement, effective protection of the tenderer must be ensured. Tenderers must be protected in any event, before the procedural errors under the principle of equal treatment, Grundgesetz für die Bundesrepublik Deutschland, 1976.

631 Thomas/Putzo, Zivilprozessordnung, 31 Auflage, 2010, S. 1275.

of the public contracting authority, such a procedural error must be given such weight that it can no longer be accepted under the rule of equal treatment[632].

It is to be welcomed that, finally, in terms of primary legal protection, opportunities below the thresholds are also opened up. So far, there has been little hope for unsuccessful bidders, and now, in the case of obvious mistakes, the award can be suspended. Thereafter, the public contracting authority must always ensure the application of free movement of goods and services, the principle of equal treatment, non-discrimination and transparency. Even in the case of procurement procedures below the EU thresholds, an effective primary legal protection must be granted.

In order to assess the primary legal protection below the EU thresholds, an overview of the possibilities of legal protection before the civil courts is outlined below.

3.3 Jurisdiction of ordinary courts

For a long time, it was disputed whether the review of award decisions for low value contracts was an administrative or civil dispute. In 2007, the Federal Administrative Court decided and opened legal channels to the ordinary courts. The ordinary courts are responsible for the infringements of the procurement rule below the EU thresholds. However, unlike above the EU thresholds according to § 169 (1) GWB, there is no prohibition on the award of a contract. Thus, despite a pending action, it would be possible for the public contracting authority to effectively award the contract and thereby undermine the legal protection of the tenderer. Moreover, for below the thresholds there is also no possibility to determine that an already awarded contract is ineffective.

§ 97 (7) GWB gives the tenderer a subjective right to comply with the rules of the award procedure. The primary legal protection would not be enforced if the tenderer learned about the award of the contract after it has been awarded and for what reasons he has not been awarded the contract. An unsuccessful tenderer would in this respect only depend on the claims for damages before the ordinary courts; such legal remedies in the public domain of procurement is incompatible with the guarantee of effective legal protection under Article 19 (4) GG[633].

In contrary, there are no similar provisions for a standstill according to § 134 GWB below the EU thresholds. The public contracting authorities are neither

---

632 Prieß/Hausmann/Kulartz, Beck'sches Formularbuch Vergaberecht, 3. Auflage, 2018, p. 536.

633 VK Bund, Beschluss vom 29.04.1999.

legally bound to provide notifications for the unsuccessful tenderers nor they are required to give reasons for the refusal decision. Unsuccessful applicants learn about the decision usually only after the contract is awarded to the competing supplier and, therefore are – in the words of the Federal Constitutional Court – de facto excluded from primary rights protection[634].

In contradiction to this, the right to effective and equal judicial protection of primary rights – regardless of the achievement of certain thresholds – defines several legal systems. On the one hand, the EU law defines general principles of law, which are common to all Member States. On the other hand, since the Treaty of Lisbon, the right to effective legal protection has become legally binding pursuant to Article 47 (1) of the Charter of Fundamental Rights of the European Union[635].

The same provisions follow according to Article 6 (1) within the scope of the European Convention on Human Rights[636], which stipulate the right to a fair trial comprehensive review and compensation for alleged violations of fundamental rights. Within the framework of the German constitution, the right to effective protection derives from Article 19 (4) GG. The effective legal protection concept in these regulations implies that the public contracting authority is obliged also for below the thresholds to inform unsuccessful bidders before the award of the contract about the reasons for not eliminating them from the procurement process. Therefore, there must be a possibility to prevent the award of the contract.

3.4 Interim legal protection

In terms of below the EU thresholds, there is no legal safeguard mechanism for the procurement procedures, which guarantees the suspensive effect on the award of the contract. If the application is dismissed by the court of first instance, it has an effect until the appellate court has decided on it. Although tenderers seeking protection may apply for the adoption of a preliminary injunction award decision, the court will usually decide on this only after the oral hearing according to § 937 (2) ZPO and taking into consideration the examination of the chances of success[637].

In the context of interim legal protection, this requires the submission of application in accordance with §§ 935, 940 ZPO. By means of the regulation

634 BVerfG, Beschluss vom 13.06.2006.
635 Charter of Fundamental Rights of the European Union, 30.3.2010.
636 The European Convention on Human Rights, 1950.
637 Hans-Joachim Musielak, Kommentar zur Zivilprozessordnung, 2013, §§ 935, Rn 5.

order according to § 940 ZPO, the public contracting authority shall be prohibited from awarding the contract. When applying for a restraining order, the bidder must make a claim, which is based on the omission of the award by the public contracting authority because of a procurement law infringement in accordance with §§ 920 (2) 936 ZPO.

The ordinary courts essentially apply the provisions for the right of disposition of the pre-contractual obligation between the bidder and the public contracting authority in accordance with §§ 241 (2), 311 (2) BGB[638]. Whether the ground for complaint exists depends on whether the court assesses the tenderer's interest higher than that of the public contracting authority[639].

The reasons for the right to complain are defined in § 294 (1) ZPO. A prima facie evidence means that the tenderer has only to provide a lesser degree of probability than proof in the main proceedings for the facts giving rise to the claim. If the bidder is able to convince the court, the court may issue the preliminary decision without consulting the public contracting authority beforehand.

The public contracting authority then only has the opportunity to raise objections and to reach a judicial review at a hearing. Until then, however, several days or weeks may pass in which the public contracting authority is prevented from awarding the contract.

3.5 Submission of a protective letter

If the public contracting authority expects to receive an interim injunction from the tenderer on the grounds of complaints or comments made during the award procedure, it can prevent this by filing a protective letter with the competent court. A protective letter is a non-statutory but generally accepted preventative defence against anticipated requests for arrest and injunction.

In the protective letter, the public contracting authority can present the facts from their point of view. With the protective document submitted, there is a possibility that the injunction will not be issued or will be issued with a hearing by the court.

The competent court for issuing the injunction is the court of the main action. If the order value is over €5,000, the jurisdiction of the district court is given. Exceptionally, in urgent cases, the locally competent district court may issue an injunction.

---

638 Wolfgang Krüger, Münchener Kommentar zum Bürgerlichen Gesetzbuch: BGB Band 2, 7 Auflage, 2015, §§ 241.

639 OLG Düsseldorf, Beschluss vom 13.01.2010.

3.6 Disadvantages of legal protection below the thresholds

In the case of the so-called secondary legal protection, the applicant or bidder who has been unlawfully treated from his point of view could obtain damages from the public contracting authority after the award of the contract. These procedures for claims for damages are handled under the civil law. In practice, these actions for damages have a very important significance. The primary legal protection will almost always take place in proceedings for interim relief and has the aim of prohibiting the public contracting authority from awarding the contract. The possibility of forcing the public contracting authority to refuse to award the contract by means of a normal action has one major disadvantage: the public contracting authority is not hindered by the award of such contract. The civil courts are responsible for such proceedings with regard to a regular procurement process in the form of a private law contracts[640].

In addition to these, the below-threshold legal protection procedure, compared to the procedure under Part 4 of the GWB, also has additional disadvantages, which are discussed below. The unsuccessful bidders in the proceedings below the thresholds receive no message from the public contracting authority that they wish to receive the contract from. However, once the contract has been awarded, it is generally effective and cannot be reversed. It is uncertain when the public contracting authority will award the contract and whether any legal protection is possible at all. In the first instance, the district and regional courts are responsible for the claims, and usually they have no experience in law. For the second instance the Land and Higher Regional Courts are responsible. The application for an interim injunction does not lead to an automatic suspension of the contract award. This gives the public contracting authority a possibility to award the contract in any case.

In the upper threshold area, the public contracting authority is prevented from awarding the contract from the moment on which the Public Procurement Tribunal informs the public contracting authority of a review procedure, § 169 (1) GWB. This protection does not exist in the below the thresholds area.

There are no legally defined deadlines for the court decisions. While applications for a temporary injunction are always given priority, they may well be at the expense of appropriate consideration of the legal problem.

The applicant has no opportunity to also inspect the underlying procurement records. The applicant has no right to access the files either – at least not

640 Mark von Wietersheim, Vergaberecht, 2 Auflage, 2017, S. 148.

according to the ZPO. The legal basis for a prohibition of the contract award largely is found in § 1004 (1), § 311 (2), 823 (2) BGB.

3.7 Damages under § 181 GWB

The damages could be applicable once the contract has been awarded.[641] The secondary legal protection provides the possibility to claim damages below and above the thresholds before the civil courts. This protection for tenderers applies without restriction for claims for damages. According to § 181 (1) GWB the tenderers can claim compensation from a public contracting authority for the costs of preparing the tender or for participating in the procurement procedure. If the public contracting authority has infringed a provision intended to protect the candidates or tenderers and if –without this infringement –the undertaking would have had a real chance of being awarded the contract, which was, however, adversely affected by the infringement[642], The applicant has to prove that an infringement of a procurement law has taken place and would have had a real chance of being awarded the contract. The procurement law infringement must have affected adversely the chances of the undertaking being awarded the contract.

There must be a condition that the undertaking seeking damages had a "real chance" of being awarded the contract. This implies that only such undertakings, whose bids did not have to be excluded from the competition for formal reasons or because of an exorbitantly low price, who fulfil the qualitative selection criteria and whose bids, when applying the evaluation criteria, could have been considered for the award of the contract, i.e. were in the top ranking of the bidders, can be considered to have had a real chance of being awarded the contract.[643]

The damages that can be obtained are limited to the costs of participating in the procurement procedure, including the bidder's cost in connection with the preparation of the tender. Thus, under this provision it is not possible to obtain compensation for loss of profit[644]. In most cases bidders are unlikely to initiate a

---

641 Steen Treumer, Enforcement of the EU public procurement rules; Marin Burgi, A report about the German Remedies System, 2011, p. 141.

642 Martin Burgi, Vergaberecht, 2018, p. 238.

643 OLG Düsseldorf, Beschluss vom 30. Januar 2003.

644 Andreas Neun, Wolfram Krohn, Marc Gabriel, Handbuch Vergaberecht, Gesamtdarstellung und Kommentierung zu Vergaben nach GWB, VgV, SektVO, VSVgV, KonzVgV, VOB/A, UVgO, VOL/A, VO(EG) 1370, SGB V, AEUV, 2. Auflage 2017, p. 1174.

long and time consuming court case against a public contracting authority that may be awarding other interesting contracts in the future, knowing in advance that, even if they are successful, the damages obtainable are limited to these costs. Therefore, it is likely that § 181 GWB will be reduced to being an alternative, secondary legal basis for claims for damages under the general provisions of German civil law.

3.8 Damages under other provisions

§ 181 GWB explicitly States that it does not affect bidders' possibilities to bring actions for damages on other legal grounds. This pre-existing case law is largely based on the initially uncodified principle of culpa in contrahendo governing the liability of potential business partners for culpable breaches of pre-contractual duties of care, which are defined in § 311(2) BGB[645]. According to this case law, relations of trust between the public contracting authority on one side and the candidates and tenderers on the other side, equivalent to those relations that are created through the conclusion of a contract, can in certain cases come into existence in connection with a procurement procedure. When such relations have come into existence, the public contracting authority and the tenderers have duties of care toward each other that, if they are breached wilfully or negligently, can give rise to a claim for damages from the other party.[646]

When a public contracting authority initiates a procurement procedure, it gives the tenderers of the procurement the reason to trust that it is going to comply with the relevant procurement provisions. Therefore, in general, it is the duty of the public contracting authority to ensure that there is no infringement. A claim for damages under § 311(2) BGB only exists when the public contracting authority has breached the procurement provisions negligently[647].

In general, the damages that can be claimed under § 311(2) BGB include only the costs incurred by a candidate or tenderer in connection with his participation in the procurement action[648]. Consequently, the damages obtainable under

---

645 § 311(2) BGB and §§ 241(2), 280(1) BGB.

646 Hanna Schebesta, Towards an EU Law of Damages: Damages claims for violations of EU public procurement law before national and European judges, 2013, P. 130.

647 Sophie Harms, Unionsrechliche Vorgaben für den Rechtschutz im Vergabeverfahren unterhalb der EU-Schwellenwerte, 2013, S. 89.

648 Julia Anna Martlreiter, Europäisierung des vergaberechtlichen Primärrechtsschutzes bei Unterschwellenaufträgen, Europarechtliche Einflüsse und Anforderungen, Verfassungsmäßigkeit, Rechtsschutzmöglichkeiten, 2011, S. 193.

§ 311(2) BGB normally correspond to the damages candidates and tenderers can claim under § 181 GWB. In this connection it should be noted that in the context of § 311(2) BGB it has been held that also the costs of legal advice in connection with the participation to the procurement procedure are refundable[649].

Usually it is not possible to claim the loss of profit. According to the case law of the Federal Supreme Court the only possibility to obtain compensation for lost profit under § 311(2) BGB is if the bidder can prove not only that he submitted the best bid but also that another undertaking was in fact awarded a contract for works, supplies or services identical to the contract for which he had submitted a tender[650].

Thus, the compensation for lost profit under § 311(2) BGB has only been awarded in very few published cases[651]. The bidder has to prove the amount of his loss. The bidder appears to have a good chance of proving that his bid was the most acceptable, if he has offered the lowest price. At least the lowest price rightly is accepted as proof that the tender was the most acceptable, when the offers were otherwise to be considered to be equal.

3.9 Conclusions

If the contract value is below the EU thresholds, bidders seeking legal protection are generally excluded from primary protection under the German public procurement rules. The public contracting authority does not provide prior information to the unsuccessful tenders. Only in exceptional cases, the bidders learn in good time of the intended award from a competitor and have the opportunity to enforce their rights guaranteed in court. In order to achieve a better regulation of the legal protection of bidders, a reform has to be implemented.

The abolition of the current fragmentation of legislation is required, as well as the reduction of secondary legislation, better compliance with procurement rules by public contracting authorities, and compliance with national and European requirements for an effective protection of constitutionally secured legal provisions. The reform mandate to the legislator is not limited to the legal position, as is often demanded outside the scope of the public procurement directives. Instead, the legislator is required to reform German public procurement law in its entirety. Law would need to be codified.

649 Martin Burgi, Vergaberecht, 2018, p. 239.

650 BGH, Beschluss vom 16.12.2003.

651 OLG Düsseldorf, Beschluss vom 31.01.2001.

The possibility of such review would incur additional staff and cost burdens on local authorities which, especially in view of the financial situation of the municipalities, is not sustainable[652]. The public contracting authorities are resistant in terms of a new reform below the EU thresholds. However, whether the alleged doubts about the necessity, the practicability and the consequences of a reform of public procurement law are indeed justified and also how the Lithuanian remedies system is established in comparison to Germany will be highlighted in the next chapter.

652 Bundesvereinigung der kommunalen Spitzenverbände, www.oeffentliche-auftraege.de (01.05.2018).

VII Advantages and disadvantages of remedies systems in Lithuania and Germany

1 Pre-litigation proceedings

When comparing the systems of pre-litigation proceedings of the Federal Republic of Germany and the Republic of Lithuania, institutional differences of pre-litigation proceedings should be emphasised. The Republic of Lithuania, unlike the Federal Republic of Germany, which has a compulsory pre-litigation stage in Tribunals before judicial proceedings, does not have a mandatory institution of pre-litigation dispute examination. In the Republic of Lithuania, the pre-litigation stage only covers addressing the public contracting authority with a claim on the decisions it has taken.

Article 160 (3) (1–3) GWB also provides for that appeals submitted to the Tribunal by the supplier are not dealt with unless the claim is filed to the public contracting authority first. This clause is analogous to Article 101(3) of the Law on Public Procurement of the Republic of Lithuania[653], which provides for that if the supplier wants to challenge the decisions or actions of the public contracting authority before a court prior to the award of the purchase contract or framework contract, the supplier has to file a written complaint to the public contracting authority first (by fax, electronic means, registered post or another appropriate carrier). Taking this aspect into account it should be noted that the law of the Republic of Lithuania focuses more on pre-litigation proceedings that involve the supplier addressing the public contracting authority than the law of the Federal Republic of Germany, however, as mentioned above, the Republic of Lithuania does not have a separate institution which would have an independent competence of dealing with such pre-litigation proceedings.

The Law on Public Procurement of the Federal Republic of Germany does not specify the scope of the obligation of the public contracting authority to deal with a complaint, therefore, a presumption can be made that the public contracting authority reviews its procedural decisions in a superficial manner. Meanwhile, Article 103(3) of the Law on Public Procurement of the Republic of Lithuania[654] defines not only the scope of examining the claim, but also the publicity. It states that the public contracting authority must examine the claim

653 Lietuvos Respublikos viešųjų pirkimų įstatymas Žin, 1996, Nr. 84–2000.
654 Ibid.

and take a justified decision, notify the supplier who has filed the claim as well as other candidates and participants concerned in writing about the taken decision, and about the changes in time limits of procurement procedure that were announced earlier within no more than 6 working days of the receipt of the claim. The first aspect to be emphasised is that the public contracting authority must provide a motivated reply to the supplier, i.e. the public contracting authority has to both review the legitimacy of the decision made and explain legal and procedural reasons of such a decision to the supplier. Another aspect is that the information about examining the claim is provided not only to the supplier who has filed the claim, but also to other concerned participants of a certain tender; it helps to ensure the publicity of the review of decisions taken by the public contracting authority.

This difference highlights the importance of pre-litigation proceedings in the Republic of Lithuania when the dispute is settled by the participants of legal relationships themselves. The third aspect to be noted is that certain provisions of legal acts provide for an obvious obligation for the public contracting authority to examine the claim. Therefore, the system of pre-litigation proceedings in the Republic of Lithuania is structured in such a way that the supplier who has filed the claim and the public contracting authority settle the dispute among themselves in detail as early as in the pre-litigation litigation stage.

The pre-litigation proceedings in the Republic of Lithuania mainly involve the public contracting authority and the tender participants or the candidates concerned, however, the Republic of Lithuania also has an institution whose function is monitoring and supervision of public procurement, namely, the Public Procurement Office. Its competence does not cover issues of examining the disputes between suppliers and public contracting authorities, therefore, it is not to be considered a mandatory pre-litigation appeal institution. It is important to note that pursuant to Article 95 (2)(1) of the Law on Public Procurement[655], in terms of inspection, Public Procurement Office is entitled to select the subject of procurement, as well as the manner, the scope and the time of inspection at its own discretion. Therefore, in certain cases, once the supplier files a claim regarding the decisions made by the public contracting authority to Public Procurement Office, it can take the initiative and carry out the inspection of a certain public tender based on suspicions about possible violations of public

655 Lietuvos Respublikos viešųjų pirkimų įstatymas Žin, 1996, Nr. 84–2000.

procurement. However, it is not considered to be pre-litigation proceedings due to the following reasons:

1) Examining disputes between suppliers and public contracting authorities is not binding on the Public Procurement Office, therefore, it is not obliged to inspect all public tenders regarding which suppliers file appeals.
2) Theoretically, the inspection of public procurement procedures and its results may result in the satisfaction of interests and protection of the supplier who has filed a claim about the decision of the public contracting authority, nevertheless, the inspection itself is not aimed at examining and protecting the position of the supplier.
3) Public Procurement Office, pursuant to the appeal, can carry out the inspection of all the decisions made by the public contracting authority, not only of those regarding which the supplier files an appeal.

Therefore, a conclusion can be made that filing an appeal to the Public Procurement Office can be beneficial to the supplier in terms of the protection of his interests only in those cases when the Public Procurement Office makes a decision to investigate a certain public tender pursuant to such an appeal, and only to a certain extent, i.e. when it overlaps with the protection of public interest. It is possible that when the supplier files an appeal against a certain decision of the public contracting authority, the Public Procurement Office also detects other irregularities relating to the decisions of the public contracting authority or in general makes a decision to oblige the public contracting authority to terminate public procurement procedures.

Meanwhile, the competence of the Tribunals of the Federal Republic of Germany covers pre-litigation appeal proceedings between the public contracting authority and the supplier; the Law on Public Procurement of the Federal Republic of Germany also regulates the procedural aspects of such proceedings. Article 163(1) GWB stipulates the scope of the appeal investigation by the Tribunal and indicates that the Tribunal only deals with the issues covered in the appeal and does not have to overstep the subject matter of the appeal. In this case it is obvious that the focus is laid on resolving specific contestable issues/problems in a dedicated administrative institution rather than leaving them merely to the public contracting authority and the supplier to be resolved. Of course, it is impossible to compare a pre-litigation dispute-resolution institution and the Public Procurement Office, because they are fundamentally different administrative bodies, which were established with different purposes.

2 Judicial proceedings

In order to compare the peculiarities of public procurement disputes in the Federal Republic of Germany and the Republic of Lithuania, yet another important institutional aspect should be stressed, i.e. after the pre-litigation appeal proceedings are closed, suppliers in the Republic of Lithuania have a right to a remedy before ordinary courts. Special or "accelerated" rules of judicial proceedings apply to such litigation, however, except for shorter and priority dispute settlement procedure, general procedural rules apply otherwise. It means that the supplier whose interests are violated can seek the protection of their rights in the courts of three instances, i.e. ordinary county courts, the court of appeal and the Supreme Court. The Supreme Court hears the cases in cassation in exceptional circumstances: when it is obvious from the case file that the hearing of such a case forms the basis of forming new rules of applying legal provisions, or in the light of significant departure from unanimous case law which is developed by the Supreme Court of the Republic of Lithuania.

The purpose of such an institutional distribution of three levels of judicial proceedings is to ensure objective defence of rights as well as the review of court decisions and the development of case law in the field of public procurement at the top level. Meanwhile, legal acts of the Federal Republic of Germany provide for only one institution of judicial proceedings, namely, the Higher Regional Court. In terms of judicial proceedings, a huge institutional difference can be seen. The model of dispute examination in the field of public procurement in the Federal Republic of Germany covers two-stage pre-litigation proceedings and one-stage judicial proceedings in the Higher Regional Court. Meanwhile, the Republic of Lithuania has one mandatory pre-litigation stage of dispute examination and three possible instances of judicial proceedings.

We can also see that both countries show special attention to dispute examination in the field of public procurement. In the Republic of Lithuania this attention manifests through special legal proceedings which aims at accelerating the hearing of such cases, whereas the Federal Republic of Germany has a specialised administrative body of pre-litigation proceedings which also has special procedural rules of hearing such claims as well as one instance of judicial proceedings. Both countries have regulated special rules of dispute examination for such disputes, which ensures more effective proceedings in comparison to other cases.

It should be noted that the setup of the review systems of the Federal Republic of Germany in terms of protection of suppliers' rights that have been violated are very different compared to Lithuania. Although Articles 161–169 GWB establish a special procedure of pre-litigation investigation of the dispute in the area of public procurement, which shows certain similarities with judicial proceedings (e.g. being bound by the subject matter, elements of submitting defence, oral hearing of the case, etc.), apparently, it is not equal to the judicial process, when parties enjoy additional procedural rights, when judges have to meet high standards of independence and impartiality, or when they can be challenged, etc. Also, a question can be raised whether one judicial instance is sufficient to ensure proper protection of suppliers and the public interest in terms of public procurement law in cases when disputes are not resolved in pre-litigation hearings.

3 Investigation of public procurement value which is below the EU threshold

An important difference which exists between investigating public procurement claims in the Federal Republic of Germany and the Republic of Lithuania is that legal acts of the Republic of Lithuania establish essentially the same procedure of dispute settlement for both public procurement above and below the EU thresholds.

In the Republic of Lithuania, differences of dispute hearing procedures in relation to the value of the public tender can only be seen in terms of the time of hearing the case, i.e. shorter pre-litigation proceedings duration, and in terms of deferrals of awarding the contract, i.e. for small value tenders, the value of which is less than €58,000 excluding VAT, the deadline of deferral of awarding the contract is not applied. In terms of all other aspects, the legislation of the Republic of Lithuania, unlike the legislation of the Federal Republic of Germany, ensures equal protection of both suppliers and the public interest irrespective of the value of the contract. It goes well with the statement that the Law on Public Procurement of the Republic of Lithuania, with an exception of small value tenders (less than €58,000 excluding VAT), provides for essentially identical procedures for public procurement, except for timelines of procedures and requirements for public procurement notice. Thus the legal system of the Republic of Lithuania ensures the following important aspects irrespective of the value of the contract:

1. An essentially uniform standard of protection for suppliers and public interest.
2. A common and uniform practice of application of public procurement provisions of the Republic of Lithuania is developed irrespective of whether it is a public or simplified public procurement;

3. An effective and straightforward application of legal acts, examination of disputes, and interpretation of principles is ensured.

Meanwhile, the legal regulation of public procurement disputes in the Federal Republic of Germany focuses on the protection of public procurement procedures and participants thereof above the EU thresholds, and general protection of rights that does include any special dispute settlement procedures applies to public tenders the value of which is lower than the EU thresholds.

4 Compensation for damages in public procurement disputes

The law on public procurement in both the Federal Republic of Germany and the Republic of Lithuania[656] provide for the institution of compensation for damages, the aim of which is to award damages for violation of the supplier's interests due to unlawful decisions of the public contracting authority. Article 107 (1) of the Law on Public Procurement of Lithuania that the Court satisfies only the claim of the supplier for compensation of damages under the following conditions:

1) Public procurement contract has already been awarded;
2) The supplier does not qualify for any grounds of his exclusion;
3) The supplier has been put on the list of proposals;
4) The supplier has been notified about the decision regarding the successful tenderer;
5) Deadlines of deferral to award the contract were met (including deadlines of filing complaints or bringing an action in the court);
6) The supplier has used the institution of pre-litigation dispute examination and has filed a claim to the public contracting authority;
7) In terms of the subject matter of the claim, the court has ruled against the termination of the public procurement contract and has applied alternative sanctions to the public contracting authority.

The presence of all afore-mentioned circumstances leads to a situation where the Court does not consider the public procurement contract ineffective, and does not oblige the public contracting authority to adopt other decisions, therefore, the protection of suppliers' interests can only be ensured by the compensation of damages incurred. It is important to note that the supplier, pursuant to Article 107(3) of the Law on Public Procurement, must additionally prove the amount of damages incurred as well as the fact that due to the contested decisions of the

656 Lietuvos Respublikos viešųjų pirkimų įstatymas Žin, 1996, Nr. 84–2000.

public contracting authority they has lost an opportunity to enter into a public procurement contract, i.e. they are the supplier who would have been the successful tenderer otherwise.

Another interesting aspect is indicated in Article 107(2)[657], which stipulates that the supplier is entitled to seek damages incurred directly and indirectly, but not both at the same time. If the supplier seeks both, direct and indirect damages, the court shall award the greater amount of damages. Indirect damages in such cases usually result from the loss of profit, whereas direct damages result from the cost of preparing the proposal and participating in the tender.

In contrast to the Federal Republic of Germany, in the Republic of Lithuania the issue of compensation for damages in such cases is resolved by courts of the same competence. Although cases of compensation for damages in the field of public procurement are rare in the Republic of Lithuania, an assumption is made that the claim for compensation for damages could be filed as an alternative requirement together with the same action for public procurement infringements. Filing such a requirement together with an initial action would lead to time savings, in comparison to the application of the institution of compensation for damages in the Federal Republic of Germany, according to which the dispute over procedural infringements of public procurement must be handled first, and only then requirements for compensation of damages incurred due to the decisions of the public contracting authority can be filed.

Despite the afore-mentioned, it can be stated that the institution of compensation for damages is more developed in the Federal Republic of Germany than in the Republic of Lithuania, because it provides for the compensation of damages that result both from the decisions of the public contracting authority and from unfair competition of other suppliers during the tender. Such possibilities were not projected when public procurement dispute examination procedures were regulated in the Republic of Lithuania. Of course, such possibilities do exist in the light of general provisions of compensation for damages set forth in the Civil Code[658], however, the practice of their application that involves proving causal links between unlawful actions and damages incurred as well as the amount of such damages is rather delicate and difficult to be implemented in the context of public procurement disputes.

657 Ibid.

658 Lietuvos Respublikos civilinis kodeksas Žin., 2000, Nr. 74–2262.

5 Proposals for revision of German remedies system

The most logical conclusion is that the legal system in Germany should ensure a better protection of rights in the tenders below the EU thresholds. The author of this thesis would like to propose the amendments to the law of Germany by several articles that are similar to Articles 102–104 of the Law on Public Procurement of the Republic of Lithuania; these articles would cover only pre-trial investigation of simplified tenders.

Another proposal would be to include into the German law the obligation for the public contracting authority to review the claim in detail and to provide a reasoned and justified response to the supplier who filed the claim as well as to other participants of the tender. The law could be amended by an additional paragraph to the article that covers the referral to the public contracting authority; this additional section could resemble the provisions of Article 103 of the Law on Public Procurement of Lithuania. It would not place an additional burden for public contracting authorities; however, it would likely reduce the number of potential claims filed to Tribunals in general, since a justified response by the public contracting authority and a reasoned explanation of their legal decision could provide reasons for the future claim.

The author would like to suggest the following amendments to the §§ 155–184 of the Act against Restraints on Competition:

1. Upon receiving the supplier's claim, the public contracting authority shall suspend procurement procedures until the claims are fully examined and a decision is taken.
2. The public contracting authority must examine the claim, take a justified decision, and inform in writing the supplier who filed the claim as well as the candidates and participants concerned about changes in time limits of procurement procedure that were announced earlier within no more than 6 working days from receiving the claim.
3. The supplier has the right to file a claim to the public contracting authority, to submit a request or lawsuit before the Public Procurement Tribunal (except for a lawsuit for declaring the procurement contract or framework contract ineffective or a lawsuit for declaring the termination of the procurement contract unfounded).
4. If the supplier considers that the decision of the public contracting authority to terminate the procurement contract because of a material breach was unfounded, he has the right to institute proceedings before the Public Procurement Tribunal within 30 days from the day of contract termination.

5. The supplier has the right to institute proceedings for declaring the procurement contract or framework contract ineffective within 6 months from the day of awarding the procurement contract.
6. Upon becoming aware of the court's judgements regarding the supplier's claim or suit, the public contracting authority shall inform in writing other candidates and concerned participants no more than 3 working days about such judgements.

Final conclusions

1. The concept of public procurement refers to the purchase of goods, services or works by a public contracting authority. In the course of public procurement, the public contracting authority must adhere to the following principles: equality, non-discrimination, mutual recognition, proportionality and transparency.
2. The legal framework for public procurement for works, supplies and services is based on Directive 2004/24/EU. For the purpose of legal regulation of public procurement, the efficient use of public funds must be ensured. The strict regulation of public funds in the implementation of public procurement restricts the arbitrariness of civil servants and reduces the chances of corruption.
3. The analysis of specificities in the legal regulation of Germany and Lithuania and an examination of different economic assessments and jurisprudence prove that both countries have successfully implemented the objectives of the Directive 2004/24/EU. The aim of the new Directive 2014/24/EU is to introduce more flexibility and provide simplification for application of new procedures. It should be pointed out that the reform did not entirely simplify the application of public procurement procedures and in addition introduced one new procedure – innovation partnership. The author analysed in detail all the available public procurement procedures established in the Directive 2014/24/EU and their transposition into the nation law of Lithuania and Germany.
4. The author is of the view that the application of the current procedures should be further simplified, providing more flexibility for increasing efficiency and transparency of procurement. Following the arguments discussed in the Chapter III above and similarities between competitive procedure with negotiation, competitive dialogue and restricted procedure, the author would like to suggest merging these three procedures into one and propose the following definition for a new procedure: "competitive procedure". Public contracting authorities may apply competitive procedure either with negotiation or without negotiation or using competitive dialogue where its use is linked to the subject matter of the public contract. Accordingly, the restricted procedure, negotiated procedure with publication and competitive dialogue could be covered in one procedure without defining such a complex process

for each of them separate. In addition, in author's view, all procedures should be applied equally without having any restriction. Such approach is already defined in the Directive 2014/25/EU. The specific conditions that limit application of these procedures create huge barriers for public contracting authorities; therefore, they mostly decide to apply standard procedures such as open procedure.

5. After examining the main possibilities of improving the legal framework for public procurement, it may be concluded that in Europe competitive procedure with negotiation, as an exceptional means of awarding contracts, has been used relatively rarely. The assessment of the current situation shows that such a procedure would be more often applied if it becomes a standard procedure. The practical impact of using competitive procedure with negotiation would be greater if such procedure could be applied in the same way as open or restricted tender procedures.
6. The analysis of major weaknesses that need to be addressed in the Member States leads to the conclusion that administrative costs in the Member States must be cut down. Importantly, the simplification of public procurement rules and creating favourable conditions for SMEs would give the latter a better chance to take part in procurement procedures on equal and fair grounds with other tenderers.
7. Legal regulation in public procurement would be more efficient if the application of the price criteria would be reduced. The most economically advantageous proposal should dominate over the lowest price principle in public procurement procedures; also in order to reduce life-cycle costs.
8. The analysis and synthesis of stakeholder responses reveals that so far, the Member States have not given adequate priority to innovations in public procurement. Innovative public procurement plays a key role in improving the quality and efficiency of public services. One of the ways to promote innovation in public procurement is the selection of adequately skilled staff and their training and qualification improvement. Therefore, the European Commission should issue guidance and subsidies projects, which would help the Member States to apply innovations in order to improve the efficiency of public procurement legislation.
9. In order to follow pre-commercial procurement practices it is necessary for the Commission to establish guidelines on how to conduct such innovations in accordance with procurement rules. Such a guide would be particularly useful for local and regional authorities, which could then successfully follow best practices.

10. The provisions of Directive 2014/24/EU show that these will help Member States to better understand the legal certainty of procurement rules and better implement them in practice. Although Directive 2014/24/EU covers a large number of legal obligations, which are clarified by the developed jurisprudence of the Court of Justice, there is no doubt that the Member States will come across with new jurisprudence and face a conflict of laws.
11. The legislation of the Republic of Lithuania adequately regulates the decision review system of the public contracting authority, which gives suppliers realistic possibilities to defend their infringed rights. However, the recent increase in the number of disputes brought before the court, which is believed to continue to grow largely due to the recent amendments in legal regulations of public procurement, leads to the consideration of how to improve the benefits and efficiency of dispute settlement procedures. It is not the regulation of dispute settlement that causes the main issues, but its failure to settle a dispute still during the stage of the public procurement procedure, which would allow parties to debate their positions through pre-litigation procedures and increasing suppliers' trust in the decisions of the public contracting authority. The regulation of pre-litigation procedures should help ensure the trust in the public contracting authority's decision.
12. The German primary legal protection is established for public contracts only above the EU thresholds. The legal capacity of a tenderer depends essentially on whether, in the case of a procurement procedure, the contract value exceeds the EU thresholds or not. The primary legal protection means that it is possible to address the claim against the award decision and aims to get the contract or to prevent a competitor from getting it.
13. If the contract value is below the EU thresholds, suppliers seeking legal protection are generally excluded from primary protection under the German public procurement rules. The public contracting authority does not provide prior information to the unsuccessful tenders. Only in exceptional cases, the suppliers learn in good time of the intended award from a competitor and have the opportunity to enforce their rights guaranteed in the court. In order to achieve a better regulation of the legal protection of suppliers, a reform has to be implemented. The abolition of the current fragmentation of legislation is required, as well as the reduction of secondary legislation, better compliance with procurement rules by public contracting authorities, and compliance with national and European requirements for an effective protection of constitutionally secured legal provisions.
14. Both countries show special attention to dispute examination in the field of public procurement. In the Republic of Lithuania this attention manifests

through special legal proceedings that aims at accelerating the hearing of such cases, whereas the Federal Republic of Germany has a specialized Public Procurement Tribunal for the pre-litigation proceedings that also has special procedural rules of hearing such claims as well as one instance of judicial proceedings. Both countries have regulated special rules of dispute examination for such disputes, which ensures more effective proceedings in comparison to other cases.

15. It should be noted that the practice of the Federal Republic of Germany in terms of protection of suppliers' rights that have been violated is differently established than in Lithuania. Although Articles 161–169 GWB of the Federal Republic of Germany establish a special procedure of pre-litigation investigation of the dispute in the area of public procurement, which shows certain similarities with judicial proceedings (e.g. being bound by the subject matter, elements of submitting defence, oral hearing of the case, etc.), apparently, it is not equal to the judicial process, when parties enjoy additional procedural rights, when judges have to meet high standards of independence and impartiality, when they can be challenged, etc. In addition, a question can be raised whether one judicial instance is sufficient to ensure proper protection of suppliers and the public interest in terms of public procurement law in cases when disputes are not resolved in pre-litigation hearings.
16. Taking into consideration the analysis, it can be stated that the institution of compensation for damages is more developed in the Federal Republic of Germany than in the Republic of Lithuania, because it provides for the compensation for damages that result both from the decisions of the public contracting authority and from unfair competition of other suppliers during the tender. Such possibilities were not projected when public procurement dispute examination procedures were regulated in the Republic of Lithuania. Of course, such possibilities do exist in the light of general provisions of compensation for damages set forth in the Civil Code of Lithuania, however, the practice of their application that involves proving causal links between unlawful actions and damages incurred as well as the amount of such damages is rather delicate and difficult to be implemented in the context of public procurement disputes.

List of figures

Bibliography

ABZ, Leaflet. (2013). *Public procurement in Germany*. Retrieved from: https://www.handelskammer-bremen.de/blob/hbihk24/gruendung_foerderung/downloads/1301404/6cf334c8b75cd488115c323207c2f5a2/Public_Contracts_in_Germany-data.pdf [Retrieved on: 06.07.2017].

Act against Restraints on Competition (GWB) – Part 4 in the version of the Act on the Modernisation of Public Procurement Law [Vergaberechtsmodernisierungsgesetz - VergRModG] of 17 February 2015, Federal Law Gazette I of 23 February 2016, p. 203. (2016). https://www.bmwi.de/Redaktion/DE/Downloads/V/vergaberechtmodernisierungsgesetz-en.pdf?__blob=publicationFile&v=6

Ambrazevičienė, R. (2004). *Viešųjų pirkimų valstybinio reguliavimo politikos raida Lietuvoje (The Development of State Policy on Public Procurement in Lithuania)*. In *Jurisprudencija* 59 (51) (pp. 105–113).

Andrecka, M. (2015). *Innovation partnership in the new public procurement regime – a shift of focus from procedural to contractual issues?* In *PPLR*, No 2 (pp. 18–31).

Arrowsmith, S. (1994). *The award of interim measures in procurement case: Implications of the recent order in the Wallonia buses case*. In *PPLR*, No 4, CS130–136.

Arrowsmith, S. (1995). *The application of the EC Treaty rules to public and utilities procurement*. In *PPLR*, No 6 (pp. 255–280).

Arrowsmith, S. (2000). *Regulating public procurement, national and international perspectives*.

Arrowsmith, S. (2011). *EU public procurement law: An introduction*.

Arrowsmith, S. (2014). *The Law of Public and Utilities Procurement*.

Arrowsmith, S. & Treumer, S. (2012). *Competitive dialogue in EU procurement*.

Average duration of public procurement trials in courts. (2015). Public Procurement Office. Retrieved from: http://vpt.lrv.lt/uploads/vpt/documents/files/Vie%C5%A1%C5%B3j%C5%B3%20pirkim%C5%B3%20byl%C5%B3%20nagrin%C4%97jimas%20teismuose%202015%20m.pdf [Retrieved on: 28.06.2018].

Battis, U. (2017). *Öffentliches Baurecht und Raumordnungsrecht*.

Battis, U., Krautzberger, M., Löhr, R. P. (2016). *Kommentar zum BauGB*.

BeamtStG, vom 17.06.2008.

Benedict, C. (2012). *Sekundärzwecke im Vergabeverfahren, Öffentliches Auftragswesen, seine teilweise Harmonisierung im EG/EU-Binnenmarkt und die Instrumentalisierung von Vergaberecht durch vergabefremde Aspekte.*

BGH, Beschluss vom 16.12.2003.

Bovis, C. H. (2005). *Public procurement in the European Union*, UK.

Bovis, C. H. (2006). *EC public procurement: Case law and regulation.*

Bovis, C. H. (2007). *The EU Public Procurement Law.*

Bovis, C. H. (2016). *The EU Public Procurement Law.*

Boyle, R. (2011). *EU procurement green paper on the modernisation of EU public procurement policy: A personal response.* In *Public Procurement Law Review*, No 5, NA171–184 (pp. 2–8).

Braun, P. (2000). *A matter principle(s) – the treatment of contracts falling outside the scope of the European public procurement Directives.* In *PPLR*, No 1 (pp. 39–48).

Brown, A. (2005). *Transparency obligations under the EC Treaty in relation to public contracts that fall outside the procurement Directives: A note on C-231/03, Consorzio aziende metano (Coname) v. Comune di Cingia de'Botti.* In *PPLR*, No 6, NA153–159.

Brown, A. (2007). *Case T-258/06: The German challenge to the commission's interpretative communication on contracts not subject to the procurement Directives.* In *PPLR*, No 3, NA84–87.

Brown, A. (2007). *Seeing through transparency: The requirement to advertise public contracts and concessions under the EC Treaty.* In PPLR, No 1 (pp. 1–21).

Buhr, B. (2007). *Die Richtlinie 2004/18 und das Deutsche Vergaberecht, Beiträge zum Europäischen Wirtschaftsrecht*, Band 51, Berlin.

Bundeshaushaltsordnung, (BHO) vom 19. August 1969 (BGBl. I S. 1284), die zuletzt durch Artikel 11 des Gesetzes vom 14. August 2017 (BGBl. I S. 3122) geändert worden ist. (2017).

Bundesvereinigung der kommunalen Spitzenverbände, 14.07.2010, http://www.oeffentliche-auftraege.de/[Retrieved on: 01.05.2018].

Burgi, M. (2011). *A report about the German remedies system*, by Steen Treumer, Enforcement of the EU public procurement rules, 2011, p. 107.

Burgi, M. (2018). 2. Auflage, *Vergaberech*. https://www.beck-shop.de/burgi-vergaberecht/product/24010547

Burgi, M. und Dreher M. (2017). Beck'scher Vergaberechtskommentar Band 1: *Gesetz gegen Wettbewerbsbeschränkungen* - GWB - 4. Teil, dazu Horn L., Hofmann, Kapitel 2, Nachprüfungsverfahren, 3 Auflage. https://

www.beck-shop.de/beckscher-vergaberechtskommentar-zweibaendige-ausgabe-band-1-gesetz-wettbewerbsbeschraenkungen-gwb-4-teil/product/16626390

Burnett, M. (2015). *Competitive Dialogue and Negotiated Procedures.* A practical Guide, 2nd edition.

BVerfG, Beschluss vom 29.07.2004.

BVerfG, Beschluss vom 13.06.2006.

BVerwG, Beschluss vom 08.03.1962.

BVerwG, Beschluss vom 13.03.1970.

BVerwG, Beschluss vom 02.05.2007.

BVerwGE, Beschluss vom 06.09.2005.

Byok, J. & Jaeger, W. (2011). *Kommentar zum Vergaberecht*, § 101 GWB, n. 602.

Caranta, R. & Trybus, M. (2010). *The law of green and social procurement in Europe*, Denmark.

Case C-18/01, *Arkkitehtuuritoimisto Riitta Korhonen Oy, Arkkitehtitoimisto Pentti Toivanen Oy and Rakennuttajatoimisto Vilho Tervomaa v Varkauden Taitotalo Oy*, 2003, ECR I-05321.

Case C-108/98, *RI.SAN. Srl v Comune di Ischia, Italia Lavoro SpA and Ischia Ambiente SpA.*, 1999, I-05219.

Case C-120/78, *Rewe-Zentrale v. Bundesmonopolverwaltung für Branntwein "Cassis de Dijon"*, 1979, ECR 649.

Case C-194/88 R, *European Communities v Italian Republic*, 1988, ECR 05647.

Case C-195/04, *Commission of the European Communities v Republic of Finland*, 2007, ECR I-03351, Opinion of Advocate General Sharpston, 18 January 2007.

Case C-195/04, *Commission v. Finland*, 2007, ECR I-03351.

Case C-21/03 and C-34/03, *Fabricom SA v Belgium*, 2005, I-01559.

Case C-21/84, *Commission v. France, 1985, ECR 01355.*

Case C-21/88, *Du Pont de Nemours v. Unita Sanitaria Locale*, 1990, ECR I-00889.

Case C-213/07, *Michaniki AE v Ethniko Symvoulio Radiotileorasis and Ypourgos Epikrateias*, 2008, ECLI-731.

Case C-220/05, *Jean Auroux and Others v Commune de Roanne*, 2007, ECR I-00385.

Case C-221/89, *Factortame*, 1991, ECR I-157; Case C-76/81 *Fearon*, 1984, ECR 3677.

Case C-225/98, *Commission of the European Communities v French Republic*, 2000, ECR I-07445.

Case C-231/03, *Consorzio Aziende Metano (Coname) v Comune di Cingia de' Botti*, 2005, ECR I-07287.

Case C-243/89, *Commission of the European Communities v Kingdom of Denmark*, 1993, ECR I-3353.

Case C-249/81, *Commission v. Ireland*, 1981, ECR 4005.

Case C-249/89; *Trave-Schiffahrtsgesellschaft mbH & Co. KG v Finanzamt Kiel-Nord*, 1991, I-00257.

Case C-250/07, *European Communities v Hellenic Republic*, 2009, I-04369.

Case C-253/95, *Commission v Germany*, 1996, E.C.R. I-2423.

Case C-263/85, *Commission v. Italy*, 1991, ECR, I-2457.

Case C-264/03, *Commission of the European Communities v French Republic*, 2005, ECR I-08831.

Case C-275/98, *Unitron Scandinavia A/S and 3-S A/S, Danske Svineproducenters Serviceselskab v Ministeriet for Fødevarer, Landbrug og Fiskeri*, 1999, ECR I-08291.

Case C-283/00, *Commission of the European Communities v Kingdom of Spain*, 2003, ECR I-11697.

Case C-299/08, *European Commission v French Republic*, 2009, ECR I-11587.

Case C-3/88, *Commission v. Italy* (Re Data Processing), 1989, ECR 4035.

Case C-31/87, *Gebroeders Beentjes BV v State of the Netherlands*, 1988, ECR I-04635.

Case C-324/93, *Evans Medical*, 1995, ECR I-00563.

Case C-324/98, *Telaustria Verlags GmbH and Telefonadress GmbH v Telekom Austria AG, joined party: Herold Business Data AG*, 2000, I-10745.

Case C-336/12, *Ministeriet for Forskning, Innovation og Videregående Uddannelser v Manova A/S*, 2013, ECLI:EU:C:2013: 647.

Case C-359/93, *Commission v. Netherlands* (UNIX), 1995, ECR I-00157.

Case C-360/89, *Commission of the European Communities v Italian Republic*, 1992, ECR I-03401.

Case C-360/96, *Gemeente Arnhem and Gemeente Rheden v BFI Holding BV*, 1998, ECR I-0682.

Case C-369/89, *Commission v. Italy*, 1992, ECR I-3353.

Case C-373/00, *Adolf Truley GmbH v Bestattung Wien GmbH*, 2003, ECR I-0193.

Case C-399/98, *Ordine degli Architetti delle province di Milano e Lodi, Piero De Amicis, Consiglio Nazionale degli Architetti and Leopoldo Freyrie v Comune di Milano, and Pirelli SpA, Milano Centrale Servizi SpA and Fondazione Teatro alla Scala*, 2001, ECR I-05409.

Case C-412/04, *Commission v Italy*, 2008, ECR I-00619.

Case C-432/02, *Commission v Trombin*, ECR I-9665.

Case C-433/03, *Commission v Germany*, 1995, ECR I-2303.

Case C-44/96, *Mannesmann Anlagenbau Austria AG and Others v Strohal Rotationsdruck GesmbH*, 1998, ECR I-00073.

Case C-45/87, *Commission v. Ireland*, 1988, ECR 4929.

Case C-451/08, *Helmut Müller GmbH v Bundesanstalt für Immobilienaufgaben*, 2010, ECR I-02673.

Case C-454/06, *Pressetext Nachrichtenagentur GmbH v Republik Österreich (Bund), APA-OTS Originaltext-Service GmbH and APA Austria Presse Agentur registrierte Genossenschaft mit beschränkter Haftung*, 2008, ECLI-351.

Case C-470/99, *Universale-Bau AG, Bietergemeinschaft: 1) Hinteregger & Söhne Bauges.m.b.H. Salzburg, 2) ÖSTÜ-STETTIN Hoch- und Tiefbau GmbH v Entsorgungsbetriebe Simmering GmbH*, 2002, ECR I-11617.

Case C-496/99 P, *Commission of the European Communities v CAS Succhi di Frutta SpA*, 2004, ECR I-3801.

Case C-507/03, *Commission of the European Communities v Ireland*, 2007, ECR I-09777.

Case C-513/99, *Concordia Bus Finland*, 2002, I-07213.

Case C-532/03, *Commission of the European Communities v Ireland*, 2007, ECR I-11353.

Case C-54/96, *Dorsch Consult*, 1997, E.C.R. I-496.

Case C-59/00, *Bent Mousten Vestergaard v. Spøttrup Boligselskab*, 2001, ECR I-9505.

Case C-599/10, *SAG ELV Slovensko a.s. and Others v Úrad pre verejné obstarávanie*, 2012, ECR I-10873.

Case C-272/91, *Comission v. Italy*, 1994, ECR I-01409.

Case C-8/74, *Procureur du roi/Dassonville*, 1974, ECR 837.

Case C-81/98, *Alcatel Austria AG and Others, Siemens AG Österreich and Sag-Schrack Anlagentechnik AG v Bundesministerium für Wissenschaft und Verkehr*, 1999, ECR I-07671.

Case C-87/94, *Commission of the European Communities v Kingdom of Belgium*, 1996, I-02043.

Case C-810/79, *Peter Überschär v Bundesversicherungsanstalt für Angestellte.*, 1980, ECR. 2747.

Case C-92/00, Hospital Ingenieure Krankenhaustechnik Planungs-Gesellschaft mbH (HI) v Stadt Wien, 2002, ECR I-05553.

Case T-203/96, *Embassy Limousines & Services v European Parliament*, 1998 II-04239.

Case T-258/06, *Federal Republic of Germany v European Commission*, 2010, ECR II-02027.

Cases C–267/91 and C–268/91, *Keck v. Mithouard*, 1993, ECR I-06097.

Charter of Fundamental Rights of the European Union, 30.3.2010.

Chever, L., Moore, J., (2012). *Negotiated Procedures Overrated? Evidence from France Questions the Commission's Approach in the Latest Procurement Reform*.

Civil Code of the Republic of Lithuania, 18 July 2000, No VIII-1864.

COM (2003) 262/02, Commission interpretative communication on facilitating the access of products to the markets of other Member States: The practical application of mutual recognition.

COM (2007) 36, Laying down procedures relating to the application of certain national technical rules to products lawfully marketed in another Member State and repealing Decision 3052/95/EC.

Comba, M. & Treumer, S. (2013). *Award of contracts in EU procurement*.

Commission Communication of 3 March 2010. Europe 2020: A strategy for smart, sustainable and inclusive growth.

Commission Delegated Regulation (EU) 2015/2170 of 24 November 2015 amending Directive 2014/24/EU of the European Parliament and of the Council in respect of the application thresholds for the procedures for the award of contracts.

Commission Delegated Regulation (EU) 2015/2462, of 30 October 2015 amending Delegated Regulation (EU) No 1268/2012 on the rules of application of Regulation (EU, Euratom) No 966/2012 of the European Parliament and of the Council on the financial rules applicable to the general budget of the Union.

Commission Delegated Regulation (EU) 2017/2365 amending Directive 2014/24/EU of the European Parliament and of the Council in respect of the application thresholds for the procedures for the award of contracts, 2017.

Commission interpretative communication on the Community law applicable to contracts awards not or not fully subject to the provisions of the public procurement Directives, 2006/C 179/02.

Commission of the European Communities, Completing the internal market, White Paper from the Commission to the European Council, COM (85) 310 final, 14 June 1985.

Commission staff working document of 23 February 2007. Guide on dealing with innovative solutions in public procurement, 10 elements of good practice.

Commission staff working document, Country report Germany 2017. Including an in-depth review on the prevention and correction of macroeconomic, SWD (2017) 71.

Commission staff working paper of 27 January 2011. Evaluation Report, Impact and Effectiveness of EU Public Procurement Legislation, Part 1.

Communication from the Commission to the Council, the European Parliament and the European Economic and Social Committee of 11 March 2008 "Towards an increased contribution from standardisation to innovation in Europe".

Communication from the Commission to the Council, the European Parliament, the European Economic and Social Committee and the Committee of the Regions – "Think Small First" - A "Small Business Act" for Europe. Retrieved from: https://eur-lex.europa.eu/legal-content/en/ALL/?uri=CELEX:52008DC0394 [Retrieved on: 05.06.2017].

Communication from the Commission to the European Parliament, the Council, the European Economic and Social Committee and the Committee of the Regions of 6 October 2010. Europe 2020 Flagship Initiative Innovation Union, COM(2010) 546.

Communication from the Commission to the European Parliament, the Council, the European Economic and Social Committee and the Committee of the Regions of 17 December 2007 "Pre-Commercial Procurement: driving innovation to ensure sustainable high quality public services in Europe".

Communication from the Commission, Europe 2020, A strategy for smart, sustainable and inclusive growth, COM (2010) 2020.

Communication from the Commission to the European Parliament, the Council, the European Economic and Social Committee and the Committee of the Regions, Making Public Procurement work in and for Europe, 2017.

Consolidated version of the Treaty on the Functioning of the European Union, OJ C 326; 26 October 2012.

Council Directive 71/305/EEC concerning the procedures for the award of public works contracts, 1971.

Council Directive 77/62/EEC of 21 coordinating procedures for the award of public supply contracts, 1976.

Council Directive 88/295/EEC amending Directive 77/62/EEC relating to the coordination of procedures on the award of public supply contracts and repealing certain provisions of Directive 80/767/EEC, 1988.

Council Directive 89/440/EEC amending Directive 71/305/EEC concerning coordination of procedures for the award of public works contracts, 18 July 1989.

Council Directive 89/665/EEC on the coordination of the laws, regulations and administrative provisions relating to the application of review procedures to the award of public supply and public works contracts, 1989.

Council Directive 92/13/EEC coordinating the laws, regulations and administrative provisions relating to the application of Community rules on the procurement procedures of entities operating in the water, energy, transport and telecommunications sectors, 1992.

Council Directive 92/50/EEC of 18 June 1992 relating to the coordination of procedures for the award of public service contracts, OJ L 209, 24/07/1992.

Council Directive 93/36/EEC of 14 June 1993 coordinating procedures for the award of public supply contracts, OL L 199, 9/8/1993.

Council Directive 93/37/EEC of 14 June 1993 concerning the coordination of procedures for the award of public works contracts.

Council Directive 93/38/EEC coordinating the procurement procedures of entities operating in the water, energy, transport and telecommunications sectors, 1993.

Council Regulation (EEC) No. 3906/89 of 18.12.1989, [1989] O.J. L375/11, last amended by Council Regulation (EEC) No. 1366/95, June 12, 1995.

Craig, P. & de Búrga, G. (2003). *EU Law, III Edition.*

Das Bürgerliche Gesetzbuch (BGB), Auslegung von Willenserklärungen§ 133, BGB, 157, 2002.

De Koninck, C., Ronse, T., Timmermans, W. (2015). *European Public Procurement Law, The Public Sector Procurement Directive 2014/24/EU explained through 30 years of case law by the Court of Justice of the European Union.*

Decision of the Government of the Republic of Lithuania 15 May 1992 No 355 On Procedure of Procurement of Goods (Services) in Budgetary Institutions, Official Gazette, 1992, No 20–604.

Decision of the Government of the Republic of Lithuania No 1079 of 29 September 1999 on goods, services or works, the value of which is lower than the one provided for in Article 1(1) of the law on public procurement of the Republic of Lithuania approving the procedure.

Decision of the Government of the Republic of Lithuania No 1473 of 19 December 1996 on the establishment of the Lithuanian Public Procurement Office.

Decision of the Government of the Republic of Lithuania No 355 of 15 May 1992 on the purchase of goods/services of the budgetary institutions.

Decision of the Government of the Republic of Lithuania No 444 of 9 June 1992 On Regulations of Tender of State Order, Regulations of Contract of State Order, Approval of Methodology of Loss Assessment due to Failure to Comply with Obligations of State Order. Official Gazette, No 24–716.114.

Decision of the Government of the Republic of Lithuania No 510 of 12 April 1995 on the Provisional Government Procurement Rules, No 33–778.

Decision of the Government of the Republic of Lithuania of 15 April 1991 No 139 On Amendment and Supplement of Regulations of State Order of the Republic of Lithuania. Official Gazette, 1991, No 13–356.

Decision of the Government of the Republic of Lithuania of 26 November 1991 No 489 On Regulations of State Order of Republic of Lithuania. Official Gazette, 1992, No 5–90.

Decree of the Minister of Economy of 29 December 2014 on the approval of innovative public procurement guidelines. Retrieved from: http://eimin.lrv.lt/uploads/eimin/documents/files/Inovaciijos/LR%20Ukmin%20isakymas%20del%20inovatyviujju%20pirkimu%20gairiu_14-12-29.pdf [Retrieved on: 21.11.2019].

Determination of the Duration of Public Procurement Proceedings in Courts. (2013). Retrieved from: http://vpt.lrv.lt/lt/statistika-ir-analize/temines-viesuju-pirkimu-analizes [Retrieved on: 07.08.2017].

Dettmers, W. *The preliminary ruling procedure pursuant to Article 267 TFEU*, http://www.ejtn.eu/Documents/About%20EJTN/Administrative%20Law%202016/AD201605%20Preliminary%20Ruling%20ERA%2019-20%20Sept/DETTMERS_The_Preliminary_Ruling_Procedure_2016.pdf (Retrieved on 14.04.2018).

Dėl mažos vertės pirkimų tvarkos aprašo patvirtinimo (implementation of simplified procedures), 2017. Retrieved from: https://www.ltkt.lt/admin/ckeditor/fileman/Uploads/Dokumentai%20parsisiuntimui/Mazos-vertes-pirkimu-tvarkos-aprasas_galioja-nuo-2017-07-01.pdf [Retrieved on: 21.11.2019].

Die Bundesregierung, Monitoring – Bericht der Bundesregierung zur Anwendung des Vergaberechts. (2017) Retrieved from: https://www.bmwi.de/Redaktion/DE/Artikel/Wirtschaft/reform-der-eu-weiten-vergaben.html [Retrieved on: 08.08.2017].

Dimitri, N., Piga, G., Spagnolo, G. (2006). *Handbook of procurement*, UK.

Directive 2004/17/EC of the European Parliament and of the Council of 31 March 2004 coordinating the procurement procedures of entities operating in the water, energy, transport and postal services sectors.

Directive 2004/18/EC of the European Parliament and of the Council of 31 March 2004 on the coordination of procedures for the award of public works contracts, public supply contracts and public service contracts.

Directive 2007/66/EC of the European Parliament and of the Council of 11 December 2007 amending Council Directives 89/665/EEC and 92/13/EEC with regard to improving the effectiveness of review procedures concerning the award of public contracts.

Directive 2009/81/EC of the European Parliament and of the Council of 13 July 2009 on the coordination of procedures for the award of certain works contracts, supply contracts and service contracts by public contracting authorities or entities in the fields of defence and security, and amending Directives 2004/17/EC and 2004/18/EC.

Directive 2014/23/EU of the European Parliament and of the Council of 26 February 2014 on the award of concession contracts.

Directive 2014/24/EU of the European Parliament and of the Council of 26 February 2014 on public procurement and repealing Directive 2004/18/EC.

Directive 2014/25/EU of the European Parliament and of the Council of 26 February 2014 on procurement by entities operating in the water, energy, transport and postal services sectors and repealing Directive 2004/17/EC.

Directive 98/4/EC of the European Parliament and of the Council amending Directive 93/38/EEC coordinating the procurement procedures of entities operating in the water, energy, transport and telecommunications sectors, 16 February 1998.

Dischendorfer, M. (2001). *Service concessions under the EC procurement Directives: A Note on the Telaustria Case*. In *PPLR*, No 10, NA57.

Dragos, D. & Caranta, R. (2015). *Outside the EU procurement directives-insite the treaty?*

Estevan de Quesada, C. (2014). *Competition and transparency in public procurement markets*. In *PPLR*, No 5 (pp. 229–244).

European Commission, Green paper on the modernisation of EU public procurement policy, towards a more efficient European Procurement Market, 2011.

European Commission. (2013). *Key facts and figures of Germany*. Retrieved from: http://ec.europa.eu/regional_policy/sources/policy/how/improving-investment/public-procurement/study/country_profile/de.pdf [Retrieved on: 05.07.2017].

European Commission. (2013). *Key facts and figures of Lithuania*. Retrieved from: http://ec.europa.eu/regional_policy/sources/policy/how/improving-investment/public-procurement/study/country_profile/lt.pdf [Retrieved on: 05.07.2017].

European Commission. (2016). *SBA Fact Sheet, Germany*. Retrieved from: http://ec.europa.eu/growth/smes/business-friendly-environment/performance-review-2016_en. [Retrieved on: 07.08.2017].

European Commission, Public Procurement Guidance for practitioners, 2018.

European Commission's Green Paper of 9 February 2011, *From Challenges to Opportunities: Towards a Common Strategic Framework for EU Research and Innovation Funding.*

European Commission notice, Guidance on Innovation Procurement, C(2018) 3051, https://ec.europa.eu/digital-single-market/en/news/commission-notice-guidance-innovation-procurement-published [Retrieved on: 15.05.2018].

European Parliament amendments (1–210) of 7 July 2011 to the report on the resolution on the modernisation of public procurement.

European Parliament and Council Directive 97/52/EC amending Directives 92/50/EEC, 93/36/EEC and 93/37/EEC concerning the coordination of procedures for the award of public service contracts, public supply contracts and public works contracts respectively, 13 October 1997.

European Parliament Resolution of 24 May 2007 on putting knowledge into practice: A broad-based innovation strategy for Europe.

European Parliament Resolution of 3 February 2009 on pre-commercial procurement. *Driving innovation to ensure sustainable high-quality public services in Europe.*

European Parliament Resolution of 25 October 2011 on modernisation of public procurement.

European Parliament Resolution of 6 October 2016 on monitoring the application of Union law: 2014 Annual Report (2015/2326(INI)).

Evers Hjelmborg, S., Stig Jakobsen, P., & Troels Poulsen, S. (2006). *Public procurement law, the EU Directive on public contracts*, Denmark.

Expert group report of September 2005, Public procurement for research and innovation, developing procurement practices favourable to R&D and innovation.

Eyermann, E. (2014). Verwaltungsgerichtsordnung, 14 Auflage.

Fernandez Martin, J. M. (1995). *Note on case C-359/93 Commission v. the Netherlands (the "Unix" case)*. In *PPLR* No 4, CS74–79.

Fletcher, G. (2014). *Minimum time limits under the new Public Procurement Directive*. In *PPLR*, No 3 (p. 95).

Folsom, R. (1993). *European Union law after Maastricht: Practical guide for lawyers outside the common market*.

Ford-Fyffe King, P. (2015). *OECD Review of the corporate governance of States-owned enterprises*. Lithuania.

Frenz, W. (2018). *Vergaberecht, EU und national*.

Geoghegan, J. F. (2014). *Gaswise Limited v Dublin City Council High Court of Ireland*. IEHC 56, February 14, 2014.

Gesetz über die Grundsätze des Haushaltsrechts des Bundes und der Länder (Haushaltsgrundsätzegesetz - HGrG), § 6 (1) HGrG, 1969.

Gesetz zur Änderung der Rechtsgrundlagen für die Vergabe öffentlicher Aufträge (Vergaberechtsänderungsgesetz - VgRÄG). Vom 26. August 1998 BGB.

Gormley, L. (1989). *Quantitative Restrictions and Measures Having Equivalent Effect: Grandfather Clauses in Community Law*. In *E.L. Rev.*, 14(3) (pp. 156–162).

Green Paper of 27 November 1996 on public procurement in the European Union: exploring the way forward.

Green Paper on public-private partnerships and community law on public contracts and concessions, COM (2004) 327.

Green Public Procurement, 2018. http://ec.europa.eu/environment/gpp/index_en.htm [Retrieved on: 21.05.2018].

Grundgesetz für die Bundesrepublik Deutschland, Article 3, 1976.

Harms, S. (2013). *Unionsrechliche Vorgaben für den Rechtschutz im Vergabeverfahren unterhalb der EU-Schwellenwerte*.

Hendry, D. (2007). *Transparency obligations in public procurement – Two cheers for Advocate General Sharpston*. http://www.worldservicesgroup.com/publications.asp?action=article&artid=1892 [Retrieved on 21.05.2018].

HM Government. *Transposition Guidance: How to implement European Directives effectively*. (2013). Retrieved from: http://ec.europa.eu/growth/

tools-databases/newsroom/cf/itemdetail.cfm?item_id=9057 [Retrieved on: 06.06.2017].

Holoubek, M., Fucks, C., Holzinger, K. (2014). *Vergaberecht.*

Hormann, C. (2007). VergabeR, Heft 4.

ICLG, Public Procurement 2018. Retrieved from: https://iclg.com/practice-areas/public-procurement-laws-and-regulations/eu-public-procurement-rules [Retrieved on 21.05.2018].

Innovation Union Scoreboard 2017. Retrieved from: https://ec.europa.eu/docsroom/documents/30690 [Retrieved on: 08.08.2017].

Jakštas, V. & Jovaišas, K. (2004). *Commentary on Public Procurement.* In *Verslo ir komercinė teisė*, Vilnius (p. 31).

Jakštas, V. & Jovaišas, K. (2005). *Viešieji pirkimai, komentaras.*

Judgment of Administrative Court of Appeals Koblenz, No 6L 26(public procurement commentary), 17/04, 31 January 2005.

Judgment of Administrative Court of Koblenz, No 7B 10356/05, 25 May 2005.

Judgment of German Federal Constitutional Court, No 1 BvR 1160/03, 13 June 2006.

Judicial practice of February 2008. Retrieved from: https://www.lat.lt/data/public/uploads/2018/01/2009-liepa-rugpjutiss.doc [Retrieved on: 07.06.2017]

Kapellmann, K. D. & Messerschmidt, B. (2015). *VOB, Teile A und B: Vergabe- und Vertragsordnung für Bauleistungen mit Vergabeverordnung.*

Katz, A. (2017). *Kommunale Wirtschaft.*

Kiiver, P. & Kodym, J. (2014). *The Practice of Public Procurement.*

Knauff, M. (2010). *Das Kaskadensystem in Vergaberecht, ein Regelungsmodell mit Zukunft?* In *NZBau* (pp. 657–659).

Knauff, M. (2016). *Strukturfragen des neuen Vergaberechts Aufsatz.* In *NZBau* (p. 195).

Kopp, O., und Schenke, W. R., (2009). VwGO, Verwaltungsgerichtsordnung Kommentar, 16 Auflage.

Kotsonis, T. (2007). *The extent of the transparency obligation imposed on a public contracting authority awarding a contract whose value falls below the relevant value threshold: Case C-195/04, Commission v Finland, opinion of Advocate General Sharpston.* In *PPLR*, No 3, NA71–83.

Kotsonis, T. (2011). *Green paper on the modernisation of EU public procurement policy: Towards a more efficient European procurement market.* In *Public Procurement Law Review*, No 3, NA51–58.

Körner, B. *Entscheidung über die Verfahrensart*, Retrieved from: https://www.vergabe24.de/blog/entscheidung-ueber-die-verfahrensart/ [Retrieved on: 27.05.2018].

Krohn, W. (2007). *NZBau*, S. 493.

Krugner, M. (2003). *The principles of equal treatment and transparency and the Commission interpretative communication on concessions*. In *PPLR*, No 5 (pp. 181–207).

Krüger, W. (2015). *Münchener Kommentar zum Bürgerlichen Gesetzbuch*: BGB Band 2, 7 *Auflage*.

Kulartz, H. P., Portz, N. (2009).Vergabe- und Vertragsordnung für Leistungen, (VOL) und VOF.

Kulartz, H. P. & Portz, N. (2016). *VOL und VOF*.

Kulartz, H. P., Röwekamp, H., Portz, N., Prieß, H. J., (2018). Kommentar zur UVgO.

Lapėnienė, J. (2017). *Neišvengiamos viešųjų pirkimų rekomendacijos įklampino į teismus (Inevitable recommendations of PPO have pushed into courts)*. Retrieved from: https://www.delfi.lt/news/daily/lithuania/neisvengiamos-viesuju-pirkimu-rekomendacijos-iklampino-i-teismus.d?id=74770212 [Retrieved on: 04.06.2017].

Law Amending Law on Public Procurement of the Republic of Lithuania, No I-1491, Article 85, 31 January, 2006. Retrieved from: https://www.e-tar.lt/portal/lt/legalAct/TAR.C54AFFAA7622/mljgfOSVqW [Retrieved on: 03.06.2017].

Law on Amendment and Supplement of the Code of Civil Procedure of the Republic of Lithuania. In Official Gazette, 2011, No 85–4126.

Law on Public Procurement of the Republic of Lithuania No I- 149, 13 August 1996.

Law on Public Procurement of the Republic of Lithuania No I- 1491, 3 June 1999.

Law on Public Procurement of the Republic of Lithuania of 1 June 2004, No I- 1491.

Law on Public Procurement of the Republic of Lithuania, No I-1491, last amended on 2 May 2017. Retrieved from: https://e-seimas.lrs.lt/portal/legalAct/lt/TAD/b63962122fcb11e79f4996496b137f39?jfwid=-wd7z6gl6o [Retrieved on: 02.06.2017].

Law on Public Procurement of the Republic of Lithuania. In Official Gazette, 1996, No 84–2000, 1996, No 84–2000; 2002, No 118–5296.

Legislative resolution on the proposal for a Council and Commission Decision on the conclusion of a Europe Agreement between the European Communities and their Member States, of the one part, and the Republic of Lithuania, of the other part (COM(95)0207 – C4-0326/95 – 95/0128(AVC)) (Assent procedure), Official Journal C 323, 04/12/1995.

Leinemann, R. (2016). *Die Vergabe öffentlicher Aufträge.*

LG München I, Beschluss vom 18.04.12, 11 O 7897/12.

Lithuania Country Study Guide. (2015).Volume 1, Strategic Information and Development.

Lithuanian Law on Public procurement, online English version from 1997, Retrieved from: http://www.who.int/medical_devices/survey_resources/medical_device_technical_specifications_lithuania.pdf [Retrieved on: 27.05.2018].

Mario Monti's Report to the President of the European Commission José Manuel Barroso of 9 May 2010. *A New Strategy for the Single Market at the Service of Europe's Economy and Society.* Retrieved from: https://www.kfw.de/migration/Weiterleitung-zur-Startseite/Homepage/KfW-Group/Research/PDF-Files/Monti_Report.pdf [Retrieved on: 21.11.2019].

Martlreiter, J. A. (2011). *Europäisierung des vergaberechtlichen Primärrechtsschutzes bei Unterschwellenaufträgen, Europarechtliche Einflüsse und Anforderungen, Verfassungsmäßigkeit, Rechtsschutzmöglichkeiten.*

McLean, S. (2006). *Choice in government software procurement: A winning strategy.* In *PPLR*, No 6 (pp. 338–351).

MEMO 06/303, Frequently Asked Questions (FAQs) on interpretative communication on contract awards not or not fully subject to the public procurement Directives (2006).

MEMO/06/482, State aid: Revised *'de minimis'* Regulation – frequently asked questions (2006).

Millet, T. (1992). *The rule of the European Court of Justice in relation to public procurement.* In *PPLR*, No 1 (pp. 70–79).

Mincienė, A. *Public Procurement by Direct Agreement: Application Problems.* Retrieved from: http://www.verslobanga.lt/lt/patark.full/4aa40d7784723.1 [Retrieved on: 05.06.2017].

Musielak, H. J. (2013). *Kommentar zur Zivilprozessordnung.*

Neumayr, F. (2002). *Value for money v. equal treatment: The relationship between the seemingly overriding national rationale for regulating public procurement and the fundamental E.C. principle of equal treatment.* In *PPLR*, No 4 (pp. 215–234).

Neun, A., Krohn, W., Gabriel, M. (2017). Handbuch Vergaberecht, *Gesamtdarstellung und Kommentierung zu Vergaben nach GWB, VgV, SektVO, VSVgV, KonzVgV, VOB/A, UVgO, VOL/A, VO(EG) 1370, SGB V, AEUV, 2. Auflage.*

Neun, A. & Otting, O. (2016). *Die Entwicklung des europäischen Vergaberechts in den Jahren 2015/2016*, EuZW.

OECD public governance review, public procurement for innovation, 2017.

OLG Düsseldorf, Beschluss vom 31.01.2001.

OLG Düsseldorf, Beschluss vom 30.01.2003.

OLG Brandenburg, Beschluss vom 17.12.2007.

OLG Düsseldorf, Beschluss vom 15.10.2008.

OLG Düsseldorf, Beschluss von 12.01.2009.

OLG Düsseldorf, Beschluss vom 13.01.2010.

OLG Düsseldorf, Beschluss von 04.03.2010.

OLG Düsseldorf Beschluss vom 07.12.2011.

OLG Naumburg, Beschluss vom 23.12.2004.

OLG Saarbrücken, Beschluss vom 29.04.2003.

OLG Stuttgart, Beschluss vom 11.04.2002.

Opinion of Advocate General Mischo, *Case C-81/98, Alcatel Austria AG and Others, Siemens AG Österreich and Sag-Schrack Anlagentechnik AG v Bundesministerium für Wissenschaft und Verkehr*, 1999, ECR I-07671.

Opinion of European Parliament's Committee on Employment and Social Affairs of 18 July 2011 on the modernisation of public procurement. (2011/2048(INI)), Rapporteur: Heide Rühle.

Opinion of the European Parliament, Industry, Research and Energy Committee of 19 July 2011 on modernisation of public procurement. (2011/2048(INI), Rapporteur: Konrad Szymański.

Ordinance on the Award of public contracts (Vergabeverordnung - VgV), 14 April 2016.

Panasiuk, A. (2017). *The court of justice of the European Union and its influence on European and national public procurement regulations: the case of Poland.* In *E.P.P.P.L.*

Pijnacker Hordijk, E. (2005). *A bridge too far: Why the European Commission's attempts to construct an obligation to tender outside the scope of the public procurement Directives should be dismissed.* In *PPLR*, No 3 (pp. 123–130).

Portz, N. (2016). *Deutscher Städte- und Gemeindebund, UVgO Unterschwellenvergabeordnung*. Retrieved from: https://www.akh.

de/fileadmin/download/Vergabe_und_Wettbewerbe/Vergabetag/Vergabetag_2017/01_Portz.pdf.

Portz, N. (2016). *Deutscher Städte- und Gemeindebund. The new rules on public procurement in 2016*. Retrieved from: https://www.dstgb.de/dstgb/Homepage/Schwerpunkte/Vergaberecht/Aktuelles/Entwurf%20%E2%80%9EGesetz%20zur%20Modernisierung%20des%20Vergaberechts%E2%80%9C%20vorgelegt/Positionspapier_%20Die%20Umsetzung%20der%20neuen%20EU%20Vergaberichtlinien.pdf [Retrieved on: 05.07.2017].

Prieß, H. J., Hausmann, F. L., Kulartz, H. P. (2018). Beck'sches Formularbuch Vergaberecht, 3. Auflage.

Professional Association of Lawyers Soloveičikas, Markauskas, Aviža, Bagdanskis. (2007). *The Study of Improvement and Development Strategy for Lithuanian Public Procurement System.*

Public Procurement – study on administrative capacity in the EU Germany country profile. Retrieved from: http://ec.europa.eu/regional_policy/sources/policy/how/improving-investment/public-procurement/study/country_profile/de.pdf [Retrieved on: 08.09.2017].

Public Procurement. (2018). Retrieved from: https://iclg.com/practice-areas/public-procurement-laws-and-regulations/eu-public-procurement-rules [Retrieved on: 12.05.2018].

Public Procurement Indicators 2015, DG Grow G4 – Innovative and e-procurement, 19 December, 2016.

Public Procurement Office. Retrieved from: http://vpt.lrv.lt/lt/teisine-informacija/viesieji-pirkimai-2 [Retrieved on: 03.06.2017].

Public Procurement Office. Yearly analysis of procurement in Lithuania. Retrieved from: http://vpt.lrv.lt/lt/statistika-ir-analize/ketvirtines-ir-metines-ataskaitos-1 [Retrieved on: 07.08.2017].

Public Procurement Office. Yearly statistics and analyses of public procurement in Lithuania. Retrieved from: http://vpt.lrv.lt/lt/statistika-ir-analize/ketvirtines-ir-metines-ataskaitos-1 [Retrieved on: 04.06.2017].

Public Procurement Reform. (2017). Who can deliver transparency? In Teismai.lt 1 (25).

Question No. 835/82, MEP R. Schwarzenberg and Commission response C-93/1, 1983.

Recital 3 of the Commission Implementing Regulation (EU) 2016/7 of 5 January 2016 establishing the standard form for the European Single Procurement Document.

Regular report from the Commission on Lithuania's progress towards accession, 1998. Retrieved from: http://aei.pitt.edu/44570/1/lithuania_1998.pdf [Retrieved on 12.05.2018].

Regulation amending Directive 2014/24/EU of the European Parliament and of the Council in respect of the application thresholds for the procedures for the award of contracts.

Report from the Commission to the Council and the European Parliament, minimizing regulatory burden for SMEs, adapting EU regulation to the needs of micro-enterprises, 2011–11–23. Retrieved from: https://eur-lex.europa.eu/legal-content/EN/TXT/?uri=CELEX:52011DC0803 [Retrieved on: 05.06.2017].

Report from the Commission, Monitoring the application of European Union law 2016 Annual Report, COM (2017) 370.

Resolution on the Commission Green Paper on public procurement in the European Union: Exploring the way forward (COM(96)0583 C4-0009/97), 1996.

Retrieved from: http://ec.europa.eu/growth/tools-databases/newsroom/cf/itemdetail.cfm?item_id=9057 [Retrieved on: 06.06.2017].

Retrieved from: http://ec.europa.eu/social/main.jsp?catId=1135&langId=en [Retrieved on: 04.06.2017].

Retrieved from: http://vpt.lrv.lt/lt/teisine-informacija/viesieji-pirkimai-2/lietuvos-respublikos-istatymai-1/viesuju-pirkimu-istatymas [Retrieved on: 08.07.2017].

Retrieved from: http://www.etsi.org/ [Retrieved on: 05.06.2017].

Retrieved from: http://www.lsdp.lt/lt/naujienos/2188-z-balcytis-ragina-europos-komisija-tobulinti-es-viesuju-pirkimu-sistema.html [Retrieved on: 05.06.2017].

Retrieved from: http://eimin.lrv.lt/lt/veiklos-sritys/viesuju-pirkimu-politika/darnieji-inovatyvus-ir-ikiprekybiniai-viesieji-pirkimai/ikiprekybiniai-viesieji-pirkimai [Retrieved on: 08.06.2017].

Retrieved from: https://www.cen.eu/Pages/default.aspx [Retrieved on: 05.06.2017].

Retrieved from: https://www.cenelec.eu/aboutcenelec/whoweare/ [Retrieved on: 05.06.2017].

Retrieved from: https://ec.europa.eu/info/business-economy-euro/economic-and-fiscal-policy-coordination/international-economic-relations/enlargement-and-neighbouring-countries/enlargement/economic-accession-criteria_en [Retrieved on: 12.05.2018].

Retrieved from: https://ec.europa.eu/agriculture/glossary/acquis-communautaire_en_en [Retrieved on: 12.05.2018].

Retrieved from: http://vpt.lrv.lt/lt/teisine-informacija/teises-aktu-archyvas/viesuju-pirkimu-tarnybos-direktoriaus-isakymai-3 [Retrieved on: 21.05.2018].

Retrieved from: http://vpt.lrv.lt/lt/teisine-informacija/teises-aktu-archyvas/ministru-isakymai-3 [Retrieved on 21.05.2018].

Retrieved from: https://verslas.lrytas.lt/rinkos-pulsas/2017/05/30/news/pirkimu-prievaizdai-spjove-i-reikalavimus-del-kuriu-skalpuoja-kitus-1477510/ [Retrieved on 21.05.2018].

Retrieved from: https://www.forum-verlag.com/themenwelten/kommunales/unterschwellenvergabeordnung-uvgo-zeitplan-fuer-die-einfuehrung-in-den-bundeslaendern [Retrieved on 22.05.2018].

Retrieved from: https://ec.europa.eu/regional_policy/sources/docgener/guides/public_procurement/2018/guidance_public_procurement_2018_en.pdf [Retrieved on 27.05.2018].

Retrieved from: https://www.gov.uk/guidance/public-sector-procurement-policy [Retrieved on 27.05.2018]. Retrieved from: http://www.vergabe.de/nachpruefungsinstanzen/ [Retrieved on 04.04.2018].

Retrieved from: http://www.vergabe.de/nachpruefungsinstanzen/ [Retrieved on: 04.04.2018].

Retrieved from: http://www.forum-vergabe.de/news-detail/statistiken-der-nachpruefungsverfahren-2016-veroeffentlicht-6806/ [Retrieved on: 04.04.2018].

Retrieved from: http://www.forum-vergabe.de/fileadmin/user_upload/Downloads/2016_OLG_Statistiken_Nachpruefungsverfahren.pdf [Retrieved on: 04.04.2018].

Retrieved from: http://vpt.lrv.lt/uploads/vpt/documents/files/Pirkimu_stebesenos_ataskaita_2017_m.pdf [Retrieved on: 04.04.2018].

Retrieved from: https://www.fdfa.be/sites/default/files/atoms/files/564_Final%20act%20in%20English.pdf [Retrieved on: 04.04.2018].

Revised Agreement on Government Procurement, April, 2014: Revised GPA 1994 enters into force(GPA), 1994. https://www.wto.org/english/tratop_e/gproc_e/gp_gpa_e.htm [Retrieved on: 06.07.2017].

Rolfstam, M. (2008). *Public procurement of innovation*, Sweden.

Rolfstam, M. (2009). *Public procurement as an innovation policy toll: The role of institutions*. In *Science and Public Policy*, 36/5 (p. 358).

Ruling of the Civil Division of the Supreme Court of Lithuania of 4 May 2010 in civil case No 3K-3-126/2010.

Ruling of the Civil Division of the Supreme Court of Lithuania of 18 April 2012 in civil case No 3K-3-170/2012.

Ruling of the Judicial Panel of the Civil Cases Division of the Lithuanian Court of Appeal of 31 August 2010 in civil case No 2A-713/2010.

Ruling of the Judicial Panel of the Civil Cases Division of the Supreme Court of Lithuania of 2 February 2009 in civil case UAB Kauno keliai v Klaipėda, case No 3K-3-25/2009. Retrieved from: https://www.lat.lt/data/public/uploads/2018/01/2009-liepa-rugpjutiss.doc [Retrieved on 06.07.2017].

Ruling of the Judicial Panel of the Civil Cases Division of the Supreme Court of Lithuania of 17 November 2009 in civil case No 3K-3-508/2009.

Ruling of the Supreme Court of Lithuania of 21 March 2011 in civil case No 3K-3-119/2011.

Ruling of the Supreme Court of Lithuania of 23 December 2008 in *UAB "ZIP Travel" v National Audit Office of Lithuania*, case No e3K-3-1-969/2017.

Ruling of the Supreme Court of Lithuania of 23 December 2008, *UAB "ERP" v State Tax Inspectorate under the Ministry of Finance of the Republic of Lithuania*, case No 3K-3-538/2008.

Ruling of the Supreme Court of Lithuania of 30 March 2016 in civil case No 3K-3-177-916/2016.

Ruling of the Supreme Court of Lithuania of 5 April 2011 in civil case No 3K-3-158/2011.

Ruling of the Supreme Court of Lithuania of 6 April 2010 in civil case No 3K-3-150/2010.

Ruling of the Supreme Court of Lithuania of 9 February 2009 in civil case No 3K-3-35/2009.

Rupnik, J., Pettai, V., Zielonka, J. (2003). *The Road to the European Union. Volume 2. Estonia, Latvia, Lithuania.*

Sanchez-Graells, A. (2016). *Reformation or Deformation of the EU Public Procurement Rules.*

Schebesta, H. (2013). *Towards an EU Law of Damages.*

Schepel, H. (2000). *Legal aspects of standardisation in the member states of the EC and EFTA.*

SIGMA paper No 45. (2010). Public Procurement in EU Member States – the Regulation of contract below the EU thresholds and in areas not covered by the detailed rules of the Directive.

Sodan, H., und Ziekow, J. (2018). Verwaltungsgerichtsordnung, 5. Auflage.

Soloveičikas, D. (2007). *The Study of Improvement and Development Strategy for Lithuanian Public Procurement System.*

Soloveičikas, D. (2008). *Neįprastai mažos kainos koncepcijos taikymo ypatumai pagal Europos Sąjungos ir Lietuvos viešųjų pirkimų teisę (Peculiarities of Application of Concept of Abnormally Low Price According to Public Procurement Law of the European Union and Lithuania).* In Teisė, Vilnius, No 67 (pp. 7–23), ISSN 1392-1274.

Soloveičikas, D. (2008). *Viešųjų pirkimų principai: jų taikymas remiantis Europos Teisingumo Teismo ir Lietuvos teismų praktika (Principles of Public Procurement: Their Application on the Basis of the Case-Law of the CJEU and Lithuanian courts).* In *Justitia*, 3 (69).

Soloveičikas, D. (2009). *Public Procurement in Lithuania: The ongoing development*. In *E.P.P.P.L.*, vol. 2 (p. 110).

Soloveičikas, D. (2014). *Viešųjų pirkimų teisės tikslai ir jų įgyvendinimas (Objectives of Public Procurement and their Implementation).* In Teisė (p. 42).

Statistische Meldungen über Vergabenachprüfungsverfahren gem. § 129a GWB, retrieved from: https://www.bmwi.de/Redaktion/DE/Downloads/G/gesamtuebersicht-vergabekammern.pdf?__blob=publicationFile&v=11 [Retrieved on: 04.04.2018].

Statistical data retrieved from: https://de.statista.com/statistik/daten/studie/214139/umfrage/nutzung-von-ausschreibungen-durch-industrieunternehmen-im-b2b/ [Retrieved on: 07.08.2017].

Statistical data retrieved from: https://de.statista.com/statistik/daten/studie/74234/umfrage/eprocurement-pre-award-process-von-behoerden-in-europa/ [Retrieved on: 07.08.2017].

Telles, P. (2016). *Public procurement financial thresholds in the EU and their relationship with the GPA*. In E.P.P.P.L. (p. 206).

The conclusions of 8 March 2011 of the European Council meeting of 4 February 2011.

The European Commission's Green Paper of 27 January 2011 on the modernisation of EU public procurement policy: Towards a more efficient European procurement market.

The European Commission's Green Paper on the modernisation of EU public procurement policy — towards a more efficient European Procurement Market, 2011.

The European Commission's proposal for a Directive of the European Parliament and of the Council of 20 December 2011 on public procurement, COM (2011) 896.

The European Convention on Human Rights, 1950.

The European Parliament, the Employment and Social Affairs Committee's opinion of 18 July 2011 on modernisation of public procurement.

The Ministry of Economy of the Republic of Lithuania. (2011). *Report of the project 'Improvement of System of Public Procurement Dispute Settlement'*. Retrieved from: http://eimin.lrv.lt/uploads/eimin/documents/files/Viesieji%20pirkimai/VPGNS[1].pdf [Retrieved on: 07/01/2014].

The new Lithuanian Law on Public Procurement, Official Gazette, 118–5296, 2002.

The official statistics of Lithuanian Courts. Retrieved from: http://www.teismai.lt/lt/visuomenei-ir-ziniasklaidai/statistika/106 [Retrieved on: 05.07.2018].

The order of the chairman of PPO of 26 February 2003 regarding the adoption of the methodology of the evaluation of the procurement value of goods and services. Official Gazette, 28th February, 2003, No. 22–949.

The PHARE programme, Annual report 1998, COM (2000) 183 final, 2000, p. 51.

The PHARE programme, twinning project "Strengthening Public Procurement Policy", No LI99/IB-FI-03, final summary of 10 September 2002.

The table provides overview of procurement values below and above the EU thresholds. Retrieved from: https://www.nbank.de/medien/nb-media/Downloads/Rechtliche-Grundlagen/Vergaberecht/%C3%9Cbersicht-Wertgrenzen-und-EG-Schwellenwerte.pdf [Retrieved on: 05.07.2017].

The table provides overview of the different thresholds established in the federal States. Retrieved from: http://www.abst-brandenburg.de/wp-content/uploads/2019/08/Wertgrenzen_Bund_-Bundesl%C3%A4nder_2019.-07.08.19.pdf [Retrieved on: 05.07.2017].

Thomas, H., und Putzo, H. (2010). Zivilprozessordnung, 31 Auflage.

Transparency International (2012). *Study regarding public procurement corruption in Lithuania*. Retrieved from: http://media.transparency.org/nis/cogs/assets/lt/pdf/Lietuva_NIS.pdf [Retrieved on: 05.07.2018].

Treaty establishing the European Coal and Steel Community (ECSC), 1951. https://eur-lex.europa.eu/legal-content/EN/TXT/?uri=legissum:xy0022

Treaty establishing the European Economic Community (TEEC), 1957. https://eur-lex.europa.eu/legal-content/EN/TXT/?uri=LEGISSUM%3Axy0023

Trepte, P. (2007). *Public Procurement in the EU*.

Treumer, S. (2011). *Enforcement of the EU public procurement rules*.

Treumer, S. (2014). *Modernising Public Procurement: The New Directive*.

Trybus, M. *Improving the Efficiency of Public 11. Procurement Systems as Part of the European Union Enlargement Process*. Retrieved from: http://citeseerx.ist.

psu.edu/viewdoc/download;jsessionid=D59784085737B5996852A94F4987B49D?doi=10.1.1.612.1406&rep=rep1&type=pdf [Retrieved on: 05.07.2018].

Trybus, M. (2011). *Enforcement of the EU Public Procurement Rules*; von Treumer, S. & Lichère, F.

Trybus, M., Edelstam, G., Caranta R. (2013). Award Procedures for the EU Institutions. Chapter 16, in EU Public Contract Law, Public Procurement and Beyond, 1 Edition.

Twelve projects for the 2012 Single Market: together for new growth, 13 April 2011.

Under the PHARE programme a twinning project 'Preparation for the implementation of the acquis on public procurement. Definition of Acquis communautaire https://ec.europa.eu/agriculture/glossary/acquis-communautaire_en_en [Retrieved on: 21.11.2019].

United Nations Commission on International Trade Law: UNCITRAL Model Law on Procurement of Goods, Construction and Services, adopted in 1994. Retrieved from: http://www.uncitral.org/pdf/english/texts/procurem/ml-procurement/ml-procure.pdf [Retrieved on: 07.07.2017].

Usai, A. (2014). *Caught between the public procurement principles and the 'public procurement function' of Directive 2006/123/EC still a 'grey zone' in search for legal certainty*. In EPPPL 9 (p. 228).

UVgO: Umsetzung in Bund und Ländern, Vergabeblog (2017). Retrieved from: https://www.vergabeblog.de/2017-08-16/uvgo-umsetzung-in-bund-und-laendern/ [Retrieved on: 08.08.2017].

Van den Bossche, P. (2005). *The law and policy of the World Trade Organisation.*

Van Iersel, J. & Cabra de Luna, M. A. (2011). *Green Paper on the modernisation of EU public procurement policy of 13 July 2011. Towards a more efficient European Procurement Market.*

Verdingundordnung für freiberufliche Leistungen (VOF), 2006. https://www.bmwi.de/Redaktion/DE/Downloads/Gesetz/verdingungsordnung-freiberufliche-leistungen.pdf?__blob=publicationFile&v=1

Verdingundordnung für Leistungen (VOL/A).2009. https://www.bmwi.de/Redaktion/DE/Downloads/V/vol-a-abschnitt-1.pdf?__blob=publicationFile&v=4

Vergabe- und Vertragsordnung für Bauleistungen Teil A, Allgemeine Bestimmungen für die Vergabe von Bauleistungen, 2016 (VOB/A).

Vergabekammer des Bundes vom 05.11.2012 - VK 3-120/12.

Vergabekammer des Bundes 29.04.1999.

Vergabekammer Nordbayern, Beschluss vom 28.10.2002 (ref. 320. VK-3194-33/02).

Verwaltungsverfahrensgesetz (VwVfG), 23. Januar 2003.

Verordnung über die Vergabe öffentlicher Aufträge (Vergabeverordnung – VgV), 2016.

Vidaus sandoriams – prezidentės veto. (2017). (For In-House Deals –President's Veto). Retrieved from: http://alkas.lt/2017/04/18/vidaus-sandoriams-prezidentes-veto [Retrieved on: 01.06.2017].

Viešųjų pirkimų reglamentavims ir teismų praktikos apžvalga, AC-38-1, 2016. (The regulation of public procurement and the review of case law).

Vinod, R (2001). *Transparency in government procurement*. In *Journal of World Trade*, 35 (4).

Von Wietersheim, M. (2017). Vergaberecht, 2 Auflage.

White Paper from the Commission of the European Communities, *COM* (85) 310 final, 1985.

Willenbruch, K. & Wieddekind, K. (2017). *Kompaktkommentar Vergaberecht*.

Williams, R. (2007). *Contracts awarded outside the scope of the public procurement Directives*. In *PPLR* 1, NA1–10.

Williams, R. (2011). *The European single procurement document*. In *§ 101 GWB*, n. 4.

Williams, R. (2016). *The European single procurement document*. In *PPLR* (p. 2).

Zubrute, V. *VPT del policijos automobilių pirkimo pasikonsulatvo su gamintojais*, (purchase of police cars). (2017). Retrieved from: https://www.vz.lt/transportas-logistika/2017/05/22/vpt-del-policijos-automobiliu-pirkimo-pasikonsultavo-su-gamintojais [Retrieved on: 21.05.2018].

Zivilprozessordnung (ZPO), 2005. https://www.gesetze-im-internet.de/zpo/BJNR005330950.html

www.ingramcontent.com/pod-product-compliance
Ingram Content Group UK Ltd.
Pitfield, Milton Keynes, MK11 3LW, UK
UKHW021921120926
8556IPUK00042BA/1097

9 783631 799765